a cold coming

PUBLISHED BY BOLL WEEVIL PRESS

acoldcoming.blogspot.com

ISBN-13: 978-0-9889568-2-7

a cold coming

By W. Jeff Bishop

Boll Weevil Press

acoldcoming.blogspot.com

To a fellow history lover!

CANTO I

Midway on my journey through life, I find myself within a forest dark. The straight path, she's lost. The forest, it's savage, rough, and stern. Don't know how I stumbled into it. I think I was asleep.

I dreamed I reached the mountain's foot. My soul ached to fly right on up that mountain, but my body, it needed to rest.

As I stood there, trying to work up some fire, before I could begin my climb, there she was. A mad dog, a ghost dog, her fur and skin white as death, she stood in my way and growled. She was all tooth, jaws snapping, head up, ravenous. I could not pass.

That dog lashed against me by degrees, thrusting me back where the sun is silent.

I need my hammer. First I will crack the skull of this mangy, godforsaken dog. And then I will kill my poor family. They will be free of me and my sins, at last. Amen.

Summer

Chapter One

1

T.J. kissed his Pappy's cold forehead. The skin reminded him of those white turtle shells he'd stumble over in the woods. The kiss was perfunctory. Best not to linger too long over the dead.

The gaunt young man straightened his tie and stiffened his spine so that his two missing buttons would not show. T.J. did not feel as sad as he thought he should. He wondered if anyone could tell about that. Or the missing buttons.

The family members all filed in the same way, with pots smelling of butter and gravy, all tucked under pale, flaccid arms; atrophied and veiny limbs outstretched to hug a neck, grasp a clammy hand.

Aunt Lillie licked her fingers as she handed off a bundled-up pot to the help at the big table. Even as she fought off 40, her lips were still plump and pink. T.J.'s admiring eyes followed Aunt Lillie's feelers as they made their way down to her wide, inviting hips to wipe themselves. Her red hair trickled down like lava from her black mourning hat.

Birdy, T.J.'s cousin, laughed at something Lillie whispered in her ear. T.J. noted that she'd gone and dyed her best dress black. It had been a spring dress, blue and white, with bows, before she'd gone and ruined it with all that black dye. Birdy had done most of the work to get the house ready. She'd found most of the old daguerreotypes in a parlor drawer and she'd propped them up on a table near Pappy's body. The Pappy in the cold, metal pictures was dark and puffy, with silver eyes and slick, black hair. He held his King James Bible upside-down in his lap. He looked like a tired man, but a man with important work to get back to. Not the broken remnant T.J. had known, the ghost who sieved milk through his long, white beard while babies dribbled spit onto his shoelaces.

T.J. took his place in the middle row with the other teenage children.

"You," said the photographer, a round, bearded man with dark complexion. T.J. had never seen a Jew that he could remember, but this little man fit the description given by Uncle Virgil: dark and hunched over, smoothed with oils, peering out of his sleepy eyes like a hungry weasel, waiting for some kind of opportunity. They and the Catholics could be in league, for all anyone knew, what with their ancient languages and secret symbols and mystic ways. It all went back to the Pope, who was out for nothing less than to regain the control of the world he'd lost centuries ago. Everyone had a theory.

"You, move back to the back. To the back. No, to the back! Back there!"

What a loud, insistent little man, T.J. thought.

T.J. had never been in the back row before, but he didn't mind much. He took his place directly behind Aunt Lillie, who smiled at him, flashing those straight, yellowed teeth of hers. Now that he was closer to her, T.J. could spot some grey ash in the lava bed, but it didn't matter to him. Her eyebrows were just like Louise Brooks', T.J. thought. Slight, slender arches. And her smell. Underneath the dime store perfume, it was all kitchens and sweat.

"Grab hold, T.J.," his father told him as the men eased back the coffin so that Pappy could stare into the camera with the rest of them.

"You men hold on," said the picture man as he took his position behind the camera. T.J. was surprised by how heavy the coffin was. Surely he must be getting a disproportionate share of the load, he thought.

About 30 people gathered around. T.J. clenched his wet right hand around the sharp corner of the coffin. He caught another quick glimpse of his aunt's bottom. His eyes darted around to make sure no one was looking.

"All right, now. All right, now. That's good. Everyone hold it right there, now," said the Jew.

Sweat rained down T.J.'s forehead, sweeping his glasses down his nose. The coffin weighed on him like a sermon. He clinched his thin fingers more tightly, trying to find his grip, but it was like trying to hold onto an oil-soaked piano. Gravity wants what it wants.

"Hold it right there!" said the camera man once more.

Just take the goddamn picture, T.J. thought.

He glanced out the lone open window, hoping for some type of divine intervention. A blond-haired girl about his age was standing there, clutching something. She looked a little timid, peering in like the negroes sometimes did before knocking at the back door. Then she was gone.

A barb shot through T.J.'s right hand like a snakebite. He recoiled, sending the coffin tumbling onto the floor with a splintering *crack*, punctuated by yelps of shock from the women in front. One of the babies shrieked.

Pappy's corpse plunked down at the feet of the children in a most unnatural position. The youngins clambered over the body to reach their mothers, clinging onto them like frightened monkeys.

T.J. looked down at his right hand. A tiny splinter protruded from the webbing between his index finger and thumb. He pulled it out and popped his bleeding hand into his mouth. He peered up at his father.

Granite.

His father motioned for the other men, mostly T.J.'s uncles, to hoist the body back into the coffin. T.J. stepped forward but his father shooed him away, shaking his head in disgust. T.J. seeped into the crevices.

A squeal of yimmeryammers announced Hoke, the Blond One, as he strode in through the foyer like a prince. Hoke hoisted a half-eaten chicken leg in one hand while his other picked at a splinter of bone lodged between his broad, white teeth. Hoke had a young girl with him, following a few steps behind. She was unusually thin, wearing a light homespun dress, pink flowers in a frayed hat. T.J. averted her eyes. *The scouts of the heart.* Was this the girl he had glimpsed in the window? T.J. didn't think so. He was pretty sure the girl in the window was Beatrice Evans, whom he had not laid eyes on for the better part of two years.

Hoke strutted across the room to help the men lift the body back into the coffin. T.J.'s father smiled and squeezed Hoke's arm, muttering something to him as he glanced over his shoulder at T.J., who pretended not to notice.

T.J. looked to his feet as a kind of refuge. His laces had come undone. He crouched down to tie them. And there, leaning against the wall opposite, was the girl with the pink flowers in her hat, pressing her scourpot hands against the wrinkles in her dress, her eyes flitting around the room like a child looking for its mama.

7

He fiddled with his laces as the blood from his wound dribbled out onto the floor. He wiped it against his pants leg and looked up to see if she had noticed. The girl's eyes pinned him to the floor like the insect he knew he was.

T.J.'s grandfather had been tucked back into the coffin now. T.J. sucked the last of the blood away, stood up, and took his place again in the back row. No one asked him to help hold up the body this time. Instead, Hoke assumed T.J.'s position beside his father.

Hoke winked back at T.J.

"How are ya, Slick?" he asked.

T.J. hated it when Hoke called him that.

In a flash it was all over. The family dispersed, with the women cackling their way into the kitchen and the children cat-and-mousing one another in and out of creaky screen doors. The men shuffled and shifted their weight, looking at their shoes, nodding, each waiting for his turn to speak. Occasionally a contemptuous snort rolled out over the steady, low rumble of mutters, grunts and farts. T.J. looked at his father. He was out of place. In a room full of doughy pastiness, Tom Latham's red skin stretched over his bony frame like a roped-down tarp.

T.J. wanted to follow his mother into the kitchen, like he used to as a child, dropping in on the gossip about cousins and uncles jumping on trains or getting into fights or drinking themselves to hell.

But T.J. went with the men today. He knew that he was no longer welcome with the women. He was too old.

So he would follow his father, but he would be thinking of Aunt Lillie's hair, the waif in the homespun dress, and Beatrice, the girl in the window.

T.J. hoped he was old enough now not to be noticed, to blend in with the other men as they paraded onto the front porch like a row of ducks. The most horrifying thing would be if one of his uncles, or most especially his father, were to tell him to "go play."

He thought he already knew what today's sermon would be. Usually a few of the brothers would gang up on Victor, who drank too much. Just as often, they would pile on Bije, who provided Victor -- and every other so-inclined man up and down the Big and Little Tallapoosa Rivers – with liquor. But today, T.J. knew, it would be his father who would have to run the gauntlet.

From what T.J. had pieced together, his father was going to be asked to take over the family farm. Now that Pappy was dead, there would be no one to oversee the stables and the crops, the Negroes and sharecroppers. All the other brothers either lived out of town or were too slack or disinterested. Tom had run all the way down to Milledgeville to get away from the boll weevils and the bullshit. Now he was back, but was that any reason to rope an educated man behind two mules? It wasn't like the old days. Farms were going under due to falling prices for corn on the one end and higher taxes on the other. People were moving to the cities or to the cotton mills and villages, just to get out, to find a meal, to have running water and electricity, to survive.

After his father and all of his uncles filed out the front door, T.J. tried to sneak his way around the corner, alongside Hoke. But Edgar, the eldest, raised his hand to T.J.'s breast.

"I'm sorry, T.J.," he said.

And the door shut.

T.J. spun around. The girl with the faded pink flowers was working her tongue around a lollipop while she waited for Hoke.

He thrust his hands into his pockets and slunk out to the back without saying a word.

3

A team of horses ker-clomped into the driveway as T.J. stepped out the back door. A dozen men unloaded a tangle of red roses, twisted into the shape of a cross.

T.J. felt obliged to stop and hold the door for the small army. He couldn't help but be amused by the oversized floral arrangement. The men hoisted it like a battering ram, heroically positioning and re-positioning, first horizontally, then vertically, and then again at a number of different and increasingly esoteric angles. But finally they had their way, with a little brute force, although the lower left corner of the floral arrangement had to be sacrificed in the process. T.J. followed the horde into the dining room.

He could hear his grandmother's gasp of approval before he even rounded the corner. Queen Victoria Brown Latham was a large woman, with dense bones and massive hands, much like her son Abijah. She had a coarse, full-bodied voice like Abijah's, too; when she spoke, the windows rattled.

T.J. recognized the red-headed captain of the men as Frank White. Mr. White served as a deacon at T.J.'s church, along with T.J.'s father and Mr. John Evans. Mr. White and Mr. Evans also served as the three trustees of the Philadelphia Church School. T.J. knew that Mr. White had never much cared for his father. T.J. knew that it had something to do

10

with his mother. Apparently Mr. White had accompanied her home from church a few times and had even been invited by her parents to have supper with the family, before Tom Latham came along and ruined everything. T.J. noticed that his mother always found an excuse to leave the room whenever Mr. White was present. Today was no exception.

Frank White also led the local chapter of the Ku Klux Klan, or what was left of it. It was in that capacity that he was here today.

"We're sorry for your loss, Miss Victoria," said Mr. White as his color guard hoisted the floral arrangement. The broken corner dangled and swayed.

"Taz was a great man," he said. "A true pioneer. A patriot."

Mr. White then motioned for one of the other Klan members to step forward. He ceremoniously unwrapped a medium-sized American flag and presented it to Gammy. She took it in her hands like a baby, offering White a polite hug of thanks in return.

T.J. had heard his father telling his mother that the Klan had asked permission to carry a flaming cross at the funeral procession, in honor of one of Haralson County's earliest pioneer citizens. Gammy had declined the suggestion, pointing out that Pappy had never been a member. John Tazwell Latham, Sr. was never known as a "joiner" and had never been a member of any organization that anyone could remember. He wasn't even officially a member of his own church. But the Klan had insisted on doing something special, and apparently they had opted for the red roses, instead.

"Would you say grace for us, Mr. White?" Birdy asked.

It was the invitation Mr. White had been hoping for. He assumed the somber, slightly slumped stance one was

11

expected to take prior to a prayer. T.J. suspected there was not a meek bone in the man's body. But just as everybody bowed their heads and Mr. White opened his mouth to invoke the name of the Lord, a sudden commotion erupted in the kitchen, at the back door.

T.J. opened his eyes to see Willie and Nattie Latham rooted in the rear doorway like possums in the lamplight.

"Oh!" Willie exclaimed, grabbing Nattie by the arm. "I'm sorry, Mrs. Latham. Me and Nattie'll come on back some other time!"

Gammy shed a thousand pounds of burden as she plodded toward the pair, her flabby arms outstretched.

"Willie! You will do no such thing, Willie! Now you get in here and have yourself something to eat! Get on in here! Help me, Birdy."

"Just like those niggers to be late," T.J. heard Virgil mumble.

Birdy offered her left arm to help Gammy lumber across the room. It was like watching someone walk on stilts through a mudhole, T.J. thought. She finally fell into Willie and Nattie's embrace and they escorted her into the dining room. Mr. White simmered.

"Now, Miss Latham, you know we can just come on back later, now," Willie said.

"We don't wanna intrude on nothin'," Nattie said.

"Y'all come on in."

Willie and Nattie were descendants of slaves that Taz's father had brought with him from Bedford County, Virginia, before the Civil War. Gammy was only 16 when she'd married Pappy, and Willie and Nattie hadn't been much younger.

12

"You should've been here 15 minutes ago and we could have put you in the picture!" Gammy said, pressing her fleshy face into Nattie's bosom. Her tears poured down Nattie's breast like spring waters down an obsidian mountain.

"We're so sorry, Mrs. Latham," said Willie. "We brought you these flowers here and we'll be on our way. Nattie and me's got to get to town today and get back before nightfall."

"Birdy, you fix up a plate for Nattie and Willie. Big helpings. You come and sit down, now. We won't have you runnin' off."

"Ms. Latham, we'd love t'but we cain't. We just stopped by on de way."

"Well," she said, wiping her nose with her fingers, "how about a plate to take with you, then?"

"All right, if that suits you, Miss Latham. We'd sure appreciate it, if it ain't much trouble."

Mr. White nodded to Willie and approached him as Birdy prepared two plates.

"Howdy, Mr. White."

"How you doin', boy?" said White. He extended his hand.

"Your crops coming in all right?" he asked.

"Just fine, thank you, sir."

White gripped Willie's hand and squeezed. He leaned in closer. Willie could smell the tomatoes Mr. White had eaten for dinner.

"I wish we had more men like you around here, Willie," he growled. "I need to talk to you about a couple of your people. Particularly that Wilson boy."

13

"He don't know nothing but trouble, do he?" said Willie, shaking his head as he tried to negotiate his way out of White's vise-like grip. White pressed in closer and squeezed a little tighter. Willie didn't think he'd ever seen that exact shade of yellow on a set of teeth before.

"I wish you'd speak to him," said Mr. White, pawing a coarse left hand against Willie's shoulder. "I'd hate to have to do it myself. Best to nip this in the bud, you know what I'm saying? I know he's a good boy. You speak to him, you hear?"

"I'll surely do that, Mr. White. I sure will."

With that, Frank White smiled, clapped Willie on the shoulder once more, and relaxed his grip. Willie smiled in return and signaled to Nattie, who was already aimed at the door.

Birdy swooped in with two heaping plates of food. Willie hoofed toward the back door as Nattie graciously accepted the victuals.

"You're sure you won't stay?" asked Gammy.

"We can't, Ms. Latham," said Nattie.

"Well..."

Gammy hugged them both once again.

"I'll see you tonight, you hear? Thank you. Thank you. Bless you."

"All right, then," said Mr. White as the screen door whacked shut. Birdy helped Gammy amble back to her chair. "Let's all bow our heads."

CANTO II

I tread down to the lowland, out the door and into the
yard, to retrieve my hammer from the shop, and before my eyes a
figure presents himself, seeming hoarse from a long silence.

When I behold him in the darkness, I cry out to him,
"Have pity on a poor sinner!" I know what I am about to do. I want
someone to stop me. Please stop me.

"Which are you," I ask, "haint or real man?"

He answers me: "Not man; man once I was, And both my
parents were of Florence, with loyalties to the Guelphs. Under
Gemini was I born, and lived during the time of a false and lying
God, although I only suspected it at the time. A poet was I, and I
sang a comedy that is often called 'divine.' But it's all rubbish,
absolute rubbish.

"But let's talk about you. Tell me, why goest thou for the
hammer? Why climb'st thou not the Mount Delectable, which is the
source and cause of every joy?"

"Great Sir," I answer, "indeed I know who you are. I have
shared your visions, and your lusts. You are my master. And I have
been to Mount Delectable. But sir, it brought me no joy. Only pain
and despair.

"And now, behold this beast, this ghost dog, which has
chased me away. Will you protect me from her, Master? For she
makes my veins and my pulse tremble."

"Teacher, it behooves thee to take another road," responds
he, when he sees me weep, "if from this savage place thou wouldst

15

escape. Because this beast, at which thou criest out, suffers not any one to pass her way, but so harasses him, that she destroys him. She has a nature so malign and ruthless, that never doth she glut her greedy will, and after food is hungrier than before."

I do not wish to feed upon that which nourished the dog, but rather to feed upon wisdom, and on love and virtue. Just like The Poet. I wish to drive that mad dog back to Hell, from which she had been loosed.

And so I need my hammer. I must set things straight. I must begin anew, free from the weight of this world, which has led me so far from the straight path.

But then the Poet says to me:

"I think and judge it for thy best thou follow me, and I will be thy guide, and lead thee hence through the eternal place, where thou shalt hear the desperate lamentations, shalt see the ancient spirits disconsolate, who cry out each one for the second death.

"And I will take you, then to the blessed people; to whom, then, if thou wishest to ascend, a soul shall be for that than I more worthy; with her at my departure I will leave thee; because that Emperor, who reigns above, in that I am rebellious to his law, wills that through me none come into his celestial city. He governs everywhere, and there he reigns; there is his city and his lofty throne; O happy he whom thereto he elects!"

And so I say to him:

"Poet, I ask you, so that I may escape this woe and worse, conduct me to the portal of Saint Peter."

Then he moves on, and I follow behind.

Chapter Two

1

Fifty yards past Philadelphia Church Cemetery, toward Rufus Goldin's house, next door to Mr. Rowland "Hobblin'" Brown, just off the Eaves Bridge Road, squatted the one-room Philadelphia School. Built by the members of the Philadelphia Baptist Church, the white, wooden shotgun box lacked a bathroom, or even an outhouse, but the children all understood the rule of "girls' woods on the left and boys' woods on the right," even if they didn't always strictly follow it. Unlike most buildings of its kind and time, the Philadelphia School was fitted with window after window: two walls of uninterrupted glass.

T.J. attended school at Philadelphia, just across the road from his family's small farm, for nearly ten years now. Every bit of that time his father had been his only teacher. On his first day of class Lois Latham took an hour to dress her six-year-old son in a special pink-and-white striped romper, with a neat jacket and bow tie, that she'd store-bought especially for the occasion. She walked T.J. up to the schoolhouse door and told him precisely what to say.

"Now, T.J., you tell him, 'Professor Latham' … you call him 'Professor Latham,' not 'Daddy,' all right?"

"I know," said T.J., grabbing his crotch and kicking his left leg in the dirt.

"You tell him, 'Professor Latham, do you have need for a new student?' Say it just like we practiced." She kissed him on his baby-soft, brown hair, tucked his primer under his arm, patted him on his back, opened the door for him and sent him on his way.

Despite all the practice, T.J, still flubbed the line, but it didn't take away from the effect. The entire school room roared with laughter.

Each day, class was called to order by a small brass bell with a cracked, wooden handle that Tom Latham kept on his desk. The bell was also rung at dinner time, when everyone went home for an hour, and then again when school was dismissed for the day. Usually Tom rang it while standing in the doorway, where the children huddled outside before school began, or as they braced for an all-out sprint home when it ended.

Tom taught everything from primary school through the ninth grade. T.J. shared a room with students Roy Lee McConnell, P.J. Dalton, Odell Stubblefield, Clarence Sloman, Tailey Goldman, Little John Evans, Russell Carter, Troy Summerville, and about 20 others, ages six through sixteen.

Tom Latham's method of teaching was, T.J. thought, quite intimate. He would sit down on an old shipping crate in the front of the room and call small groups of students in turn -- older students studying geography would take 15-minute quiz on capitals, followed by a group of first and second graders going over their spelling words, succeeded by eighth and ninth graders needing an advanced lesson in mathematics. The small groups, assembled into clusters by age and subject matter, gathered in the front row for the quick sessions, then moved back to their regular seats to work individually.

T.J. had many memories of his father sitting on that little wooden box, and he wondered how he could stand it. Thomas Jefferson Latham was a slight and bony man, weighing 165 pounds sopping wet, and T.J. marveled at the fact that his father never used a cushion all those hours he spent squatting on that unforgiving crate. He wondered why his father had never brought in a more comfortable chair from home. He supposed it was because the box put Professor Latham just where he wanted to be. Crouching on that box, Tom did not tower above the students at some imposing height, pouring out knowledge from on high into the little vessels beneath him. Instead, he was right there with his students, turning the pages in their primers, going over each line, eye to eye. Intimate.

Even when the young scholars were put on the spot, as was the case during the weekly spelling bees, they weren't singled out for humiliation or punishment. Tom assigned a word to each student as he went down the line, by the blackboard. Tom then directed any student having trouble to sit at the bench at the side of the room, and then, while the rest of the students progressed to the next assignment, he took a primer in hand, sat down with the student who needed extra help, and spent up to half an hour sounding out letters, talking about words and their meanings. The older girls and the prettier ones usually had the most troubles and needed the most help.

Of course, even in an intimate setting such as this, there were the occasional discipline problems. That's why the professor kept four hickory switches standing in the corner. Anyone who got into trouble knew they had to tell the professor which switch to use and exactly how to use it. Again, it was often the older girls who got the switch. T.J. couldn't understand why the prettiest ones gave his father so much trouble so much of the time.

The whole time T.J. had been a student, he could only recall one or two times that his father had been forced to give boys the switch. Usually a wayward glance was enough to

19

settle the boys down on even the rowdiest of days. Tom Latham could make children feel as if he were looking straight through them.

But there was this one time, T.J. recalled, involving Albert Previtt, who was hare-lipped, with his upper lip slit right up to his nose, red gums all exposed. The children spent many of their most creative hours trying to devise ways to get Albert to speak, never failing to draw a cheap laugh from the boys and reproofs from the girls. Young Mr. Previtt could never seem to whisper but, in order to be understood, due to his struggles with his harelip, felt compelled to bellow.

Carl Bishop, always a troublemaker, had whispered something to Albert, trying to provoke him, and when that failed he resorted to throwing spitballs. Albert had responded to him in kind.

"Albert Previtt!" Professor Latham said, writing at the blackboard, without even turning around to look at him. "Come up front right now!"

Albert -- never the brightest student in the class – could not deduce how he'd been apprehended.

"Professor Latham?" he'd asked. "How did you know it was me whispering?"

"Albert," Tom had said, with a look of parturient gravity. "Don't you know I have *eyes in the back of my head*?"

It was something many teachers had said, the worst kind of cliché, but Albert had actually believed it. Professor Latham certainly didn't need eyes in the back of his head to know who was behind Albert's delinquency. Albert Previtt no longer attended classes at the Philadelphia school house. Carl Bishop was disciplined by Professor Latham so many times and so severely that, by age 12, he stopped coming to school.

When Professor Latham returned to his teaching duties after his father's funeral, he acted as if nothing had changed, as if the discussion with his brothers had never taken place. T.J. was not privy to the outcome, but their grave expressions told him all he needed to know.

For a long time, Tom was silent. He stared out of one of the rows of windows and rubbed his face with the palms of his hands.

"What's wrong, Professor Latham?" one of the younger girls finally asked.

"I..." he said. T.J. squirmed in his seat as his father cleared his throat.

"I won't be continuing in my position as your teacher. I came here today because I thought you deserved an explanation. My father died, and ... and I'm going to work his farm. I've enjoyed being your teacher but Mr. Clarence Sloman, a graduate and former classmate whom I trust some of you will remember, will arrive here tomorrow and will assume my duties as professor of this school. For this I ... I am deeply, deeply sorry. Please forgive me."

He looked around the room once more and bit his lower lip.

"Forgive me," he mouthed silently.

With that, T.J.'s father cleared his throat again and began the school year's first lesson.

"Open your primers to page one, please," he said.

T.J. could not make himself hear the lesson. He sat in disbelief. What had his uncles said to his father? Tom Latham was no farmer. Couldn't they see that?

T.J. wondered what had made his father agree to it. Was it guilt? Obligation? Tom was the only brother who hadn't gone into the service. No one ever let him forget it,

21

either. Taz had worked the mail service for General John Pershing. Edgar had fought as a colonel with the Rough Riders in the Spanish-American War, alongside his brother Henry. Virgil still suffered from his trench sores from the Great War in Europe. But the service had no need for Tom, with his thin frame and high blood pressure and other ailments. Had his brothers made him feel guilty about it? What kind of leverage did they have?

T.J. had been taught by his daddy all his life and he wondered what it would be like to be taught by someone else. Mr. Sloman, it turned out, lived up to his name. The second day of the semester lasted an eternity. And, for the first time, T.J. felt small in a classroom, very small, as Mr. Sloman took his place behind the only new piece of furniture that classroom had seen in decades: a lectern.

He felt even smaller when he saw who was waiting for him outside the school in a new 1931 Ford Phaeton Model A.

2

T.J.'s unpleasant experiences with Carl Bishop stretched all the way back to the Dominicker chicken incident.

Carl had been about 12 years old, and T.J. a year older. Tom bought 15 black-and-white feathered Dominicker chickens from a farmhand who was loading up his wagon and heading north, looking for work in the mills. Removed from their own yard, the hens never successfully reoriented themselves and they developed a habit of wandering off. They especially liked to toddle across the road to the school at dinner time, when the students often threw scraps from their pails after they finished eating. This wasn't a huge problem since the chickens were expected to forage for a good part of their living. Tom's biggest concern was not that they wandered, since they never seemed to go far, but that the children might think it funny to feed them gum or buckshot.

But then the 15 dwindled to 12 – not so unusual, since there were dogs roaming the neighborhood. But soon two more went missing, and then three more. Tom scoured the surrounding woods for clues to their whereabouts and it wasn't long before he ran across a corn-baited trap near the schoolhouse. All he had to do, he thought, was hide in the bushes and wait for the owner of the trap to come along and claim his prize. But the chickens by that time had become experts at avoiding the trap -- or maybe only the clever hens remained -- so Tom had to catch one and put her into the trap himself. Soon enough, Carl Bishop and his stepbrother Legs McDowell came along.

Professor Latham escorted the boys home and tried to talk to their father, Oscar, about the missing hens. "Now, Tom Latham, you know that's not so," said Mr. Bishop, a sharecropper for Mr. Goldin who was known as an extremely polite, reserved man. "Them chickens went wild from my hog pen," he said. Tom's first instinct was to smack the man in the nose. But instead he told Mr. Bishop, with all the civility he could muster, that this was difficult to believe, since the Bishops' hog pen was three-quarters of a mile away from the school, with the Brown farm in-between.

"I don't have your chickens, Tom Latham," he answered.

"You're a goddamn liar," Tom Latham told the man.

Frank White and John Evans, as trustees of the school, were called in to help settle the dispute, since the alleged thefts had occurred on the school grounds. Mr. Bishop would have to pay for the chickens or his boys would have to stop coming to school, they decided. So, after voicing his protests, Mr. Bishop grudgingly paid for the missing birds with eggs, some sugar, and a hen of his own. Oscar, a widower with a gentle soul who usually shied away from confrontation, didn't have any real money. The boys probably trapped the chickens simply because they were hungry. But that didn't matter to Tom Latham. Right was right.

The settlement allowed Carl and Legs to come back to school, but they couldn't manage to stay out of trouble. One day Carl stuck out his foot to trip T.J. as they lined up after recess to enter the school house. T.J. fell off the steps, scratched his nose and broke his glasses. "What's the matter, T.J.? You been drankin' from your Maw's closet again?" Carl had said, sniggering. Seeing Carl negotiate the business end of a hickory stick was little consolation to T.J. and his brother Grady. "Don't pay any attention to them," Tom told T.J. "Don't invite them to play the games you play. Just ignore them. If you get hurt, I'll take up for you."

Most afternoons right after dinner the students played marbles until T.J. and Professor Latham returned from across the road and the bell rang school back into session. But Fridays were different; those were baseball days. The school day ended early and usually students from another school in the county would come to play. A team was assembled and those who weren't picked to play sat on a rock or under a tree and watched the game while eating a sandwich with their parents. Sometimes they'd play a round of marbles.

Carl and Legs were always picked for the team and were considered more or less regular players. Legs was the team's best pitcher while Carl was good at bunting his way on base and stealing his way home.

The visiting team from Lindale had a one-armed pitcher whom everyone had heard about. Scouts from as far away as Tuscaloosa had been following him. He had no left arm, but his right arm was pure gold. A knuckleball was his specialty, and it was un-hittable. He would tuck his glove under his stub of a left arm and let the right arm do its work.

Carl wouldn't be bunting that day. Mr. Sloman, who had just recently graduated school at the time and volunteered as the umpire, called him out after the ball fouled off Carl's leg. Carl got into Clarence Sloman's face, kicking the dirt and screaming to the world. As he sauntered back to the bench, Carl muttered something under his breath that sent Clarence Sloman into a rage, which shocked everyone. In fact, the reason Sloman had been asked to umpire was because of his easygoing, even-tempered personality. But on that day his fist sent Carl flying into two somersaults. The trustees immediately stepped in, of course, and Oscar talked of suing the school.

John Evans, a well-liked blacksmith and a man of constant moderation, calmed everyone down and halted the game long enough to find out exactly what had happened.

"Mr. Evans," Clarence said, "I don't know whether I'm right or whether I'm wrong, but when someone calls me a 'son of a bitch' he's gonna get everything I got."

That ended the whole thing. No one seemed to take into account that Carl was only 12 at the time while Clarence was 18. Carl was big for his age and had a surly reputation, so that was that. Clarence Sloman was a respected young man who often helped at the school and even substituted for Tom on occasion. So, soon after that incident, whatever friends Carl and Legs had at the school dwindled to almost nothing. Carl's nickname soon became "S.B." Everyone knew what

25

that meant. The girls, many of whom were Lathams by name or by blood, were especially merciless.

It wasn't long after that that Carl Bishop quit coming to school altogether.

3

So T.J. was understandably a little suspicious when Carl showed up at the school, offering him a ride in his brand new Model A. Where had someone like Carl Bishop made the money to buy something like that? Was it stolen?

Beep! Beep!

Carl dusted up the road as he cruised into T.J.'s path and kicked it out of gear to let it purr. Carl's dark hair was slicked back like some of the gangsters T.J. had seen at the picture show in Bremen. He had dark eyes and a swarthy complexion.

"Hey, T.J.! Want a ride?"

"Naw, I just live across the road, Carl."

T.J. motioned to his sister Beryl to follow him as he tried to maneuver around the car. Carl inched up, blocking their path.

"Aw, come on! I won't bite ya. Yer pretty little sister can come, too. Come on!"

Even from the road, T.J. could smell whiskey. He didn't know whether it was on Carl's breath or from somewhere in the car, but the smell was pungent. He had heard talk that Carl had gotten mixed up in Uncle Abijah's moonshine business, making runs to the Atlanta restaurants with Hoke and Black Charlie Summerville.

"We can walk, Carl," T.J. said.

He grabbed Beryl by the arm and led her around the rear of the vehicle. Carl tried to swing the car into reverse but the gear stuck.

"Hey!" he said, taking a quick glance around and hoisting a bottle. "I got some corn liquor. Want some?"

Carl opened the back door and winked at Beryl, who blushed. T.J. shook his head.

"We're going home, Carl."

Carl shut off the engine and hopped out, galloping after them.

"Aw, come on now, T.J.! You know you want to go for a ride! You ever been for a ride in an A model? It's smooth as a baby's bottom. Come on!"

T.J. kept walking, dragging his sister behind him.

"What about you, Beryl? Don't let Mr. Stuffy stop ya. I won't tell yer daddy. Come on!"

Beryl flushed red again. She dealt Carl a look that was difficult to decipher, then shook her hand loose from T.J. Beryl squinted her eyes at her brother, stuck out her tongue and followed a beaming Carl to his fancy new car.

"Beryl?" T.J. said. "What are you doing?"

"At least somebody knows how to have a little fun around here," Carl said, ushering her into the car.

"You can't go with him, Beryl!" T.J. said, stomping the dust. "He's drunk!"

"He ain't drunk," said Beryl, smiling.

"You can't go with him! Get out of that car! Beryl!"

Carl started the engine. He looked at himself in the rearview mirror and slicked his dark hair back into place.

"Ain't she purty?" he said. "Climb on over into the front seat so's you can see."

"Beryl!" said T.J.

27

"It's all right!" she said, climbing into the seat beside Carl. "He ain't gonna do nothing but give me a ride. You shush!"

Carl put the car into gear and gave T.J. a sideways glance over his shoulder.

"Well, you comin' or not, T.J. Latham?"

Carl revved the engine and grinned while Beryl giggled and motioned for T.J. to hop aboard.

T.J. looked back helplessly to his house, which was only a couple of hundred yards away, then back to Beryl, who was motioning ever more frantically as Carl began to inch away.

T.J. sighed, shook his head, shouldered his sack full of textbooks and walked over to the car.

No sooner did he land a hand on the door, though, than Carl gunned the engine again, popped out the clutch, and lurched forward. T.J. jumped back, frightened, prompting a laugh from Carl.

"You skeert I'm a-gonna hit ya, Mr. Latham?" Carl said, grinning. Beryl tittered in appreciation. Here was someone finally keeping her older brother in line.

T.J. smiled politely, trying hard not to over-react. After all, he was about to put his life into this boy's hands.

T.J. stepped onto the running board.

Carl revved up the car again and lurched it forward, tossing T.J. into the dirt. Beryl laughed even louder this time. She was getting a kick out of seeing her big brother get knocked around. And Carl had several reasons to savor this, too, but he wasn't thinking about that just now. Seeing Beryl enjoy it was enough for him.

T.J. got up, gathered his books and dusted himself off. He smacked the soil off his texts one by one and carefully placed them back into his sack.

"That's really mature, Carl," he said.

T.J. spun around and marched back toward his house.

"Aw, now, come on back here, T.J. Latham. You know I didn't mean it like that. Hey!"

Carl threw the car into first and pulled up beside T.J. as he walked back up the hill.

"Ah, now, I'm sorry, T.J. What I gotta do to make it right? Come on, now. I'll do anything you say."

"Just go and leave me alone. I don't want nothing to do with it," T.J. said.

"Now, T.J., don't be a crybaby! You know I was just cuttin' up. Look, now, I'll even shut 'er off."

Carl pulled up in front of T.J., turned off the engine and waited. Beryl motioned to her brother to slide into the back seat.

"What? What is it? Come on and get in," Beryl said as T.J. just stood and stared at the two of them.

"Where are we gonna go?" T.J. asked.

"Oh, Lord sakes, T.J., I don't know that!" said Carl. "Where you wanna go to?"

T.J. took one last look at his front porch, sighed again and tossed his sack into the rear. He clambered in and tried not to be seduced by the oily-smooth leather upholstery on the rumble seat.

"Dad's not going to like this," T.J. said, tucking his legs in under him as Carl put the car in motion.

4

T.J. had to admit that he was thrilled by the speed and the smoothness of the ride. He was used to mule wagons and horse-drawn buggies. He'd been in the T models a few times, but they were nothing at all like a new Ford Phaeton.

As they toured the back roads, turning up the dirt, whizzing by cows and oaks and pines and pastures, dodging chickens, Carl launched into a song:

I'm just a country feller from way out in the sticks.
I have a lot of trouble, I get a lot of kicks!
I raise my cotton and corn, I never owned a Ford.
I run the boardin' house where folks don't pay no board!
My boardin' house, my boardin' house, it sets up on the hill,
Now come along and join the throng, you're welcome if you will.
Eat corn bread and taters too, and drink out of a gourd,
My boardin' house, my boardin' house, where folks don't pay no board!

Carl laughed, tickled with his own performance, while Beryl crossed her arms and grimaced.

"Sounds better with my gee-tar," said Carl. "But I don't reckon I kin drive and play gee-tar at the same time. You know that ol' tune, don't you, T.J.?"

"Naw, don't think so," T.J. said. He hadn't been listening. He was taking in the whirling countryside.

Carl looked back over his shoulder, mouth open, incredulous.

"Don't you know nothin', man! That's ol' Gid Tanner and the Skillet Lickers! Ain't you never heard 'Corn Licker Still in Georgia'? My brother Preston got all 14 sides."

"We don't have a phonograph," said T.J.

"Aw, we cain't afford one, neither," said Carl. "We gotta go plum up the road to the Stubblefields; they let us listen to theirs."

T.J. ran his hands over the leather interior as his eyes soaked up the yellow sun and the galloping green.

"If you can't afford a record player, how did you wind up with this car?" T.J. asked.

Carl laughed and spat into a coffee can that he pulled out from between his legs, then laughed again. He looked at Beryl, who was forcing a smile and crossing her arms, not knowing what to do. Then Carl fell quiet.

"Don't y'all even know yer own uncle?" he asked. "This is Bije's car. Ain't he showed it to ya?"

"Bije?" said T.J. "All he ever had was an old T model."

"Naw, man!" said Carl, spitting again. "He went and settled up fer thissun five days ago. He ain't took you fer a ride in it?"

"I don't reckon," said T.J.

"You wanna see how fast she goes?" said Carl.

"Naw, I don't aim to see that," said T.J. "Carl, we gotta get home. I done told you. And we're going the wrong way!"

Beryl began to look worried. She drew her sweater close in around her. Carl took note and shook his head.

"Y'all wanna go home? All right, I'm takin' yer ass home!" said Carl. "I'll take yer ass home, then. I was just trying to -- I just gotta drop something off with Bije first thing. It'll only take a minute or two."

Carl kicked up dust and gravel as he floored the accelerator and swerved left off of Eaves Bridge Road.

Abijah Latham lived in an old one-room slave shack that had been the sharecropper quarters before Henry Latham, T.J.'s uncle, had died. Abijah kept talking about plans to build a proper house, but somehow he never got around to it.

As they pulled up in the driveway, T.J. saw Hoke peek out from a window, then step to the front door. Carl kept the car running as he grabbed a box in the floorboard and ran up to meet Hoke.

T.J. leaned forward and whispered to Beryl.

"Don't ever do this again, Red," he said.

She rolled her eyes and clenched her sweater tighter around her shoulders.

Hoke waved to T.J., who nodded in return as he leaned back in the rumble seat.

"Slick!" T.J. heard him shout over the patter of the engine. T.J. wondered if Uncle Bije wanted his vehicle back, and if he and Beryl would be forced to walk home.

T.J. saw that Hoke was carrying a shotgun. Carl handed the box to him, smiled and apparently cracked a joke of some sort, motioning to the car. Hoke laughed and nodded in agreement, then stepped back inside. Carl waved and made his way back to the vehicle.

"All right," he said, climbing back into the car and pushing the gearshift. "Let's get you yungins home."

CANTO III

And so we approach the Gates of Hell, me and the Poet, on that dark hillside, just outside my house, and I begin to doubt whether I'll be man enough for the task ahead. I am so unworthy, so weak.

Maybe this whole thing is ill-advised, I tell him. Can I unwill what I have willed? Can I summon new thoughts, and change my intentions? Can I withdraw from my designs?

And the Poet, whom I had hoped would grab my shoulder and pull me back from the Abyss, whom I had expected to give a knowing smile and a pat on the back, turning me around and sending me back to bed, what does he do instead?

He calls me "coward."

"Thy soul," he said, "is tainted with cowardice, turning you back from this honored enterprise -- as false sight doth a beast, when he is shy."

And he is right. I am a coward.

But my feet keep on marching relentlessly forward, taking me to the shop, where the hammer is.

Chapter Three

1

Uncle Virgil was always the first to the mailbox. It didn't matter whether or not it was his mailbox, his brother's mailbox, or someone else's. He wanted to be in the know. He was always especially on the lookout for newspapers and bulletins. He would spread the newspaper out on the floor like a war map and blast his opinions like cannon fire. He hated President Hoover, like most folks did. And not just because of the Depression, although that was part of it. And not just because Hoover was a Republican, although that, too, was a big strike against the man. Mostly he hated Hoover because Hoover had cost him his old Model T. Virgil had lost it in a bet against old man Elijah Rice when Hoover ran against Al Smith, the Pope-loving Catholic, in 1928. Virgil nearly got into a fist fight with Elijah Rice every time he saw him driving his old car. Virgil had said it was the "way that man smiles at me." In fact, Sheriff Richards had been called in to subdue or warn Virgil on more than one occasion.

Virgil hated a lot of things almost as much as he hated Elijah Rice. He hated Communists, for one. Strikers, unionists. They were mostly controlled by foreigners who wanted nothing more than to tear the country down, just like they'd done in Russia, Virgil had said. He hated Jews and Catholics. Both had aims similar to the Communists and were even more clever in the ways they disguised their true, sinister intentions. Henry Ford had known all about it and tried to warn everyone, but no one would listen. Virgil could recite nearly every word of William Jennings Bryan's "Cross of Gold" speech. Virgil had thought all along that Sacco and

Vanzetti were guilty of the vile crimes of which they had been accused, and did not doubt the guilt of Leo Frank, the Jew who had killed that little girl who worked for him at the pencil factory in Atlanta. Not only did he hate and distrust foreigners of all stripes, but Virgil also hated the goddamn railroads and the devils who set the freight rates, as much he hated the hobos who huddled together in those freight cars, sad sacks going God knows where. He hated the goddamn banks and the fatcats who used them to grind farmers like his father and brothers into the dust. He thought all niggers were lazy and too clever for their own good. He hated drunks and he hated women who voted. Ever since the War, he hated God, even if he didn't believe in him most of the time. But most of all he hated to work.

If you asked him about it, it wasn't the work that he hated so much as the physical pain involved in carrying it out. Virgil, like thousands of others who fought in the trenches of the Great War, had come down with "trench fever," which he repeatedly told T.J. had "ruined him for life." In a way it certainly had, because it made him bitter and stole his God.

T.J. admitted he never could understand all of his uncle's ailments. Something to do with body lice. He remembered Virgil telling him that some of the lice were as large as his thumb. The disease used to give Uncle Virgil terrible headaches and a fever, and still caused sores on his legs from time to time, and pain, always the pain. At least he had said so. T.J.'s father sometimes had his doubts, but he hadn't gone to serve in the trenches, so what could he say?

So Virgil watched Tom work on the farm and kept him entertained with stories about what was going on in the world. Lately their discussion had centered on a new building being constructed in New York City called the Empire State Building. It was supposed to be the tallest ever constructed by man. Except for maybe the Tower of Babel.

Virgil puttered up into the yard with an old beat-up fifth-hand T-model his father had managed to scrounge up to replace the T he'd lost to Elijah Rice. T.J. could hear him coming for a mile or so away. He could, of course, hear him crossing the bridge over the river, but the engine was what made the lasting impression. It made an ungodly *chugga-chugga* racket because a previous owner had poured cement into one of the cylinders. But it was the only form of transportation the family had, unless they wanted to saddle up the horses or wear out a pair of shoes.

"What's the news, young man?" Virgil said as he idled, waiting for T.J.'s father.

T.J. shrugged and waved, seemingly in a single motion.

"Nothing much," he said. "You waiting on Dad? You want me to fetch him?"

Virgil shook his head and shouted over the roaring rattle of the engine.

"Nah," he said. Virgil took off his hat and waved it at the porch. T.J. turned around and saw his mother in the doorway, holding Erlene on one hip and Collier on the other.

"Where y'all headed to?" asked T.J., putting a foot on the running board, moving in close to Virgil so they could talk over the engine din.

"What's that?"

"I said where y'all headed?"

"Where are we headed? We're headed to your uncle's house, young man. Bije's house."

T.J. nodded. He wasn't surprised.

36

"Does Uncle Bije have an A model?" he asked.

"A model? Who told you that?" said Virgil.

"Someone at school," said T.J.

"Shit," Virgil muttered.

T.J. jumped when a firm hand pushed him aside. It was his father, who offered a silent apology as he sprinted into the vehicle. He was carrying a shotgun.

"You ready?" said Virgil. Tom nodded.

"Can I go with you?" T.J. asked his father, who shook his head and motioned to his brother to start driving. Virgil furrowed his brow.

"Shit, Tom, we don't need that, do we? I got my pistol if we need it."

Tom's cold, grey eyes settled on Virgil, then on T.J. He half-stood and handed the gun over to his son, patting him on the shoulder.

"Run this in there to your mama, all right? Be careful, now. Don't run."

T.J. took the gun and paced back up to the house. Erlene began to cry, flinging her tiny hands to her head and clamping her ears.

"What's going on?" asked T.J., laying the gun on the kitchen table.

"Nothing," said his mother. "Go get us some water, would you, T.J.? Your sister's hungry. And don't dilly-dally. If you think you're old enough to go with your father on things like this, then you're certainly getting old enough now where I should be able to *depend* on you for--"

"I know!" snapped T.J., jerking up the water pail and marching down the hill to avoid another lecture.

Marching to the well, T.J. listened to the corn fields. The husky sound of a guitar drifted over them. He let the coarse chords dance in the folds of his mind as he drew the water. A soft breeze blew from the east. As he turned to face it he could feel the cold beads of sweat gather on the back of his neck. T.J. thought of Zipporah sometimes when he went to the well. Not many people remembered that Moses had met Zipporah at a well. Usually when the preacher went on about a well he referred to Rebekah or maybe Joseph, but never Zipporah.

T.J. hefted the full pail and cut through the cornfield to Willie and Nattie's place. He wouldn't take long.

Willie and Nattie Latham lived in an old, converted corn crib on the edge of the Latham estate. They were descendants, T.J. had been told, of slaves his great-grandfather Henry Latham had inherited from his father and brought down with him from Virginia before the Civil War. Willie's mother had continued on as a house servant after the War. Freedom doesn't mean much when you have no means, T.J. had heard Willie say, attempting to explain why they hadn't simply left. The ex-slaves kept on doing pretty much as they always had. T.J.'s great-grandfather hadn't even bothered to tell them about the Emancipation. They eventually caught the news, of course, but it would have been gratifying to have heard it come from the lips of Henry Latham himself, Willie had told T.J. many times.

T.J. didn't know exactly what generation Willie and Nattie represented, or how many there had been in the Latham family, but he did know that they were all that were left of a group that had once exceeded 40. Most had moved north. Willie and Nattie remained behind to help Taz, T.J.'s grandfather, with what was left of the old farm. For a time, they raised a family on the land. T.J. had played with Willie and Nattie's son, Briscoe, when they were both babies. But Briscoe died of a fever when he was nine. For some reason, Nattie was never able to conceive again.

Willie's latest passion was the guitar. Someone had traded a six-stringer for an old, half-dead mule Pappy had given Willie in lieu of pay on a crop two years ago.

He wasn't good at it. Willie could often be heard banging away, on into the night, particularly when Tom went off and Willie knew he wouldn't be bothering anyone. Tom didn't care for Willie's guitar playing, or anyone else's.

It was always the same song, with variations here and there. T.J. couldn't make out the words. They were all slurred and slushed together. Willie seemed to strike the instrument as much as he was plucking it; almost like the guitar was percussion rather than a string instrument.

T.J. could hear Willie croon as he cozied up to the front porch:

"Baby, set my pony, settle my black bear
Ready set my pony, settle my black bear
I won't pay no rattle where it's worth-o-while."

Or something close to that. T.J. couldn't make much sense of it.

"You're getting better, Willie," said T.J.

"Hello, son!" said Willie. "Your daddy let you stop workin' long enough come down here?"

"He don't know. Don't tell," T.J. said, putting his finger to his lips. Willie winked at him. T.J. put the water pail to one side.

"Where's Nattie?"

"She don' wanna listen to no guitar," he said, thrusting a large black hand in no particular direction. "She don' much care for the blues, son. You see I got all six strings, now? Them is catguts, you see that?"

T.J. nodded and smiled. He'd always liked Willie. The spring on the screen door creaked as Nattie ambled out onto the porch.

"Hoo! I can finally come outside. We finally gets us some peace and quiet out here!" she said, wiping the sweat from the folds in her forehead. "Why, hello, Mr. T. J. Latham!"

"Hello, Nattie. Is Willie bothering you with all this racket?"

"Child, ever since this nigger heard that ol' Charley Patton song he just cain't get it out of his fool head," she said. "What's that song called, Willie?"

"*Pony Blues*," he grunted. She knew damn well what song it was.

"Pony Blues! That's the one," she said. "Lawd! Them ponies oughta be dead by now, he's beat 'em plumb to death! It's all I hear."

"Don't you listen to her, T.J." said Willie, winking at T.J. and leaning in conspiratorially. "She just don' like that one part that say, um, '*Brownskin woman —*'"

Nattie crossed over and popped Willie on the shoulder with the back of her hand.

"I tol' you don' be singing that damn foolishness in my house!" she said.

Nattie wrenched away his guitar tossed it over T.J.'s right shoulder. Willie winced as it skidded across the dirt.

"Ain't nothin' but a bunch of noise, nohow. You don't even know what to do with it, old man!"

Willie sighed and lifted himself from his rocker, shaking his head as he shuffled off the porch and into the dust.

"She keeps chunking it and I keep fixing it up," he said, picking up the guitar and brushing it off. He held it up to the sunlight to inspect it and gave Nattie the evil eye.

"That's two strings you done broke," he said.

Willie tucked the guitar under his arm, patted down his overalls, and began to sing *a capella* as he plied his way back to the porch:

"And a brownskin woman like something fit to eat,
Brownskin woman like something fit to eat.
But a jet black woman, don't put your hands on me!"

Nattie slapped him again and tugged at his guitar, landing a few more strikes before throwing up her clenched fists in a snarl of frustration.

"And I won't, neither, you old fool!" she said, slamming the screen door on the way back inside.

Willie put his large hands on T.J.'s back as he leaned over and whispered.

"T.J., I done tol' your daddy, when this next crop comes in I'm goin' to Chicago and be a singer. Or a worker. Get a job. Something. I gots to have me something. I cain't work on shares no mo. There ain't no profit in it."

41

T.J. nodded but didn't say anything. Willie had been talking of leaving ever since he'd known him. He knew it was all bluster.

As Willie eased back into the straw-bottom chair, his eyes locked onto something in the distance. He squinted as T.J. turned around to get a look.

"Is that old Peg Leg? That's Peg Leg, ain't it?" said Willie.

T.J. shielded his eyes from the setting sun.

"John Davis? What's he want?" said T.J.

"Another handout, most likely. Your mama knows how to handle folks like Peg Leg. He should know better than to come around here."

T.J. looked back to his house, where his mother was hanging clothes. She gesticulated to John Davis, who looked pitiful with his wooden leg poking out of his tattered, blue trousers. T.J. wondered what the old man wanted this time. He always had some sort of sob story.

T.J.'s mother motioned for the children to go inside as she pointed Peg Leg down the road. T.J. couldn't hear what was being said. But he could see Peg Leg, hat in hand, still on the approach. Even though he couldn't decipher the content, his mother's tone was clear, even from this distance. T.J. could hear his mother raise her voice.

He could also hear his little sister, still in the midst of her squall. Shit.

"I'd better go," T.J. said.

"One of these days I'm gonna learn you how to play, T.J. You like that?"

"I sure would," he said. "But I'm afraid I don't have much talent."

"Never stopped *him*," Nattie said as she clanged a pot on the table and whipped out the potato knife.

T.J. grabbed the pail of water and ran back up the hill as fast as his legs could carry him. The scowl on his mother's face spoke volumes, although she said not a word.

"I'm sorry," he said, meekly handing over the water. His mother sighed, nodded, and snatched the offering, then hurried into the house to tend to the baby.

T.J. slumped down in the porch rocker and hit the back of his head repeatedly against the chair.

3

When Tom returned home he didn't want to talk about what happened that afternoon at Bije's house. But his slouched shoulders and shortness with the children told everyone what they needed to know.

Erlene started wailing again at supper time. T.J.'s mother had to smuggle her out of the room as Tom massaged his temples.

Collier, 8, was oblivious to his father's frustration as he kept tugging at his shirt, asking the same question repeatedly. *The motorcycle story, Daddy. The motorcycle story. Tell us the motorcycle story. The motorcycle one. Please, Daddy.*

T.J. didn't like the motorcycle story. Besides being told too often, it was never told well. T.J. felt that something important was being left out.

Collier squeezed his father's shoeshine box between his thighs and thrust up his gangly arms as if he were astride the now-legendary bike.

"Brrrrrrrmmmm!" he said "Brrrrrrmmmmmrrrrm!" Beryl laughed and pushed Collier playfully. Tom rose from

43

the supper table, scraped his scraps and dunked his dishes in the wash bucket. He splashed some water on his face and fumbled for a rag. Tom muttered something under his breath as he wiped his delicate, hairless hands on his trousers.

T.J. eyed Tom intently. His father's icy eyes scanned the countertops.

"Did Virgil take the goddamn newspaper again?" he finally said.

The children froze. Collier's eyes dilated. Grady, 14, swallowed the penny he had been wrapping under and around his tongue. He told no one.

Tom knew he would have to make amends for the swearing. He asked Grady to call Lois and Erlene back into the house. There was a long sigh and a bit of quiet as their father picked up the poker and prodded the embers and hot orange ash. For a moment his mind wandered lost in the flicker of the flames.

"I am that I am that I am that I am," he mumbled. Tom tossed the poker aside with a *clang* and squatted into his checkerboard chair.

"Well," he said, warming to the fire, "y'all remember what I said about Leo Frank, the Jew."

The children took their usual spots on the floor. Lois came in from the cold with a giggling Erlene on her hip. They shared a seat in a rocker opposite Tom.

"Oh, are we listening to the Leo Frank story again?" she said, smiling.

Tom raised his chin to the rafters and opened his throat.

"Leo Frank was the Jewish manager of a pencil factory. The building is still there, in Atlanta, going out towards Austell, right across the river, up on the hill, on the right. And

44

little Mary Phagan worked there, y'all remember, at that same pencil factory."

T.J. inhaled the sweet smoke and put his eyes at rest. He wished to leave. He didn't like this story.

"Anyway, the girl – she was a beautiful little girl; they ran her picture in the newspapers for weeks -- she came in on a Saturday to get her pay. And I believe it was a Sunday they found her … they found her…"

T.J. opened his eyes again as his father stopped and stared into the fire.

"You know about Dinah," he said. This pricked T.J.'s ears. He'd never heard his father mention Dinah before, or at least not in connection with the Leo Frank story.

"Jacob's daughter, Dinah. A beautiful girl. She was out like Mary Phagan, running errands. And Schechem, a foreign prince of the country, he took her and lay with her, and defiled her, so the Book says."

"Tom — " said Lois, her face contorted into a frown of disapproval.

"And little Mary Phagan, she was strangled to death, with a cord wrapped around her throat, in the basement of that building. Leo Frank, her boss, the manager of that pencil factory, that little Jew, was the only one that was in the building at the time."

T.J.'s father stopped again, squinted, and placed his palm flat against his forehead.

"Tell about the motorcycle," Collier said.

"Shh!" said Grady, pulling his brother onto his lap.

"And you remember," Tom said, "what happened to Schechem? He told his father he had to have Dinah. She had to become his wife. And so his father sought out her father, Jacob. But Jacob heard what had happened. So here comes

45

Schechem's father, saying, 'My son longeth for your daughter: I pray you give him her to wife.' Give us your women and we will give you ours. We'll dwell here together as brothers in this land.

"But Dinah's brothers, they answered Schechem's father deceitfully. This prince had defiled their sister, and this they could not forgive. They were not brothers, after all, but a separate people. So they said to him, 'We cannot do this thing, to give our sister to one that is uncircumcised,' for that was forbidden by God.

"But, if ye will be as we be, that every male of you be circumcised; then will we give our daughters unto you, and we will take your daughters to us, and we will dwell with you, and we will become one people.'

"So every male in that city of Schechem's was circumcised. And on the third day, when they were sore from the circumcisions, Dinah's brothers took up their swords. They came to the city...

"Leo Frank, the Jew, he was sentenced to die on June 22, 1915. To die. And the governor, John Slaton, commuted that sentence to life in prison. Well, the people all over the country jumped the governor about it. His word to them was, 'I remember a man who was hanged who was absolutely innocent, and I would never have that kind of a charge lain against me. Therefore I'm commuting his sentence.' And they laid siege to the governor's mansion and ran him out of the state of Georgia.

"And Dinah's brothers, what did they do? They entered Schechem's city and they smote all the males. They slew Hamor, Schechem's father, and they slew Schechem with the edge of the sword, and they took Dinah out of Schechem's house, and they spoiled the city, because

Schechem had defiled their sister, you see. Schechem had defiled their sister.

"And the Book says they took the sheep, and their oxen, and their asses, and that which was in the city and that which was in the field. All their wealth. All their little ones. Their wives. They spoiled them, and took them with the edge of the sword. Killed them.

"Thomas," interrupted Lois with a look of concern. Tom nodded and gazed into the fire once again.

"It's all in the Bible. It's Bible stories. Jacob reproved them," he said. "But his sons said, 'Should he deal with our sister as with a harlot?'

"So, then, what about Leo Frank? Twenty-five men, most from Marietta, went down to Milledgeville, in Baldwin County. That's the state prison where Leo Frank was being held. And me and your mama and Eloise were down there. I was the superintendent of the state boy's reformatory at that time. Juvenile delinquents."

"Uncle Edgar got you that job, didn't he?" asked T.J. Tom nodded without comment.

"The boys from throughout the state were sent there for correctional training. But that wasn't my philosophy. I treated it like it was a regular school. And they respected that. They called me Professor. 'Professor Latham.' That's how I got my name, see, that the boys and girls all still call me to this very day. The boys had a certain number of hours they had to study. And then I let them work. They cultivated the area. And the prison official furnished guards to watch them when they were out in the field.

"Anyway, those men came down there and cut the telephone wires and knocked out the transformers so there'd be no lights in the prison.

47

"And they went to our place -- we were in our nightclothes -- and they took me to the prison with my keys and went in the gate, because they had a big gate, a big fence all the way around the prison. And that's where the reform school was, you see."

"Were you scared, Mama?" asked Grady.

"I was," she said. "You can imagine waiting there, not knowing what was going to happen to your father. Yes, let me tell you, I was scared."

"And the men, they went in the front door of the prison and into the guard room," said Tom. "And there they found the guard asleep. And they aroused him and they put the guard and me in a cell right next to the guard's office. And they took the key, of course, and yanked out Leo Frank, and they carried him up to Marietta. He tried to put his clothes on, but they said not to bother with that.

"Now, the guards weren't stupid. They thought this kind of thing might happen. And the guard showed me where they kept a real stiff wire that they laid alongside of the cell in the guardroom, in the guard's office. And we got that thing through the bars and we used it to open the drawer in the desk and drag out the keys where we could get out of the cell.

"I had one of those red, high-wheel, Indian V-twin motorcycles, with white wheels. She was a thing of beauty. And I rode that motorcycle all the way over to Barnesville to notify the sheriff that Leo Frank had been kidnapped from the prison. And—"

"Tell us about the curves!" Collier said.

"The curves!" giggled Grady, like a boy five years younger.

48

Tom smiled for the first time that day and leaned Collier over to the left. Erlene squealed and clamored down from her mother's lap and over to her father, her chubby arms outstretched.

"Well, they had curves to negotiate, of course," said Tom, scooping up Erlene and plopping her down on the knee next to Collier, "and I had to LEAN THAT THING IN —"

He jolted Collier and Erlene, first in one direction, then another.

"I had LEAN IN to the left, and LEAN IN to the right!"

Tom could barely hear himself now over the roars and giggles.

"And I had to LEAN BACK IN thisaway, and LEAN IN thataway."

Collier doubled over in laughter. He smiled to his mother and T.J. noted that Collier had lost another tooth.

"And I was negotiating thisaway and negotiating thataway," Tom said.

Erlene, in her enthusiasm, flopped off her father's knee and onto the wood floor. After a befuddled scratching of her head and a look of slight disorientation, Erlene howled as she ambled back to the safety of her mother's arms. Lois scowled at Tom as she scooped up Erlene and kissed her head.

"But you didn't save him," T.J. said.

His father sobered and straightened.

"No, I couldn't save him," he said.

"Leo Frank was hanged on a tree in an oak grove right outside Marietta. They tried to get him to confess, but he wouldn't do it. There was 25 or 30 men, including a sheriff, some clergy men. He said he was innocent. He asked the men to take his wedding ring back and give it to his wife. They

49

threw a rope over an old oak tree and hung him right there. No one was ever arrested."

"I remember," said Lois. "Picture postcards of the lynching were sent out all over the state."

"And that's when we moved back to Haralson County," said T.J.

"That's when we moved," said Tom.

"Were you scared?" asked Grady. "Were you scared they'd come again and lock you up?"

"I recognized one of them. You could tell by the shoes. I knew that man's shoes. And he knew I knew it. We couldn't stay there. I turned in my resignation and your uncles helped build us this house here. And that's the end of the story. And now it's bed time."

"And what happened to Dinah?" asked T.J.

"What?"

"I said what happened to Dinah?"

Tom thought about the question for a moment, searching his mind as if he were rifling through an old desk drawer.

"You know, son, I don't know," he said. "I don't know that the Book ever says what happened to Dinah."

T.J. nodded.

"That's all right," he said. "Good night."

4

It wasn't fall yet, so T.J. was able to stay warm with just some long underwear and a single blanket.

"I wish we still had that motorcycle," said Grady. "I'd drive it all over the place, T.J. I wonder why Dad didn't keep it?"

"I don't know," T.J. said. "It probably got tore up or something."

"T.J., you reckon we'll ever get a car like Uncle Bije?"

"I don't reckon we ever will get a car," T.J. said. "We don't have no need for one. We live right across from the school and the church. Everyone we know lives within a mile."

"We could use it to go into town," said Grady. "Think about how fast we could go! I wonder if Uncle Bije will take us on a ride?"

"It ain't much," said T.J.

Grady perked up.

"You been in his car?"

T.J. quickly realized he'd made a misstep.

"Naw, but I heard Everett Sloan talking about it."

"Everett Sloan's daddy's got one?"

"Naw. He just got to ride in one. It didn't sound like much to me."

"Well, T.J., when I get grown, I'm getting me a car. Or a motorcycle. Maybe both. I'll get rich in the railroad like Uncle Taz or be a lawyer like Uncle Edgar and I'll buy me a car and a motorcycle and we'll go riding, T.J. We'll go all over Georgia. We'll go down to Savannah and see the beach. The ocean. How about that, T.J.?"

"Hm?"

"I said how about that?"

"Sounds nice, Grady," T.J. said. "It's time you got to sleep, now. Shh!"

T.J. waited patiently for signs of sleep from his little brother. It was always difficult to get him to shut up, but once Grady's mouth ceased, all outward signs of activity soon

51

subsided, as if the mouth powered the body instead of the other way around.

Then, cautiously, when T.J. heard the breathing slow, he arched his head up and peered over at Grady. He listened for his father, who had been keeping ever later hours since leaving the school. T.J. heard nothing but low murmurs and the occasional punctuated laugh from the kitchen.

He reached up under his hay mattress and felt around in the darkness. T.J. felt the sharp edge he was looking for and pulled out a large envelope, emptying the contents onto his mattress.

There were three worn pictures. T.J. had committed all of them to memory -- every line and curve.

The first was a post card T.J. had received from a friend who moved to California two years ago. It showed a striking young woman with a dark, bob haircut, severe, no bangs, hair swept back but curving in gracefully at the cheekbone, piercing gaze, no hint of a smile. T.J. felt as if she were looking straight through him. Her hands were bent at the wrists and tucked into her coat pocket, playfully. She wore a black coat, much like a man's, with a handkerchief tucked into the front pocket. She wore a white shirt under the jacket, but the collar was rumpled like she'd just rolled out of bed.

T.J. had only ever seen two picture shows at the Buffalo matinee, and one of them had starred Louise Brooks. *Beggars of Life* it had been called, an old silent. He'd liked it so much he'd snuck back to see it a second time. He remembered it was about her hoboing across America. She had killed some old man who had wanted to get a little too friendly with her, and she went on the lam. But even though

52

she posed as a boy, it wasn't long before she was found out and more men wanted to rape her.

The second photo in his secret envelope was one he'd torn from a copy of the *San Francisco Chronicle*, a newspaper his Uncle Edgar had brought back from his many travels. "Ankle Watch Introduced for Femininity by Movie Folks," the headline read. Louise Brooks sat there with a different kind of haircut, this time with bangs, still staring right at the camera with wide open eyes, but this time she had a more relaxed pose, showing plenty of leg. The legs had to be revealed to properly display the product, the ankle watch. How convenient, T.J. thought. He had never heard of a woman wearing such a thing, but he was fascinated with the idea. *"Louise Brooks, film player, and her latest, the ankle 'wrist' watch, or ankle watch,"* said the caption to her left. An inset photo showed a close-up of her lovely foot. "All she has to do to check the time is bow down or hold her foot high in the air."

The third photo was his favorite, and the one he could get in trouble for having if his parents ever stumbled across it. Albert Previtt had stolen it from his father, who had it stashed away in the bathroom under a floorboard. The photo was all tinted blue. At the top it said, "Artists and Models Magazine." It was page 15. But T.J. didn't have the magazine, just the one page. The caption under the photo read, *"LOUISE BROOKS ... Miss Brooks's beauty is a nightly pleasure to patrons of Ziegfield's Follies."* T.J. had heard that she had been a Follies dancer before going to Hollywood. She'd played a role like that in the other movie he'd seen of hers, *Canary Murder Case.* She'd worn a dress of feathers and had a nasal 'New Yawk' accent, which had sullied the image T.J. had constructed of her in the temple of his mind, but not entirely. In this photo,

53

she was in profile, her right arm extended with some type of long, flowing robe or curtain draped over it, her hand fending off some invisible intruder. She covered her breasts with a large fan held in her left hand, but other than that she was nude. She stood on her tippy toes like she was wearing high heels, and her jutting hip was divinity itself. She wore a pearl necklace choker around her neck. T.J. studied this picture every night, if he could manage it, until the footsteps came from the kitchen and his dad checked in with his nightly lamp-in, or until Grady coughed unexpectedly, or Erlene woke up the household with her squalling. There were always interruptions. But this was the closest thing to private time T.J. could manage. Not every night was successful. Some nights there wasn't sufficient moonlight to see the pictures, and candles made his mother suspicious. She could always smell them.

But tonight everything was working in his favor. The moon was out, the parents were still laughing by the fireplace, and Grady was fast asleep.

So T.J. held the picture at a slant with his left hand to catch the moonbeams as his right hand reached under the bedsheets and he grew warm with his thoughts.

CANTO IV

I enter on the deep and savage way.

Chapter Four

1

The Philadelphia Baptist Church was four bare walls,
16 pews, and a pulpit. The whitewashed boards were as
naked and splintered as the souls saved there each Sunday.
The church smelled of mildew, dust, and sweat.

The main reason T.J. looked forward to church each
Sunday had little to do with God or Jesus or the Holy Spirit,
although he rejoiced in all holiness and looked forward to the
day he could count himself among the saved. His thoughts
lingered mostly on Irene McConnell, who sat two pews up
and to the right. He had committed every mole and freckle on
her watermelon-smooth skin to memory.

Preparing for church as a child had been a relatively
simple affair – two scoops of pomade and a pair of Sunday
overalls. But these days T.J. wore a tie and button-up shirt,
which made him sweat in the tight confines of the sanctuary.
He was always careful to stay at arm's length of Irene so as
not to offend her with his bouquet.

Irene had curly, chestnut hair and brown eyes that
were three miles deep. Aunt Lillie startled T.J. when she
tapped him playfully on the shoulder as she and Uncle Victor
took a seat one pew back. T.J. nodded politely, without
looking. Irene was searching for a hymnal. T.J. wanted to
offer his but was too far away from her to make the offering
seem anything but desperate. So he watched, helpless as a
cuckold, as Carl Bishop smiled at her and offered his.

*Now, of all people to be in this place. What was Carl Bishop
doing here? And why was he sitting behind Irene?*

56

Brother Griffith, a bloated, red man with trousers two sizes too small, leaned over the pulpit to Rufus Goldin on the first pew and whispered, placing his puffy right hand on the old man's shoulder, squeezing as his left hand remained on the Bible.

Rufus Goldin began to sing "The Old Rugged Cross" and everyone gradually joined in. T.J. watched in silent satisfaction as Irene shook her head politely and passed Carl's hymnal back to him.

Preacher Griffith ambled back to the pulpit. T.J. didn't understand how he could still ride the circuit after all these years. The man, so far as T.J. could tell, didn't have a real home. He would just stay overnight in the houses of his congregations as he went from town to town. He made it to Philadelphia Church about once a month. Brother Griffith stayed with the Lathams a number of times and usually entertained the children with Bible stories for hours at a stretch. It was like he had the whole word and world of God at his immediate command, T.J. thought. Person-to-person, Brother Griffith could mesmerize, but the Sunday sermons were much less impressive. T.J. guessed he delivered pretty much the same sermons from Sunday to Sunday, town to town.

"Good morning my brothers and sisters and, hallelujah, are we here to praise the Lord? Am I in church this morning? *I said who is here to praise the Lord Jesus Christ this morning?* Who is here to praise their Lord and Savior Jesus Christ this morning?"

The answer came back in the form of nods, grunts, hands thrust into the air with open palms, and a chorus of "yes sirs" and "amens."

"I knew there was a few people awake in here," said Brother Griffith.

Today the sermon was on Deborah, but it might as well have been on anything. Brother Griffith spoke on the latest news from Australia, where some lady in a de Havilland Moth had flown from England in just 19 days. That segued into Deborah and her battle against Sisera, but by that time T.J.'s mind had started to wander back to Irene. She was wearing a blue bow and white lace in her hair. T.J. wondered if she intentionally tried to match the bow to the color of her eyes.

T.J. kept looking over at Carl, usually during the "amens," when no one would notice. Strangely, he couldn't catch Carl stealing a glance at Irene, not even once. Instead, Carl seemed to be looking back in T.J.'s direction, but never for long. It was almost as if he were stealing glances, too -- only T.J. couldn't figure out what he was looking at.

"God said, '*Show me a woman who's got some guts!*'" T.J. heard Brother Griffith shout. He wondered what the chapter and verse for that quotation might be.

Irene scratched her nose exquisitely.

"The stars in their courses fought against Sisera! The river of Kishon swept them away! *O my soul! Thou hast trodden down strength!*"

The people of Philadelphia frothed, getting genuinely excited now, standing up in the pews and clapping and rattling the rafters. T.J. shouted out at all the appropriate cues.

"The mountains melted-ah from before the Lord-ah!" sang Brother Griffith, spitting and sweating and panting like a dog in the summertime.

"Awake, awake, Deborah! Awake, awake! Even if we can get the credit, it costs more to grow the cotton, yes Lord, than we can get for it - can I hear someone praise the Lord in here? And it pays more to turn that corn into whiskey than it does to sell it to eat - *do I have a witness?* My Lord, they are burning corn for fuel in the county courthouse down the way because it's cheaper than buying the coal! But never doubt that we can still defeat the enemy!"

T.J. continued to monitor Carl, who looked pale, in stark contrast to the red, wet bodies chanting all around him. White Charlie Summerville, Jr., who was standing next to Carl, clutched his shoulder as Carl appeared to falter, but Carl shook his head and shrugged him off. Carl pounded a clenched fist against his chest as chants of "Power! Power! Power!" pulsed through the pews and pulpit.

Carl stooped over, stroking his throat, then collapsed onto the cold, pine floor.

Brother Griffith, suspecting that another of his flock had succumbed to the sweet power of the Lord, swept through the throng, who cradled Carl and fanned him with their hymnals. But T.J. could tell that this was not just another young man overcome with the Holy Spirit. Something was genuinely wrong.

Brother Griffith kneeled over Carl and pressed his buttered-up hands against Carl's cheeks. He whispered something to Carl, but all Carl could do was nod and point to his throat.

"It's all right, brother," T.J. heard Brother Griffith tell him.

Without saying another word, Brother Griffith hoisted Carl over his hunched shoulders and hurtled them both through the front doors.

He laid Carl down on the front steps and commanded the congregation to stand back. T.J. caught a glimpse of

59

Brother Griffith unbuttoning Carl's collar to lay his sweaty palms against Carl's naked chest. T.J. tried to find Irene to see if she was watching all of this.

Dr. Sanford clambered through the crowd and knelt down beside Brother Griffith. He put an ear to Carl's chest and told him to relax and breathe. T.J. suddenly remembered that Carl had suffered a number of asthma attacks in school. Most of the other children with asthma had grown out of it at an early age, but not Carl. He would often miss school because of it, even as he got older.

T.J. wasn't close enough to hear much of the conversation between Griffith, Dr. Sanford, and Carl. But he did hear Carl say one thing as he struggled for breath.

"The Lord's been dealing with me," he said. "The Lord, he's been dealing with me, Brother. Amen."

2

T.J. crept behind Beryl as she made her way through the throng to kneel at Carl's side.

"Hey."

"Hey, Beryl," said Carl, closing up his collar. Carl smiled weakly at Beryl as his labored rasps rattled his thin frame.

"You want some water?" she asked. He shook his head. Carl motioned to T.J., who still had his eye fastened on Irene as she followed her mother back inside the church.

Carl swatted Beryl and motioned to T.J. again. She turned around and elbowed her brother.

"I think Carl wants your attention, if you can quit looking at Irene long enough," she said.

T.J. frowned in embarrassment.

60

"I wasn't looking at her," he protested. He knelt down beside Carl, who laid his hands on T.J. and drew him in.

"You got any whiskey?" Carl wheezed.

"What are you talking about? Do you still know where you are, Carl?" T.J. said.

"Naw, not here, at your house!" Carl said.

"Mama's got some, I think," said T.J. "She keeps it in the kitchen cupboard."

Carl nodded and patted T.J. on his forearm.

"Help me up, son," he said.

T.J. glanced back at the church steps as he tugged Carl's arms. Irene was no longer there, but his parents were. Lois cackled as a grinning Uncle Virgil whispered something in her left ear. Tom ushered his other brother, Uncle Victor, through the church door, eyeing him with a practiced earnestness.

Uncle Victor was a man of average height, thick middle and thinning hair, with an oblong face that rested upon his wide, wet neck like an upright egg. He took after T.J.'s grandmother, after whom he had been named. Victor was not a fat man, but his body was yellow and bloated, like a festering breakfast sausage. His legs were thin and pencil-like. Uncle Victor was almost always on the verge of tears, or so it seemed to T.J. Today was no exception. He had a lot to cry about. Not only was he a drunk, but the latest rumor was that he had fathered a child out of wedlock. Victor's daughter Birdy followed close behind, keeping a wary eye on Tom.

Tom draped a thin arm over Victor's bulbous shoulders and stared deeply into his eyes, saying words that only Victor could hear. Victor accepted the words with small nods of agreement, silent grace and humility, like a convicted man standing before his judge, piously awaiting his sentence.

61

Lois cackled again and pushed Virgil away playfully as Irene exited the church with her mother. The mother's eyes locked in on T.J. like a cat ready to pounce. T.J. instinctively evaded her hungry gaze. Carl shuffled to his feet and smiled again at Beryl, who busied herself with slapping the grass and dirt from Carl's church pants. She seemed to like it just a little too much.

"T.J. Latham!" Mrs. McConnell shouted. T.J. smiled and nodded, thrusting his long, thin hands into the tight shallows of his pockets. He didn't know what to do with the upper half of his hands, which were left to protrude awkwardly at the wrists as the fingers stiffened in the confines. His stomach contracted. Irene followed her mother to T.J. like an obedient yellow duckling.

"Carl Bishop. Are you all right? You smotherin' again?"

"Yes'm," he said. "Brother Griffith's preachin' knocked the stuffin' outta me, I reckon."

Mrs. McConnell smiled politely. Her teeth looked cold and yellow.

"It's good to see you at church," she said to Carl. She didn't squeeze his arm, which would have been the friendly thing to do. "You tell your father we miss him since he started going to – where does he go now, Carl? Mt. Zion?"

"Mountain View, ma'am," said Carl.

"Mountain View, that's right. Ever since that unfortunate dust-up you boys caused with Mr. Evans. You boys should have known better and should have kept away from those hens. But that's all water under the bridge, I guess. You tell your daddy we miss him since he started going to Mountain View. You tell him there's plenty of women here who need a good man like your daddy. You make sure and tell him that."

"Yes ma'am," said Carl. Beryl smiled absently at no one in particular.

"T.J., I need to speak with you when you can sit a spell," she said, squeezing his right hand with her dry, painted digits. "Maybe you could come over for supper or sit down and help me and Irene with the preserves."

T.J. shot a nervous glance at Irene, who was studying a nearby oak tree.

"We could make you some real nice homemade ice cream, T.J.," said Mrs. McConnell. "You think about it. You let me know when you get a free afternoon. We have things to talk about."

"Yes ma'am," he said. Mrs. McConnell flew to the preacher to say a good word about the sermon, but Irene lagged behind as she continued to study the bark pattern on the oak. It seemed to T.J. as if she were inviting him to speak a word or two to her. He had nothing to say, but he couldn't allow himself to miss his opportunity.

"That's a nice tree," T.J. said. He immediately felt stupid for saying it and wished he could suck the words back into his mouth. But they were gone out into the world now, it was too late.

"It's okay, I guess," she said, shrugging. "They's ants on it."

"Really? Where?" asked T.J., moving in closer. He was sweating out his stench of yellow awkwardness in tiny little beads and he wondered if Irene could smell it on his skin.

"Right there," she said. "I can't tell if it's the red ones or if it's the black ones. Them black ones, they don't bite."

"Really?" said T.J. "I thought it was the red ones that didn't bite."

Irene rolled her eyes and smiled.

"Don't you know anything?" she said.

"Guess not," said T.J., shrugging. "Sure is a good tree. Reckon how old it is?"

Irene shrugged and raised herself up onto her toes.

"I heard you can count them rings in the trunk and that'll tell you," she said. "But then you'd have to chop it down."

"Wouldn't want to do that," said T.J. There was a long moment of awkward silence. T.J. felt compelled to fill it, so he took a deep breath and blurted out the first thing that came to mind.

"You know, I reckon oak is my all-time favorite kind of tree," he said. He once again regretted having said anything. He winced inwardly. But Irene didn't notice.

"I guess mine is maple," she said breezily. "I just love syrup. Not molasses syrup, though. I can't stand molasses syrup. Only the store-bought kind. That's the kind I like. But I guess most of the folks around here like the molasses kind just fine."

Her mother approached after finishing with the preacher and motioned for Irene to follow. At the same moment, Carl snuck up on T.J. from behind.

"You ready, boy?" asked Carl, tugging at T.J.'s shirtsleeve. T.J. nodded, glanced once more at Irene's laces and bows, and said his goodbyes to Mrs. McConnell. Carl walked T.J. and Beryl back to the Abijah's Model A, which had drawn more than a few admirers, including Virgil and Lois. Virgil orbited the vehicle like he was circling the Kabah.

"Ain't she purty?" Carl said. "Bije got it at a fair price, too."

"This is Abijah's car?" said Virgil.

"Yes sir," said Carl. "He still ain't showed it to y'all yet?"

Virgil didn't answer. He reached out to the smooth, black metal and brushed it piously with his fingertips. He opened his mouth to say something and then stopped, pursing his lips.

Lois spoke softly to Virgil, who gave silent acknowledgment. Beryl pinched lint from Carl's jacket. T.J. silently wondered where his father was.

"Come on, T.J.," Virgil said. "You walking or coming with me?"

"T.J.'s a-goin' with me," said Carl. "And Beryl, too."

"Is that so?" said Virgil. "Where y'all headed?"

"Same place as you, Mr. Latham," said Carl.

"Where's Dad?" T.J. asked his mother.

"He went with Victor," she said, scooping up Erlene just as she was crouching down to retrieve a grasshopper carcass.

"You can go with me to fetch him after dinner," said Virgil. "Beryl, T.J., y'all come on."

"Mr. Latham, there ain't enough room in that T for all y'all," protested Carl. "It's just right across the road yonder. I promise won't nothin' happen."

Virgil sighed and glanced back at his old T. He knew he couldn't squeeze Lois and all her children in his car without making two trips. And even though the distance was short, it had rained the night before and the roads were inches deep in mud.

65

"Mama, I want to go in Uncle Bije's new car," said Collier. "Please, Mama! Can I?"

Grady pinched the upholstery between his fingers and smiled as Collier kicked the tires and pleaded some more.

"You sure you don't mind, Carl?" she asked.

"Naw! Ma'am, you and Mr. Virgil go on up in the T and I'll box up all these tatersacks. We'll get 'em up there."

"All right, then. Keep it slow, Carl, with them children," said Virgil.

"I'm taking Erlene with me," said Lois as she, Virgil and the baby headed to Virgil's Model T.

"Yes sir," said Carl. Beryl beamed as she leaned down to pick up a stick to scrape the mud off the bottom of her shoes before getting in.

T.J. opened the door for Grady and Collier and all three took seats in the rumbleseat as Beryl slid into the front passenger side and squealed with glee.

"Go fast," she urged.

"No, please don't," said T.J. "You'll scare Collier."

"No he won't!" Collier insisted. "I like fast."

"Me, too," said Grady, pressing his palms against the cool leather interior.

"T.J., just try to sit back and relax," said Carl, revving up the engine as some rocks crunched underneath the tires. "Me and you, we're gonna cut loose this afternoon."

"Cut loose?" said T.J. "I gotta go get my Dad with Virgil."

"Naw, fergit about that," said Carl. "I'm gonna show you around some. Let's have some fun!"

"I don't think I can, Carl."

"Leave it to me," said Carl, smiling at Beryl. "I know how to put it t'yer Mama jes right."

3

By the time the Model A pulled up into the Latham driveway, Collier and Grady were engaged in a shoving match over who had nicked the door interior. Carl promised not tell Abijah about it since it was hardly noticeable. But the fight went on, anyway, because it was as good an excuse as any for two brothers to shove and slap one another. T.J, quietly threatened to show their mother the rip and have his little brothers explain to her exactly how it got there. With that, the argument was all over.

Carl and his crew were the first to arrive at the house. The five ambled out of the car and onto the porch. Carl closed in on T.J. as they approached the front door. Lining the porch were empty buckets of various sizes.

"Is the door open?" Carl asked, grabbing the latch. T.J. nodded and they moved inside.

"What is it?" T.J. asked as Carl gave the kitchen a quick perusal.

"Is this the cupboard?" he asked. Suddenly T.J. remembered the whiskey. Carl offered a toothy grin and pried open the cupboard door.

"What are you gonna do?" asked T.J. Carl put his hand over his lips to shush him.

The whiskey bottle was half-empty. Carl removed the top and tilted back his head as he raised the bottom of the bottle to the roof and washed down its contents.

"Stop that!" T.J. said, slapping the bottle. Two or three swallows sloshed to the floor. Carl shot T.J. a diabolical grin.

"Now look whatcha done," he said. "Yer daddy's gonna smell that, I guarantee."

T.J. reached for the bottle, but Carl yanked it away. T.J. sighed in frustration and reached for the bottle once again, and once more Carl moved away.

"You want this?" he asked.

"I would appreciate it if you would put that back," T.J. said.

"Why, sure," said Carl. "All you had to do was ask."

Carl smiled broadly, fastened the lid back onto the bottle, and placed the bottle back into the cupboard just as Lois entered the front door with a napping Erlene.

"Shh! We drove down the road to get her to sleep so let's don't wake her," Lois whispered. She looked up and saw T.J. fuming at Carl, who stood by the cupboard awkwardly.

"Is something wrong?" she asked.

"Naw, ma'am," Carl said. "T.J. was just volunteering to help me and my daddy git his old wagon out of the mud but I told him he already promised Virgil he'd ride with him to Victor's to git his daddy, so I'll just be a-goin'. It's awful kind of you to offer, though, T.J. I'll just be gittin' on before Daddy thinks I'm tryin' to lay out."

Carl patted T.J. on the back and moved past the cupboard to the front door.

"Can we ride in your car again, Carl?" asked Collier.

"Maybe some other time. I got to git on," he said, scruffing up Collier's hair.

As he moved to the front porch, Lois closed the door and followed him out.

"So your daddy's wagon got stuck last night?" she said.

"Yes'm. He was out picking up ol' Paig Laig. You know John Davis?"

Lois nodded.

"Well, Daddy pulled him outta the ditch again. Drunk, as usual. Daddy gave him a fire to sleep by so he could dry out. That rain came down awful hard last night. But the wagon stuck on the way back. Daddy just threw him on the back of the ol' mule and took him on home."

Lois cracked open the front door and motioned for T.J. to come outside. He was crouched by the cupboard with a wet rag in hand.

"What are you doing?" she asked.

"Nothing," he said, tossing the rag into the sink.

"Why don't you run along with Carl and help with that wagon," she said, dusting off his shoulder.

"But Mama, Carl just—"

"T.J., keep your voice down. I told you Erlene's sleeping. Now you run on and help like I told you. I'll explain to your Uncle Virgil. You go."

T.J. shook his head and descended the steps, making his way to the passenger side. Beryl was still sitting in the passenger seat.

"Get up," said T.J.

"Where y'all going?" she asked, pulling a few strands of red hair behind her ear.

"Nowhere," T.J. said. "Move out. Come on!"

"Can I come?"

"Naw," said Carl. "We're gonna pull a wagon out the mud. You might dirty yerself up."

"Move!" said T.J., opening the door and fuming.

"All right, all right!" she said, thrusting out her leg and kicking T.J. in the shin as she rose. T.J. winced. Carl watched Beryl appreciatively as she folded her arms and stormed up the steps, pouting like a girl half her age. He smiled and got behind the wheel. T.J. slammed the passenger side door shut.

69

Carl started up the engine and drifted down the hill. T.J. simmered.

"Aw, come on, T.J. That was slick, weren't it?"

"What do you mean?"

Carl turned onto the Eaves Bridge Road without saying a word.

"You mean your daddy doesn't have a wagon stuck in the mud?" T.J. asked.

Carl laughed as he pulled the bottle of whiskey from inside his coat.

"Hey, Simon!" T.J. said. "I thought you put that back!"

"I did," said Carl, opening it up and taking another sip.

"You want a swaller?" he asked.

"Take me back," said T.J.

"Now, just hold on a minute, T.J.," said Carl. "This is for my asthma, that's all. Yer mama would understand, if I put it right. And, besides, I got somethin' to show you."

4

The Bishops lived in an old sharecropper house near a spring, about a half-mile from the Lathams. The two-room post-and-beam crouched under the shadow of an ancient, dead walnut tree. The northwest corner of the home was sunken and rotten, and the front porch sagged in the middle like an old pony with a broken back. The house was supported underneath by slim columns of pink and grey rock. Under the home lie a litter of half-completed metal contraptions, termite-infested boards, broken toys and play-purties, snakeskins and rat droppings. The fireplace had begun to separate from the structure in a manner that seemingly defied physics, arching away from the rusted tin roof in a prolonged, sweeping surrender.

John Davis sat on the front porch with an old quilt pulled in close around his shoulders. He was talking quietly to himself as T.J. skipped over the puddles lining the foot trail to the house. Carl just sloshed right through them.

"Daddy let Paig Laig stay here last night on accounta that storm, and my sister Bernice just had a fit, man," Carl said. "She was out this morning beatin' the sheets he slep' in and just a-scrubbin' the pallet. She didn't get no sleep last night a-tall."

"My mama just chases him off," said T.J.

"I can't blame 'er, I guess. Yer mama's a good woman," said Carl. "She's just lookin' out fer you kids."

"She gives him a plate of food every now and then. One time she gave him some of Dad's old clothes," T.J. said.

"It's like this, T.J.," Carl said. "If ya ain't got nothin', ya ain't gotta worry about nobody takin' nothin' from ya."

"You know, we aren't rich, Carl. My dad's a farmer now, just like yours."

"Naw, you ain't like us, T.J.," Carl said.

T.J. followed Carl to the front door. He stopped and nodded at Peg Leg, who nodded in return, still muttering to himself like he was trying to think up some new Riddle of the Sphinx for a new age. Or maybe he was just crazy, like everybody said.

The house, which appeared so hopelessly dreary from the exterior, was resplendent with people and the dance of light. Carl was right: it was nothing at all like the Latham bunker, which was dark, clean, quiet, and cold. Sunlight flittered in through the wallslats, which were papered over with newsprint. Two of Carl's sisters were fussing over how

71

to make a pie. One of his brothers was playing his fiddle while the other tuned his banjo. T.J. recognized the song, *Down Yonder*, a popular tune at the local socials. He also recognized Legs from school, and Nathan Bishop, Carl's younger brother.

The home vibrated with energy and demented chaos. Nothing was in its proper place. Someone had set a fire in a tin bucket in the middle of the room. Carl later explained that was because the fireplace was too dangerous to use anymore. A rusty Coca-Cola sign hung on the wall next to a picture of Jesus that someone had torn from a magazine. The sofa was the back seat of an old touring car.

"Why, hello, young Latham!" shouted a lovely girl who Carl introduced as Alphie. She and Luler were the ones making the pie. It turned out that the pie was just the capper being put on the after-church dinner, and T.J. was welcome to come fix himself a plate when it was all ready.

Legs was making a dulcimer. He asked T.J. if he played.

"Aw, no, no," said T.J. "My mother taught me how to play a few tunes on the piano. That's about all I know how to do."

"That's all right," said Carl. "You know they say all fiddle players and banjo players is going straight to hell."

Carl introduced T.J. to Preston, his oldest brother. He towered over the rest of his siblings and seemed to possess a quiet kind of intelligence that T.J. immediately respected.

"Sit with us a spell and we can help you study on it," Preston said. "It ain't hard to pick a banjer."

T.J. politely declined but said that he'd love to listen in a time or two, if they didn't mind.

Their father was still at church, it turned out. He had stayed for a men's Bible study class while the kids walked back to the house. It was three miles to Mountain View by road, but the family shaved a mile off the trek by cutting through the woods. On muddy days like this one it was actually far easier to take the path through the forest, anyway, since the roads were almost like quicksand. It was tough to keep your shoes on your feet on mornings like this – the mud just sucked them plumb off.

As Nathan launched into a tune T.J. hadn't heard before, Carl motioned for him to follow outside.

"Ever play of Mumbly Peg?" he asked, removing a knife from his pocket, flashing the whiskey.

"Mumbly Peg? What's that?" T.J. asked.

"You got a knife?"

T.J. shook his head.

"Yeah, that figgers." He trotted back inside and T.J. remained on the back porch alone for a moment. Something smelled like shit. Chickens pecked at the grass in the back yard. One of them looked T.J. over, checking to see if he had brought any food out with him. Seeing none was to be had, it moved on. The green hills stretching out toward the horizon looked like piles of dirty laundry.

The back door slammed shut and Carl emerged with a jackknife in each hand. He handed the larger one to T.J.

"All right, let's go," Carl said.

T.J. was a little concerned. Was he going to be asked to skin some animal? To whittle something? To fight it out with Carl to some kind of bloody end?

"Awright, now lissen here," Carl said. "We start at the tip of yer pointy finger. Like this."

73

Carl held his knife vertically, from one index finger tip to the other.

"You just flip it on inta the ground, see," he said.

The knife sailed through the air, turning 180 degrees, and the point landed straight down in the sod between T.J.'s feet. T.J. jumped back and adjusted his glasses.

"Hey, watch it!" he said. Carl laughed as he bent down and retrieved his knife.

"Now you try," he said. T.J. took the knife and tried to hold it just as Carl had, but the blade slipped and he nicked himself, dropping the knife to the ground.

"Damn!" T.J. said, shoving the finger into his mouth.

"S'allright. We won't count that 'un," said Carl, picking up the knife and handing it back to T.J.

"Let's jest start over," he said. "Now, whatcha do, T.J., is you move up from the fangers to wrist, then the elbow, then the shoulder. If I miss one, it's your turn, then. If I get through the whole thang before you, I win."

"That doesn't seem right," said T.J. "If you start first, doesn't that give you the advantage?"

"Yeah, I reckon, but it don't make no sense fer you t'start, 'cause you don't know what in the hell yer doin'," said Carl. "So's you jest foller along, awright?"

Carl sailed through the left and right index finger positions and the left and right wrists. The blade sank straight into the ground like a knife into bread.

"Sometimes I hunt like this, believe it or not," Carl said. "I got me a rabbit once, throwing my knife like 'at."

Carl bent over and retrieved the knife from the soft ground, wiped the blade against his pants, then prepared to advance to the next level, steadying the blade on his elbow.

"You believe 'at?" Carl asked.

74

"That's a purty good shot, that's the truth," T.J. said.

"Naw," said Carl as T.J. repositioned his knife and studied the mark. "I mean you believe I hunt rabbits thataway?" Carl flipped the knife into the air.

"Well, that's what you said, ain't it?" T.J. said.

The blade plunked against the topsoil, landing flat on its side. Carl grimaced as he reached over and plucked up the knife.

"Yer go," he said. "Have at it."

Carl crossed his arms as T.J. grasped the knife precariously between his index fingers, whispered something to himself, and sent it into the air, where it thumped against a rock and skidded across the ground near his feet. Carl barely suppressed a giggle.

"Hrmpf," Carl said, shaking his head. He readied his knife at his elbow again with the confidence of a winner in the making.

"You'd better scooch over, son," he said, motioning with his hand.

T.J. stepped aside just as Carl let the blade fly, finding its mark where his feet had been.

"Wooo!" said T.J. "I think you about got this won, Carl."

"Aw, now, don't give up that easy," said Carl. "Don't you know what the loser hasta do?"

"What?" said T.J. "You didn't say nothing about that."

Carl smiled as he prepared to flip the blade from the opposite elbow.

"What's the loser got to do?" T.J. asked.

Carl stared at T.J. with his dark eyes. "Why should I tell you? You ain't even answered my question."

"What question is that?"

75

Carl let the blade fall. It twisted in the air and fell flat on the ground. Carl scowled.

"Do you believe me or don't you?" he said, picking up the knife and motioning for T.J. to take his turn.

T.J. considered the question, balanced his knife between his fingers, then sent it into the air. The blade took flight with a purpose, arcing through the air with graceful certitude. It sliced the ground neatly, prompting a look of mild surprise from Carl.

"I guess I'll believe what I want to believe," said T.J. "The way you catch your rabbits is your own business."

Carl rolled this over in his mind for a moment then let out a chuckle. He pulled out the whiskey and chugged down the last of it. Carl then wiped his mouth on his dirty sleeve and chunked the bottle off into the woods.

"Mama's gonna notice that's missing, Carl," said T.J. He picked up his knife and set it up against the opposite index finger.

"Naw she ain't," he said. "She'll think yer Daddy drunk it."

"My dad doesn't drink," said T.J. He threw the knife. It fell on the handle with a *clunk*.

Carl smiled again and flung his blade from his elbow. It was as close to a perfect shot as one could hope for.

"That's what you think," Carl said, picking up his knife and preparing for the next-to-last shot, from the right shoulder.

"My dad's a deacon at the church," said T.J. "He hasn't ever took a sip of liquor in his life."

"Is that right?"

"That's right."

"You sure about that?" said Carl, lobbing the blade into the soil once again. It landed perfectly.

"I'm sure," said T.J.

"You're positive?"

"I reckon I know my dad better than you."

"Do you?"

"I'd say so."

"Then say it."

"What?"

"Say it."

"My dad doesn't drink!"

"All right," said Carl. "I'm glad that's cleared up, ain't you?"

T.J. suddenly wondered what he was doing here and how he'd been snookered into it.

"Now, tell me," said T.J. "What does the loser have to do?"

Carl laughed and hit T.J. playfully on the arm.

"Why?" he said. "You thank yer gonna lose?"

With that, Carl's knife plunged to the earth and hit its mark. Game over.

"Okay, it's like this," said Carl. "My knife stays there. But I get three more licks at it, with your'n. Then you gotta crouch down and pull it out whitcher teeth."

"With my teeth?" T.J. said. "I ain't pulling that thing out with my teeth, Carl! There's chickens all in this yard!"

"That's the game, son!" said Carl. "Why you think it's called 'Mumbly Peg'? Yer about to git a mouthful of dirt an' that'll set you t'mumblin' sure enough, son."

With that, Carl extended his hand, motioning for T.J. to give up his knife.

77

"Why do you call me 'son'?" T.J. asked, turning over the blade. "You know I'm a year older than you, Carl."

Carl laughed as he took the knife in hand and let it drop one, two, three times, pounding his knife deeper into the soil with each strike. It was no so deeply embedded in the dirt that it couldn't be seen.

"Why are you doing this, Carl?" asked T.J. "You really expect me to—"

Before T.J. could finish, a slim figure emerged from the woods holding a whiskey bottle. The crooked mouth and severe eyes, in another man, would have seemed fearsome. But in Carl's dad they were just signs of the suffering of a gentle soul.

"Does this belong to one of you boys?" asked Oscar, hoisting the empty bottle.

Carl stood in stunned silence. T.J. saw the fear in Carl's eyes. He knew it wasn't fear that he'd get whipped. This was worse. It was fear of disappointing someone he deeply respected.

T.J. stepped forward.

"Yes sir," he said. "I reckon that's mine, Mr. Bishop."

Oscar nodded and handed the bottle to T.J., but his eyes never left his son.

"I trust you'll put this where it belongs," said Oscar.

"Yes sir," said T.J.

"Carl," he said, moving to the back porch and sliding off his coat. "Come inside when you get a chance. I need to talk to you."

"Oh, he'll be right in, Mr. Bishop," said T.J. "We just have to finish up a game of Mumbly Peg."

"Mumbly Peg?" said Oscar. "Son, haven't I told you about that game? Yer gonna slice off one of yer toes."

"The game's over, anyway, sir," said T.J. "I just got my final three licks and Carl was about to pull up the peg."

Carl's eyes darted to T.J.

"Ain't that so, Carl?" said T.J.

Carl didn't answer. He stared at T.J. for a moment, sizing him up.

"Yeah," he said. "I reckon so."

"Well then, crouch over on all fours and get that peg so's you can come on inside," said Carl's father. "Don't be a sore loser."

"Yes sir," said Carl, slowly getting to his hands and knees.

He looked up at T.J. again with a sneer.

"Go ahead, son," said Oscar. "Don't drag it out. Say, don't you boys know any better than to play this game where the chickens do their business?"

Carl closed his eyes and sank his nose into the dark sludge. He rooted around until he could clamp his teeth around the knife handle. When he came up with it, he spit the knife and a mouthful of shit-soaked dirt at T.J.'s feet.

"That's good," said Oscar. "Now come on inside. And make sure you give that boy his knives back."

"Yeah," said T.J., extending his hand. "Give me back my knives."

Carl's father gently closed the screen door behind him as Carl handed T.J. the two knives.

"I'll just walk home," T.J. said, grinning from ear to ear.

"You gonna walk home totin' that whiskey bottle for everyone to see?" Carl asked.

"Naw," said T.J. "I don't reckon I will."

He handed it over to Carl and smiled.

79

"I reckon you're gonna fill it back up with whiskey and bring it by the house tomorrow."

"Where am I gonna get whiskey?" Carl said.

"Oh, I think you know where to find it," said T.J., turning and walking down the muddy path to the road.

"What'll I tell your mama?" Carl shouted after him.

"Hm?"

"I said what's my reason for showing up at yer house?"

"Oh! Just tell Mama you've come to see Beryl!" shouted T.J.

"What!"

"Beryl!" said T.J. with a wide grin. "Ain't that what you've been comin' by these last few days for, anyhow?"

T.J. spun around and began whistling a tune he was sure Carl wouldn't recognize. His feet were coated in mud but lighter than ever.

5

By the time T.J. trudged up the trail leading to the front porch, his father had returned from Uncle Victor's house. He heard someone shouting as he rounded the corner, and then everyone fell suddenly silent.

His father, his mother, and Virgil were all on the porch. Tom stood facing Lois, hands on his hips, stern. Lois was crying. Virgil sat on the steps, massaging his right leg.

T.J. immediately caught on to the fact that he had interrupted something, but didn't know what to do other than pretend he hadn't noticed. He moved to the door without skipping a beat, careful not to look anyone in the eye.

His mother wiped her nose and called out to T.J. as he put his hand on the latch.

"Wait," she said, pointing at his shoes. "My Lord, T.J. He must've been in six feet deep."

"Six feet deep?"

"Your shoes," she said. "The wagon. You were going to help Carl's father with…"

"Oh!" he said. "Yes, it was, it was stuck in deep. But I didn't – well, they almost had it out by the time I got there. We got there."

T.J. took off his shoes and shook the mud off the edge of the porch.

"Where do you want me to put them?" he asked his mother.

"Just leave them out here for now," she said. "We'll get to them when we can."

T.J. went inside but wished he could remain on the porch. He wanted to know what they were fighting about, after all. But now they were finished, and the silence was deafening.

6

T.J. was surprised to find two of his cousins, Eurinee and Dora, sitting at the kitchen table while Beryl gave them a hair treatment.

"It's called a permanent," Beryl explained.

"A permanent *what*?" T.J. asked.

"A permanent hair style. It curls up your hair."

"*Permanently*? What if you mess it up? She did tell you girls this is the first time she's ever tried anything like this – didn't she?"

Dora and Eurinee exchanged nervous glances. Beryl put a calming hand on Dora's shoulder. They had good reason to be jittery. They and their older sisters, Birdy included, had never been too kind to Beryl as they were growing, so she had good reason to take out her revenge however she pleased. The cousins had always known Beryl was frightened of the water and they often threatened to throw her in during their frequent swims down at the creek. One time the older sisters, Birdy and Peggy, actually succeeded in hoisting Beryl's thin frame up over their heads, but she launched into such an otherworldly, Maenadic fit that they never tried it again. Birdy had described Beryl's reaction as "feral," T.J. recalled. ("Feral," she proudly explained, was a word she'd learned in one of her school lessons just two weeks before.) It was like nothing they had ever seen. Even in church.

Beryl had always had her fits. T.J. attributed it to her red-headedness. He remembered the first time he'd seen one. One day his father and Uncle Virgil went into a swamp near the house to retrieve a black gum tree that had been downed in a storm. They dragged the tree back to the shop and cut sections from the trunk to make a set of wheels. T.J. remembered his father using an auger with a huge wooden handle to drill the holes while Virgil built the body of what would become Beryl's first and only wagon. T.J. remembered that they didn't put a tongue in it, but instead used a small sack, fastening it over one side on the front of the cart. Virgil then dropped a heavy brass yoke on the opposite side.

Tom had purchased a baby bull from a neighbor, and he and Virgil had somehow hit upon the idea of hooking that bull up to a cart to let it pull the little ones around the yard. Beryl had barely begun to walk but she was eager to ride. T.J.

remembered his older sister Eloise putting Beryl in the cart while T.J. begged to pull the bull. He ran along one side while Grady ran along the other and Beryl rode in the cart. T.J. remembered thinking that it was his job to keep the cart from running into the pecan trees and the well shelter. He and Grady would take turns pushing the bull's head to keep it on the straight path. It was so hot and humid that day that the smell of the bull filled the air like a heavy fog.

It didn't take long for the bull to outrun both T.J. and his brother. The cart toppled as the calf kicked up the side of a hill, and Beryl came tumbling out the back, screaming. Tom ran up to retrieve her, brushing her off but finding no scratches. T.J. remembered hearing laughter coming from the house. He turned to see his mother and Uncle Virgil bent over in a raucous belly laugh. T.J.'s father smiled and waved to let them know Beryl was all right. The sun had been bright that day.

Beryl soon learned that she could command quite a bit of attention from her fits, and it didn't take much from then on for her to launch into a wail. But it didn't keep her from being switched a time or two.

The thing that would cause T.J.'s sister to make the most fuss was when he and Grady would peek in on her and Eloise at bath time. Their mother would heat the water in a large tub and place it behind the pantry door to separate the girls from the boys. But T.J. and Grady would peek around the corner, sending Beryl into a high-pitched squeal. Eloise and their mother were constantly trying to settle her down, but it was no use.

Beryl had read all about how to apply permanents in one of her magazine subscriptions, but apparently something essential had been left out. Despite a whole afternoon of trying, the permanents did not take.

"That's all right," said Dora. "I wasn't sure I wanted one, anyway."

Beryl promised to take them to Wallace's store at the earliest possible opportunity to get the job done properly. She would pay for it out of her own money that she'd been saving from her home-made tufted work for the folks along Peacock Alley.

"Every girl deserves to look beautiful for her man," said Beryl.

"But we ain't got no man," protested Eurinee.

Eurinee always said that it was her name that scared the boys away. It sounded too much like 'urine,' a fact that did not go unnoticed by the other children and proved to be an interminable source of derision. She swore that, when she was old enough, she was going to change her name to Eunice and be done with it.

"It don't have nothing to do with your name, Eurinee. You ain't got a man because your hair don't look purty," said Beryl. "But we'll fix that. You wait and see."

7

Any dinner that included buttermilk, corn bread, and slices of fresh tomato and onion was okay with T.J. He loved his mother's cooking and was nearly always the first to sit down at the supper table. Like most boys his age, he could eat twice as much as his parents and still not gain a pound, much to his chagrin.

The table itself was an antique from Old Man Pink Cook's place. When his wife died and he moved back to

Arkansas, he had a huge rummage sale, putting nearly everything he owned out for bid. Lois, who loved "antiques," begged Tom to buy it for her. It hadn't come cheaply. The table was one of the most valuable items in the Pink Cook estate, or at least according to Pink it certainly was, especially after he noted just how badly Mrs. Latham coveted it.

The construction of the table was simple and plain. But it was larger than most tables – so large, in fact, that the kitchen was barely wide enough to accommodate it. Only a bench built into the kitchen wall made the situation tolerable, since the chairs on that side could be dispensed with.

The tabletop was smooth and polished, as slick as glass. The cracks between the boards that made up the table had been filled and smoothed, too. The legs of the table were wide and stout. Other than perhaps the piano, which was a family heirloom, the kitchen table was more impressive than any other single item in the Latham household. This made it all the more unfortunate that T.J., on this particular night, while reaching over to grab a tomato slice, spilled his large glass of buttermilk with cornbread crumbles. The glass rolled across the table and into his father's lap. Tom cursed the glass, then cursed T.J., and proceeded to curse the cost of the table, then the table itself, then T.J.'s mother, and finally the house and everything and everyone in it.

It was an early night to bed for everyone, which was all right with T.J., who longed to spend some private time with Miss Brooks, still safely tucked away between the hay and the feathers in his mattress.

But it was too early for Grady, whose head, as usual, was full of too many questions.

"How far have you read in the Bible, T.J.?" Grady asked.

"I've read Genesis lots of times," T.J. said. "I've read First and Second Kings and First and Second Samuel, the Psalms and Proverbs, Job, of course Exodus, and most of the New Testament. But it's time to go to sleep, Grady."

"I know," he said. "I was just wondering if you've read Deuteronomy."

"I don't think anyone's read Deuteronomy much," said T.J. "Now go to sleep."

"Did God intend for us to follow all those rules in there?" Grady said.

"I reckon He did," said T.J. "Except then Jesus came and took away some of 'em. Most of 'em, I guess."

"Then why did God give all those rules in the first place, if Jesus was gonna come along and say nobody had to pay any attention to them?"

"I don't know," said T.J. "But I do know it's time for bed. Good night."

Grady was silent for a second, but his head was too full to stop just yet.

"T.J.?" he asked.

"Mmm," said T.J., pretending to drift off to sleep.

"T.J.? Are you awake?"

T.J. didn't answer.

"T.J.!"

"What!" T.J. said, hammering his pillow and rolling over.

"Why do you reckon Dad's so mad at us?"

"He's not mad," said T.J.

"Then why did he yell at us?"

"He's not mad, Grady. He just … It's nothing. He's frustrated. He doesn't want to oversee Grandma's farm, I think."

86

"Oh," said Grady. "But he's got seven sharecroppers."

"That's what makes it so hard," said T.J. "Dad has to plan out everything for them and be there for them, to make sure the crops and everything come in. I think he'd rather still be teaching us in school."

"Yeah," said Grady. "I wish Daddy was teaching us, too. Maybe he wouldn't be so mad then."

"He's not mad at you, Grady."

"But he is mad at you."

T.J. rolled onto his back and stared up at the rafters in the ceiling.

"No," said T.J. "He's just tired. He needs rest. And so do we. Good night."

"T.J.?"

T.J. let out a loud, long sigh.

"Is this gonna be the last question, Grady?"

"Yes," he said.

"Are you sure?"

Grady nodded.

"What?" said T.J.

"Do you think that God knows that Dad is just tired?" he asked.

T.J. thought about this for a moment, threading through the theater of the mind all of the events of the past three to four months.

"God knows everything," said T.J. with a tinge of uncomfortable finality. "Good night."

"Night," said Grady, rolling onto his side.

In T.J.'s mind, the sinuous jazz music begins to play and he is treated to his own private dance. Louise Brooks is in the green room, ready to seduce her patron. She is the goddess and this bed, like the picture show, is the place of T.J.'s idolatrous worship.

And God, like a cat, knows everything.

CANTO V

As I cross the threshold into my shop, I think I hear a noise, a lament in the winds. "Abandon all hope," it seems to say. And so I have, I suppose.

But I ask the Poet, "O Master, what is this I hear?" I think I must know the answer, already.

He sighs and says, "These have no longer any hope of death; and this blind life of theirs is so debased, they envious are of every other fate, that no fame of them the world permits to be; Misericord and Justice both disdain them. Let us not speak of them, but look, and pass."

So at least I know where I belong. But I keep it to myself, as always.

Fall

Chapter Five

1

Abijah Boggess Latham, the eldest son of Henry A. Latham of Bedford County, Virginia and Vesty Boggess of Meigs County, Tennessee, was born March 10, 1836, exactly sixteen days before his parents' first anniversary.

After the removal of the Creeks and the Cherokee Indians, Henry Latham followed the rivers of the Appalachian foothills south to what would become Haralson County, Georgia and traded a pocket knife for 400 acres of bottom land off the Tallapoosa River. He, his brother Silas, and his slaves cleared the land and built a log house and stables on a red clay hill overlooking the waters. There Henry bred horses and mules and planted enough food for his family, which soon grew to include sons Thomas Simon Latham, Farris, Taz, and Victor, and daughters Amanda, Jennie, Mary, Vesty, Virginia, and Ellen.

Abijah, being the oldest, was expected to do much of the work on the farm. One of his pastimes on the farm was going on excursions with his Uncle Silas, who loved to fish for jack fish. If a fish died before he got home with it, Uncle Silas – being superstitious -- wouldn't eat a bite of it. But those jack fish that lived all the way home made for more than a few good suppers.

When Abijah turned 10, Silas taught him how to use a hunting rifle and the two began going on hunting trips together. Uncle Silas taught Abijah how to use a green leaf for a turkey call. Squirrel and wild turkey were plentiful in those days. Silas stressed that a true hunter is always calm and not easily surprised.

In his late teenage years Abijah became restless and grew consumed with the notion of finding a wife. Abijah didn't much care for the rural, pioneer stock who lived in Haralson county, so he began to make regular trips to surrounding towns like Cedartown, Carrollton, Rome, and even Atlanta. On his field investigations he would always take note of the young women as well as the land. He finally met and married Surphronia Brooks of Brooks' Station, on the eve of the Civil War. They settled in Coweta County, just south of Atlanta. Their first child, Ector, was born just as the first shots were fired at Ft. Sumter in South Carolina.

Abijah, even as a young man, developed a reputation in the community as someone who was honest, trustworthy, and just. His towering appearance at 6'2" probably helped to solidify his standing as one of the leaders of the community. Abijah was one of the best rail-splitters between Palmetto and Campbellton and could out-chop any man in the area. Abijah Latham was honest and never made a promise he couldn't keep. He knew the ways of men, had many friends and few real enemies, and always paid his debts before they came due. Abijah Latham commanded strict obedience from his family and seldom had to tell his children to do something twice. He was a man of natural leadership abilities who was called in to settle many disputes between neighbors, giving his judgment in many cases of hog stealing and property boundary disputes. Although he carried no official title, everyone in the community recognized him as a sort of Justice of the Peace, and the punishments he devised were always carried out, even when they included whipping or banishment.

Abijah was an unusually calm man and his wife said she had only seen him uneasy once, when the great storm of

1860 swept through the community. There were no clouds in the sky that strange day, but the wind was blowing down the trees, everyone later remembered. The roof was blown completely off of Abijah's home, but if he indeed had looked worried that day, as his wife alleged, Abijah insisted that it was purely for her sake.

Abijah planted a crop in the spring of 1862 to see his family through the next year. He then volunteered for service in the Confederate Cavalry, serving as a 2nd Lieutenant. He journeyed to Richmond, Virginia, bringing with him a grey mare bred from his father's stables that seemed to hate Yankees as much as he did and could hear or smell them from miles away. His company made the horse an honorary scout.

When Abijah would go to sleep at night, looping the bridle rein around his arm. If the horse nudged him with its nose while he slept, Abijah immediately awakened and notified the colonel to wake the camp. The horse would look in the direction from which the Yankees were stealing upon the sleeping cavalrymen, and then the men quietly slipped away. Early the next morning the Yanks would tear into the camp, only to find it abandoned. Six times the horse spared them a Yankee surprise. The colonel was so impressed with Abijah's horse that he told him to be sure and let the camp know what the horse was thinking at all times. In fact, the colonel offered to buy the horse from Abijah. With much reluctance he accepted so that he could send the money directly to his wife, who was barely scraping out a living back home with no one but toddlers and two sharecroppers to help her on the farm.

Often the troops were underfed to the point of near-starvation, although the officers rarely went without. Abijah felt for his men and tried to help them whenever possible, sometimes in novel ways.

At one point during a march from Richmond to Columbia the troops came to a place called Kelly's Crossroads. The officers occupied a big plantation house there and feasted on the food the occupants had been forced to leave behind – collards, fat meat, country ham and gravy. Abijah suggested that they share with the enlisted men but the colonel and his underlings were hearing none of it. There wasn't enough, they said, and it would only lead to a fight among the men, who were little more than brutes, anyway.

Abijah had made many friends among the enlisted men and didn't care for the colonel's tone. So he took leave of his fellow officers and made his way to the armory.

Within minutes shells began to fall around the house, catching everyone by surprise. The order was given to leave at once, but the colonel hadn't finished his plate and didn't want to leave it behind, so he continued to feast while his men scurried away, until a shell struck the house, ripping a hole in a room adjacent to the kitchen. The colonel jumped onto Abijah's horse and it reared up, refusing to budge. As the shells continued to fall, the colonel tried again to spur the horse into action, to no avail. Only then did the colonel notice that the reins were entangled in the horse's feet. He cut the reins and made off, but not before his enlisted men witnessed him "charging the kitchen," as they described it. Many laughs were had over the comedic scene, and one private was even inspired to write something of a ballad, *The Kitchen at Kelly's Crossroads*, which was quickly learned by all the others and soon became the outfit's most popular marching tune. It almost made it worth all the grief the men had suffered by serving under such a severe man for so long. Almost.

95

Mysteriously, the shelling stopped as soon as the colonel left the building. Just as mysteriously, the enlisted men, led by Abijah Latham, showed up about two minutes later and absconded with everything that remained.

On another occasion, the colonel confiscated a turkey shot by a young private and instructed the private to take the bird two miles down the road to a black woman he knew who would cook it for him.

"And tell her not to forget the cornbread," he told the private as he headed out the door.

Abijah Latham heard the enlisted men grumbling about the injustice of it and he stopped the private, saying that he would take the turkey to the black woman himself. Putting the bird into a clean haversack, he carried it to the woman and waited for it to cook. When it was finished he told her that the colonel thanked her for her time, and he left, instructing her to send the cornbread by her small son. Abijah took the turkey back to the private who had shot it and he and his tent mates promptly ate the golden bird, with some help from Abijah, who buried the bones in the sand under the shade of a nearby pine tree. Just as they were finishing, the boy came by with the bread, looking for the colonel.

"Thank you for your trouble," said Abijah, giving the boy a penny. He took half to the private and the other half back to the colonel, who couldn't understand why his turkey was taking so long to prepare. He began to get emotional about it, storming out of his headquarters and searching the camp. Abijah hoisted a $10 bill and offered it to the first person to identify the turkey thief. No one said a word. The private, when questioned, said he had taken it to the woman, just as he had been instructed.

"Well, colonel," said Abijah after a full night's search, "I guess some poor, hungry soldier got to your turkey." And so he did.

Abijah finally managed to get his horse back by spreading rumors around the camp that the Yankees were looking to kill both the horse and its owner for constantly spoiling their surprise attacks. Word was that a $1,000 ransom had been placed on the horse and that the first person to kill its owner would be given a personal commendation from President Lincoln. But Abijah knew he wouldn't get the horse back for nothing.

So, during a skirmish with the Yankees, Abijah made off with one of the Union officer's horses under heavy fire. When he got into a clearing he found that the officer had left his pistol in the sack on the back of the horse. When he was surprised by a Yankee patrol he spun around and aimed the pistol squarely at the heads of the two Yanks. He urged them to surrender, which they promptly did. He took his two prisoners, along with their horses and the officer's horse he had stolen, and approached the colonel with a trade offer: three horses for one. It was an offer the colonel couldn't refuse.

Only later that night, when Abijah was getting reacquainted with his old mare, did he inspect the pistol he had used to overtake the Yankee patrol and discovered that it hadn't been loaded.

Abijah soon learned in the letters from home he received from Surphronia that all was not well. Yankee patrols were becoming more and more common, and more brazen, and she had been forced to fashion a trap door in the stable to hide their sweet potatoes and turnips from the hungry troops, although she let them have much of the corn

97

without a struggle. She had taken their best horse and hidden it out in the woods, and had held onto another one by pushing its head through the window and holding its four feet flush against he doorstep, keeping a tight hold on the reins and threatening to stab the hand of any Yankee who dared to reach in and try to take them from her. On one occasion she had been forced to defend her honor with an ax.

Still, he trusted in Surphronia's ability to hold her own, until he received a devastating letter in the summer of 1864 about a fire the Yankees had set which had destroyed everything they had. Only two quilts were saved, and the lives of the children. But a June 20 letter informed Abijah that his family was now homeless and helpless.

The enlisted men knew something was wrong and asked Abijah what was bothering him. When he finally told them, under much duress, they insisted that he get a furlough. The colonel, he said, wouldn't agree to it. The times were growing more and more desperate and he was needed on the front.

But the men said they would get Abijah the furlough he needed. The private whose turkey the colonel had once coveted, as it turned out, had struck up something of a friendship with the officer after saving his life on the battlefield one particularly hairy day. So he devised a plan.

The private, who had since been promoted to corporal, wrote out a furlough but left it unsigned. He visited the colonel, who had grown fond of him, and told him the men had laid down bets on how he signed his name. The paper was folded in such a way that the colonel could not see the furlough written on it, and the colonel, who was engaged in other business at the time, just laughed and quickly signed his name to settle the bet.

The men didn't bother to tell Abijah the manner in which the furlough had been obtained, because they knew he wouldn't have taken it. But, grateful for the chance to return home to his family, he asked few questions and saddled up his grey mare, heading back to his homestead in Coweta County.

The war ended just three weeks after he returned home. When Abijah died unexpectedly in a hunting accident 10 years later, Taz Latham, his younger brother, thought it only fitting that his second son should be named after him.

2

So it was from this great man that Bije Latham, Tom's brother, took his name. And it was generally said among the populace that never before in the history of mankind had two men, so identical in name, been so vastly, hopelessly different in appearance, demeanor, or reputation.

Abijah B. Latham had the hair of an onion, the shape of an onion, the skin of an onion, and, T.J. thought, the smell of an onion, too.

He conducted his affairs from a shack that had once served as a slave quarters. The tumbledown straddled a lonely, treeless hill on the outskirts of Latham Town.

Bije, as he was called, always wore the same pair of overalls, with the pockets worn away and one of the shoulder straps sewn together with a bit of twine. He preferred to travel barefoot, but he did wear shoes on special occasions.

Bije had always been an overweight, disturbed child with an angry streak that often drove his father to the edge of violence. Still, it came as a shock to the community when Bije killed his 68-year-old uncle, Thomas Simon Latham, and tossed his body into the Tallapoosa River.

Everyone agreed that Bije, like his Aunt Vesty -- whose right foot was six inches shorter than her left, leaving her stance as unbalanced as her poor mind -- had never been mentally sound, so they shipped him off to the lunatic asylum in Milledgeville for a time to see if he could reform himself. His younger brother, Tom, soon moved to Milledgeville, as well, to keep an eye on his brother as much as anything else, taking a job as director of the state boys' reform school.

Bije Latham was eventually sent home and the murder of his uncle gradually receded into a vague memory. But he had never truly reformed. He just learned to smile at the appropriate times and never keep a loaded gun within easy reach. And now that Tom was back from Milledgeville, too, he still kept one eye out for his brother. But Bije could never accept the pompous, patronizing piety of his younger sibling. He hadn't accepted it in Milledgeville and he wouldn't do it now, the good name of Abijah Boggess Latham be damned.

3

Tom Latham's mule, Grace, was a sixth-generation direct descendant of the famous Yankee-sniffing grey mare. Of course the old mule looked nothing like her majestic forebear. The only giveaway was Grace's keen intelligence. "That mule's got more sense than most kids I know of," T.J. once heard it remarked as a neighbor watched his father and Grace lay down corn with a 30-inch sweep.

T.J. noticed that Grace had several gears, and she knew which to shift to, depending on who was behind her that day. Dad was high gear, and Grace would clop along at a fast trot without complaint for hours on end. At the other end of the spectrum were the young children like Collier, who were still in training. T.J. was right in the middle, aspiring to his father's speed but still lacking the physical endurance. T.J. noticed that the slower Grace went, the more she shook her head and flopped her ears.

T.J. often plowed behind Grace while his father went to the well for water or while he went into town to get some supplies. He almost always said the same thing when returning.

"Well, you've been a burden to this poor old mule long enough now, T.J.," he would say, taking the reins. "I'm going to get some plowing done."

Whether it was T.J. or Grady or their father doing the plowing, Grace knew better than to step on the cotton like the other mules. Grace straddled the rows of cotton with feet on each side. When it was time to turn around and do another row, Tom or T.J. would tell the mule, *Whup! Whup!* and she would raise her feet up and step over the cotton. No one had ever seen anything like it. Grace, with her "cotton skip jump," quickly became the most famous mule in Latham Town. Not that there were that many.

She treated Yankees and Southerners with the same disinterested contempt, however.

4

The Latham house was 100 yards from the road, on the north side. Most of the property was given to Tom by his father after his return from Milledgeville in 1915, but Tom had to chip in a little money to purchase a pie-shaped cut of land belonging to John Cason to extend the property all the way to the road. Tom believed in straight lines and square boundaries.

One of the first things he did with the property was plant pecan trees in a line from Rufus Goldin's line at the south end all the way up to the northernmost tip, all along the side of the hill to the woods. Another short row started just below his workshop. A third row of pecan trees he planted on a terrace going across the field, eastward to the pasture fence. He planted 36 in all and sowed in grass between them. The Lathams were one of the few families to have grass planted in their front yard. Most had yards of clay, mud, corn or cotton. A few had sand. Only the most prosperous farmers could afford and maintain grass on valuable crop land.

In the spring and summer the Lathams tied their calves out front and let them eat the grass to keep it from growing too high. The children regularly picked up the pecans as they fell to the ground and eat them on the way to school. Their mother also kept peach trees, which provided a sweet snack in the afternoon. The spotted peaches would load the tree so heavily that they would often break the limbs of the tree. The children hated to help their mother pickle them in the summer, but loved to break them out in the winter months and eat them. Fried peaches were also a family favorite.

The Lathams planted an orchard behind their house, in the hollow next to the pasture. There they kept three rows of grapevines and a row of apple trees. Between the terraces they kept raspberries and blueberries and planted four apricot trees.

Tom would often grab a handful of blueberries and grapes and sit on the front porch during his lunch hour while he still taught school. If Virgil hadn't stolen the paper he would read about the day's events while he sucked on the

102

berries. Usually he would doze off after reading the headlines and he would lay the paper on his face to keep the flies away. T.J. would often have to wake his father up to start the trek back to school. Even after he quit teaching, he retained the lunchtime routine. On at least two occasions T.J. would awaken him so that he could go back to work in the fields and he would start to head back down to the road with his son, only to remember that he no longer taught at the school. After gazing for a moment or two out at the school yard, where the children were still outside playing at recess, he would turn around and head back to the fields, hooking the plow to Grace for another go-round, while T.J. continued down the driveway.

Grace was just one of the scores of mules Tom's father had raised in his cavernous barn over the years. There were 20 stables in the barn, which Tom was now charged with maintaining. T.J. helped his father when he could. Tom took the box he used to sit on to read to his pupils and set it in the stable to allow T.J. to buckle collars on the mules that they used in the fields.

"That box is the only thing keeping you from losing your toes," Tom told T.J. as he showed him how to hook a collar over a mule's neck. "Don't be in too big of a hurry with these mules. Let them take their time."

One cold Saturday in early November, just after Grady's 13th birthday, Tom sent T.J. out to haul fertilizer from his grandfather's stables in a Weber one-horse wagon, with the reliable Grace out front, pulling the load. The hill was steep and Grace was now 20 years old. T.J. noticed her sweating and foaming at the mouth, so he drove her along the fence, past where his mother kept her wash pot, to the well by the side of the road. T.J. drew water out of the well for her and she drank it quickly. Then she looked at T.J. one last time, fell over and died.

His father told him that he shouldn't have let her drink the water without allowing her to cool down first, that he'd made a terrible mistake. Virgil came to the house to help Tom drag the mule's carcass out to the woods to rot.

"Did he let her cool down first before giving her the water?" Virgil asked.

Tom shook his head without saying a word and grabbed the two front hooves. T.J. asked if he could help but they shook him off and headed to the woods.

T.J. sat down by the well and wondered, when Rebekah offered water to the camel of Abraham's slave, if the camel had died, would the whole story have turned out differently?

CANTO VI

As I pick the hammer up and head back out the shop door, I see a long train of people in my yard, all dead and hollow. These miscreants, who never were alive, are all naked, and stung all over by gadflies and by hornets. The pests irrigate their faces with blood, commingling with their tears and falling at their feet, to be gathered up by the vile worms.

They're the lucky ones.

Chapter Six

1

On the day that Grace died, T.J.'s grandmother fractured her hip. She walked out of her back door when a cat darted underfoot. Gammy wrenched her hip and fell to the ground. Birdy didn't find her until six hours later.

Tom felt such guilt over spending the afternoon in the woods with Virgil that he insisted his mother move in with his family until she recovered. He borrowed a wheelchair from Doc Sanford after her examination and he took her home in Virgil's car.

T.J. didn't find out that he would have to give up his bed until later that evening, at the supper table. His mother scrubbed the curdled remnants of buttermilk still left, weeks later, in the small pores of Pink Cook's old table. The table smelled rank, a constant reminder of T.J.'s ineptitude.

"Go and change the linens on your bed, T.J.," his mother told him. "That's going to be your Gammy's room for a while."

His grandmother insisted that a pallet in the fireplace room was good enough for her, since the fire would help keep her warm, but T.J.'s father said that her hip couldn't heal properly unless she were allowed to sleep in a proper bed with hay and feathers. She acquiesced without much further trouble, leaving T.J. in the unenviable position of figuring out how to smuggle out his contraband before anyone noticed. Luckily his mother's instructions gave him just the excuse he needed to make his way to the bedroom. Not so luckily, Grady followed.

106

"Did you know that in the Bible God tries to kill Moses?" Grady said.

T.J. was only half-listening, trying to devise a way to slip the pictures out with the linens without Grady spotting them.

"Who told you that?" T.J. said.

Grady shrugged.

"Everybody knows that," he said.

"That's the first I ever heard of it," said T.J., reaching under the mattress and feeling for the pictures.

"What are you doing? Just pull it," said Grady.

"It's all right," said T.J., finding the photos with his hand. "The sheets were just hung up on something."

He carefully lifted the sheets, tucking the pictures inside them.

"Moses was God's chosen servant," said T.J. "I seriously doubt he'd want to kill him."

"But it's true. It's in the Bible," said Grady, proud of himself for knowing something that T.J. did not.

"Where in the Bible?" T.J.'s asked, bundling up the sheets.

Grady shrugged.

"I ain't got to tell you. Look it up your own self."

T.J. smiled as he wrapped up the covers and headed for the door. But the smile faded when his mother met him there, arms extended.

"Thank you, T.J.," she said. "I'll take those outside."

T.J. had to stall a moment to think up a getaway plan.

"Mama, tell Grady that God never set out to kill Moses," he said.

"Well, I imagine if God wanted Moses dead, it wouldn't have been much trouble for him to do it," she said.

107

Just that one sentence gave T.J. the time he needed to come up with an idea.

"Don't worry, Mama, I'll take these out. You put on the new ones," he said.

"No, that's all right, I'm going out, anyway to take down the clothes before it gets dark," she said, reaching for the sheets.

"I'll get 'em for you, Mama," said T.J. "I think Gammy's gonna want her bed as soon as we can get it ready."

His mother smiled and nodded, patting T.J. on the shoulder.

"God bless you, T.J. Thank you," she said. "That's so sweet."

As soon as she left the room Grady moved in closer.

"What you got in those covers?" he said.

"Nothing," said T.J. "Don't you have something to do?"

"This one fell out," said Grady, handing him the shot of Miss Brooks in the man's jacket. *At least it wasn't the nude one*, T.J. thought. He nodded and grabbed it from his little brother, then stepped outside.

"Don't tell Mama, all right?" he said. "Or especially Dad."

Grady nodded in a disinterested manner.

"Can I have your dessert?" he asked.

T.J. rolled his eyes and nodded. Grady lit a smile and took off down the hallway, yelling for his mother.

T.J. looked down at Miss Brooks as he pocketed the lovely photo. He wondered if she was worth a cold night with the laundry and a missed slice of pecan pie. He thought so, but it was a close decision. At least, now that Gammy was around, if she healed up all right, there might be some homemade pudding to be had from time to time.

2

The next day was a Sunday, a church day, and Brother Griffith was preaching on Ezekiel, Chapter 13, concerning false prophets. Grandmother went with them, although they pleaded with her to stay home. Irene McConnell was home sick and Carl didn't bother to show up. Since T.J. didn't have that much to occupy his thoughts, he wound up listening to the sermon. The fact that his grandmother sat on his left side and his father sat on his right helped him to maintain his focus.

Griffith went on his usual rants against the railroads and the banks and President Hoover and the Republicans, denouncing them as the false prophets and devils of a new age. They build empires upon foundations of lies and tricks, on the backs of the farmers. Such an empire could not but crumble, he said.

"I will even rend it with a stormy wind in my fury!"
"Yeah!"
"There shall be an overflowing shower in mine anger!"
"Yeah!"
"I will break down the wall that ye have daubed with untempered mortar, and bring it down to the ground, so that the foundation thereof shall be discovered, and it shall fall, and ye shall be consumed in the midst thereof, and ye shall know that *I am the Lord!*"

A little later in the sermon, Brother Griffith quoted a line of scripture that caught T.J. in its snare.

"Ye have not gone up into the gaps," shouted Brother Griffith, "neither *made up the hedge* for the house of Israel to stand in the battle in the day of the Lord!"

It wasn't until later in the day when T.J. accompanied his grandmother back to her home to attend to her garden that he understood what the preacher had meant. Gammy was concerned about the rabbits coming into her garden and eating her cabbages while she was away. The rabbits had chewed a hole into the fence at the right side of her garden gate. She had fashioned a temporary means of keeping the rabbits at bay with a four-pronged weight and a small hoe pressed against the rabbit hole. She knew her rigging wouldn't hold up if she were gone for an extended period of time. When his grandmother took him to the other side of the fence he could see the problem plainly. The fence had rotted away in two different spots, and the rabbits had an easy time of chewing their way through.

"T.J., I want you to come up here one evening after school and you and Grady go out and cut a tree and get us a pretty big chunk of wood," she said from her wheelchair. "Clean out these holes where the wood is rotten, then lay the wood in these holes. Then I want you to take some staples and staple some wire to it to keep those rabbits out of my garden."

As he crouched down in the dirt to get an idea of just how big the pieces of wood would have to be to plug up the hole, he remembered the day's sermon. "Ye have not gone up into the gaps and made up the hedge for the house of Israel…"

So that's what I'm expected to be, he thought to himself. *That's what I am. A chunk of wood.* But even a lowly chunk of

110

wood could make all the difference. That's what Brother Griffith had been trying to say. Or at least T.J. thought so.

When he returned home he could tell his mother and father had been fighting again because of the uncomfortable silence that hung in the air when he and Virgil walked in, pushing Gammy in her wheelchair.

"Did you fix that hole?" his father asked.

"Gammy said I didn't have to do it today."

His father cast his newspaper aside.

"Isn't that the whole reason you took the boy over there, Virgil?"

Gammy tried to defuse the situation, explaining that she had shown T.J. the problem and asked him to fix it after school one day. She hadn't wanted him to do it this afternoon because she wanted to come back and lie down in the bed and rest, she said.

"It shouldn't have taken him but five or six minutes, at most," Tom said, standing. "Come on, T.J."

"Where are you going?" asked Lois, bouncing Erlene on her knee.

He didn't answer.

"I said where are you going?" Lois asked again.

"Where do you think we're going? We're going to fix Mama's fence, like he was supposed to."

"You don't have a car," she said. "Are you going to walk him back over there?"

"Walking a mile or two never hurt anyone," said Tom. "Some of us don't have—"

He stopped short.

"Don't have what?"

"Nothing."

"Don't have what? Money? *A car?*"

111

Tom stared at her long and hard but said not one word.

"You won't be taking him back out into that cold when there's no need," she said, standing up to her full six-foot height and slinging Erlene onto her hip. Lois towered over her husband by a good six inches, and sometimes it really showed. "He's just one week past a cold. Your mama's already explained the situation. T.J., you run along now. It's Sunday, after all, Tom. A man got stoned to death for picking up sticks on Sunday and the Lord condoned it, so we're not going to have our son mending any fences on the Sabbath, either. He can do it after school tomorrow, like your mama said."

She pressed T.J.'s forearm between her thumb and index finger and patted him on the back. Tom went out to the porch without saying another word.

T.J. headed back into his room and lay on the pallet his mother had made for him on the floor while his grandmother wheeled herself in and lay down beside him. He could tell that she desperately wanted to tell him something, but couldn't think of the proper way to say it. She eventually drifted off to sleep without saying anything.

T.J. opened his Bible to Ezekiel and began to read. He came to the verse about the hedge again. It spoke of going into battle. T.J. tried to imagine a battlefield, with troops of light lined up on the one side and the demons of darkness on the other. There was to be a war, the most massive, horrific war ever in the history of the world, worse than the Great War or even the War Between the States. On the side of all that was good and Holy were God's chosen people, but there were gaps in the line, thin places through which the devils might break through at any time. Who would go up into

112

those gaps? Who would make up the hedge for the house of Israel to stand in the battle in the day of the Lord?

The door cracked open and T.J.'s mother poked her head in. She saw the tears streaming down his cheeks and opened her mouth to comfort him when she saw his Bible lying open on the pallet. At that, she simply bowed down and kissed him on the top of his head, placed a reassuring hand on his shoulder, and then silently walked out, closing the door behind her.

T.J. closed his eyes and knelt by his brother's bed in prayer as his grandmother began to snore. He wondered why Grady shouldn't have the pallet and he could take Grady's bed. He thought of Irene McConnell and her green eyes and his father's stern, red face and Aunt Lillie's voluptuousness that spilled out of her dress this Sunday morning and of the scandalous, slim, boyish figure of Louise Brooks, whose photographs were now hidden under a rock behind the woodpile until he could think of a better place to put them. He hoped it wouldn't rain. And he thought of God and his infinite mercy, which surpasses all understanding. And, for one fleeting moment, he thought he understood. He thought he understood everything.

3

The next morning T.J.'s father left early and missed a surprise morning visitor, one of his former students.

"Hello, Beatrice," said T.J. "I haven't seen you for ... what's it been? Two years? Was that you at the funeral the other day?"

"I went off to high school in Felton," she said. "Is your daddy home?"

"He's not here," said Lois as she put aside her apron and walked in from the kitchen. "Can I help you with something, dear?"

Beatrice froze at the sight of Lois and grasped the hand of the little one standing beside her. T.J. hadn't even noticed him until Beatrice reached for his tiny hand.

"Well I'll be! Hello, little man!" said T.J., reaching out. The boy hid behind the girl's gangly legs.

"He's my little brother. Don't pay him no mind," said Beatrice. "Do you have any idea when Professor Latham will be back home?"

"He's not a professor anymore," said Lois. "Do you have a message for him? Is that it?"

Beatrice bit her lip and shook her head.

"No, ma'am," she said. "I'm sorry to have bothered you, ma'am. I just wanted to speak to the prof—- to Mr. Latham."

"Well," said Lois, drying her hands on the apron, "as you can see, he's not here."

There was a moment of uncomfortable silence, followed by a quick curtsy on the part of Beatrice.

"I'm sorry to have bothered you, ma'am. T.J."

With that, she took the boy by the hand and turned to walk back off the porch and down the muddy driveway. The blonde-haired cherubim turned and waved as they descended the hill.

Lois closed the door and grabbed T.J.'s forearm.

"Don't you ever let that girl in this house, do you understand me?" she said. T.J. nodded but didn't understand.

"She didn't go off to school, T.J. And that's not her brother, either. She's trouble. She just wants to bother your father about Uncle Victor. I'm sure you've heard about all the

114

trouble Uncle Victor gets into from time to time. Well ... this one has come back to haunt him, apparently. I guess she's not going to go away quietly like the others. You stay away from her, you hear me?"

T.J. nodded once again and took another glance out the window. It all made sense. He remembered when Beatrice was a student at his school. He remembered his father giving her extra lessons when she fell behind, which must have been due to all the trouble Uncle Victor had caused her. It must be awful to have a no-account brother like that, he thought. Grady was bad enough.

4

Thomas Jefferson Latham met Lois Eunice Jones at an all-day singing in the fall of 1911. Tom was nearing 30 and was getting a little long in the tooth for bachelorhood. He had seen his older brothers Edgar, Taz, and Abijah waste their youth on career-building or idleness, and he didn't want to meet the same fate -- lonely days and nights spent in empty bachelor apartments or one-room shacks. Tom had always wanted a family, a large one, like those of his parents and grandparents and of the brother closest to him in age, William Henry Latham. So, even though he didn't care for such social events like ice cream parties and all-day singings and tried to avoid them whenever possible, his mother and brother Henry had convinced him that this was the place to meet eligible young ladies. So he dressed in his best suit and hat, slicked up one of his father's largest, most imposing black studs, with long, pointed ears and thick mane, and took the family buggy out to the singing. He had to pass through the swamp to get to the church, where the path was so narrow that he always felt the best course of action was to let go of the reins for fear of steering the horse into the trees that closely guarded the path. It was always a little frightening to Tom to put his faith in a horse like that, and he hated to do it, but he couldn't risk wrecking his father's expensive, store-bought buggy. So the horse would speed unhindered and unrestrained down the narrow path until it opened out on the banks of the Little River, where a shallow place in waters allowed travelers passage on most days, if it hadn't rained recently. Usually Tom would speed down the narrow passage on the hill at such a clip that the horse had no time to slow before hitting the water, sending a heavy spray of ice-cold water into the buggy.

Lois wore her long, brown hair down in those days. She was a full eight years younger than Tom, who made a queer impression on most of the young ladies at the singing that day. He was awkward, wet, skinny, and short, with a severe, hungry look that scared most of the eligible young ladies away. But Lois didn't mind his short stature since most of the men in the community were shorter than her, anyway. And even though she was a handsome woman, she wasn't a typical Southern beauty, which meant that, like Tom, her prospects were limited. Besides her imposing height, she had a darker complexion that the other women, due to the Cherokee Indian blood she had inherited from her father's side. Though she wasn't by any means fat, she was often characterized as a "big-boned" girl. And her fierce intelligence was intimidating to most young men, but immediately sensed and appreciated by Tom.

They spent the afternoon under a sweetgum tree, speaking of places they wished to visit and things they wished to see and people they wanted to meet. Tom was still

116

stiff and awkward, but that made Lois laugh, and he was not offended, or didn't seem to be. Tom tied the horse to an oak tree, where some children were playing Jacob and Rachel (a church-endorsed variation on "Marco Polo"), and the discussion continued even after the singing was long over and the moon made its first appearance.

The children grew more boisterous as shadows lengthened and attention spans shortened. One of them decided it would be a fun idea to try to frighten the horse of the "funny, short, scary man." The child snuck up on Mr. Latham's horse, tickling the stud's prized testicles with a stick. Tom watched helplessly as his father's buggy tumbled after the runaway horse, splintering and shattering into thousands of spinning fragments. Tom Latham had made an impression, all right, if not quite the impression he had intended.

Twenty years later, Lois and Tom had not seen the Pyramids of Egypt, and neither had they met the Sultan, even though they had managed to get as far away as Milledgeville for three years. In fact, they had staked out their little existence on a plot of land not even a mile away from where they had met. Tom never owned a buggy anywhere approaching the elegance of the one his father had lent him that day. But they had three boys and three girls, and life seemed full, and even if they lacked some of the finer things, they were certainly better off than most.

But there were some things about Tom that Lois still did not fathom. She didn't know, for instance, that he had been putting money aside for years now in the hopes of improving their lot. He had hoped to build a bigger house with the money, one closer to Buchanan, with indoor plumbing and electricity. He had hoped to become a principal

117

at one of the larger, better-funded schools closer to town. But that wasn't going to happen now. So he was going to close his eyes and let go of the reins, as he had in younger days.

Everyone was surprised when a gaunt young man in a pressed, seersucker suit showed up at the door that morning, asking for Tom Latham. Tom, who was out in the field harnessing a mule with a drag to smooth out the field in preparation for turnip planting, left with the man without explaining anything to his family other than that he was departing for Bremen and would be gone for most of the day. He abandoned them in such a flash that he hadn't bothered to stop and free his mule.

Tom returned with the sunset, announcing his arrival with a few goose-honks from a car horn. Everyone stopped and dropped whatever canning, threshing, or playing they were engaged in and looked to the horizon. They saw Tom coaxing a 1919 Maxwell touring car up the driveway like a war hero on parade. And he was greeted as such by his family.

T.J., without being asked to do so, had taken the mule that his father had left harnessed earlier in the day and had finished the work his father had planned to do. When T.J. spotted the car, he thought it was some salesman or some other visitor and was shocked to see his father emerge from the driver's seat. He began walking, then running to the car. His mother burst into tears and hugged Tom, and his father grinned with the pride that can only come from providing for a family's happiness. The little children squealed with glee and hugged their father's legs. Grady ran his hands across the upholstered interior like he was petting a prized stallion.

The white, canvas top was pulled back to reveal an interior that was lush despite being slightly used. Whoever

118

had owned the car before had apparently taken superb care of it, although the engine did make strange rattling and wheezing noises that caused T.J.'s mother some concern.

"But she made it back from Bremen fine," Tom told her. "I'm sure I can tinker with it some and straighten her out."

As T.J. circled the car in amazement, he noticed the left rear fender pressed up against the wheel, a wooden 30" by 3" clincher.

"I had a little accident on the bridge on the way home," said his father, shrugging it off as Lois frowned at him with some concern. "It was getting dark. But it's all right. I can smooth that out."

They sat around the large family table that night – and *Mother must have done something*, T.J. thought, because the table no longer smelled of rotten buttermilk -- and they had a small feast in a kind of celebration as they discussed all the ways their lives were now about to change for the better. This was the turning point, they all agreed. All except for Beryl, who was strangely silent. She had fallen ill earlier that day with a fever and appeared not to be excited at all, which T.J. thought was strange, since she always appeared impressed with the Model A Carl drove all over the place. When their father asked Beryl what was the matter, since she wasn't eating her dinner or joining in the conversation, she just shook her head, clutched her throat, and cried.

5

The next afternoon, on a Tuesday after school, the children got their first chance to ride in the family's new Maxwell. The corn had been harvested and shucked the

119

previous weekend and Lois had put it on a rack out back to dry. The early cold spell and rains had slowed the process, so the corn still wasn't as dry as it should have been, but it would have to do, Tom said, and they piled sacks of it into the back of the vehicle and headed out to the Abernathys, who had a corn mill and cotton gin.

This was the family's first good look at the car in the daylight. Now that the sun was out they could see it was dinged and nicked a bit more than they had thought. Beryl was unimpressed, but the boys didn't let the imperfections spoil their excitement at finally having their own family automobile.

The car was black and boxy, with an open top, two rows of seats and a sleek, rectangular windshield with rounded, metallic edges. The front of the car looked like the face of a spectacled old man, with perfectly circular headlights spaced out over a square grill. The running boards, which appeared to have suffered the most under the previous ownership, extended down the entire length of the vehicle.

Tom still wasn't entirely comfortable behind the wheel, but Virgil had let him drive his T models from time to time. The Maxwell was different enough to cause him some anxiety. Lois made him promise that he wouldn't run off the road again as he had the previous night.

"It was dark," he said. "I'll be fine."

Gammy smiled and waved as the family piled in. *She seems sad*, T.J. thought. He wondered if anyone had asked her if she had wanted to ride, too – not that there was any room for her. It was probably just as well that she stay home and rest. Besides, she had said something about Nattie and Willie paying her a visit sometime in the afternoon.

T.J.'s mother had insisted for years that Tom needed glasses like his brothers, Taz and Virgil. T.J. wore wire-rimmed glasses, too, ever since he was a young boy. But his father refused to wear any. Now Tom's eyesight would be put to the test. Tom cranked up the car and the wheezewhir of the engine sputtered into a friendly rhythm.

Collier and Grady sat on a bag of corn with T.J. and Beryl squeezing into niches on either side in the back seat. Erlene sat between her mother and father in the front. She giggled as the car careened down the driveway and onto Eaves Bridge Road.

"Y'all ever hear of Alice Ramsey?" a smiling Lois shouted into the back seat as she clutched her hat in the wind. The children all shook their heads.

"She drove a Maxwell touring car from New York City to San Francisco, California in 53 days back in 1909," Lois said. "Not many of the roads were marked then. They changed their own tires. A group of women, just her and her three friends. I remember reading about that."

"Don't you get any ideas," said Tom as he shifted gears.

When they pulled up into the Abernathys' place, Mr. Abernathy was threshing wheat. T.J. helped his father lift the corn sacks out of the back of the car while Mr. Abernathy paced up the drive and admired the new purchase with T.J.'s mother.

"So you finally went and got yourself a car?" he said. "A Maxwell, ain't it? I hear that's a good 'un."

"Just got her last night," said Tom, barely able to contain his enthusiasm. Beryl crossed her arms sullenly and refused to get out of the car.

"Beryl, come say hello to Mr. Abernathy," said Lois with a forced smile.

"Hello," she said.

"Beryl's been a little under the weather this past week," T.J. heard his mother whisper to Mr. Abernathy, who nodded and winked at her knowingly.

"You boys want to help me crush that corn? Collier? You ready?"

"Yes sir!" said Collier, running to the mill full-speed.

Grinding the corn didn't take long, so soon it was time to turn around and go home. But the wheat straw caught Tom's eye and he asked Mr. Abernathy if he'd be willing to part with a car full of it in exchange for some of the corn.

"T.J., maybe we can get you off the floor and make your Gammy a bed for herself, what do you think?"

T.J. nodded and smiled.

"Come on, T.J.," Tom said, patting him on the back. "Let's fill the back full."

T.J., Grady, and Collier all pitched in and packed the back of the car full of wheat straw within just a few minutes. When they were finished they all climbed in with a rash of barely-contained excitement and sat on top of the massive wheat straw mountain.

The sun bathed the family in a warm glow as T.J. enthroned himself on his wheat straw perch, watching the light shimmer across the pastures. The cool winds whipped the sweat from his skin, and he knew that this is what people meant when they said that they felt like a million dollars. His mother began to talk about Thanksgiving and cakewalks, telling jokes that only his father understood, and for a brief moment, as his father and mother broke into spontaneous laughter, all seemed right with the world.

122

6

That same night, God's hammer fell.

In the early morning hours, when everyone was asleep -- it must have hit between 3 and 4 a.m., the people later surmised -- a cyclone thundered in from the direction of Mt. Zion Church, missing the main building by a mere 50 feet, then proceeded south over the river to the Philadelphia school. Farms flooded all along the Little River and the Tallapoosa. For two hours or more the waters mirrored the Mighty Mississippi, at a width of a mile or more in places. Latham Bridge had been swept away, last spotted somewhere in Alabama. The schoolyard was full of people with reports of reports, sometimes conflicting and sometimes corroborating, but all quite dire. The excited chatter awakened T.J. from a dream about Tybee Island. He reached out for his wire-rimmed glasses, stood, and looked out the window.

Scores of scared neighbors scattered out among the ruins of the Philadelphia schoolhouse, which lay on its side like a dead, white elephant. The surrounding forest reminded T.J. of the time he had spilled his father's matchsticks all over the grass. Trees had been ripped up from their roots and flattened, the bark stripped away, leaving splintered, bone-like remains.

T.J. dressed and walked outdoors, picking up three primers and a box of chalk from the yard before reaching the road. Layer upon layer of leaves and limbs littered the schoolyard and the adjoining Philadelphia Baptist Church cemetery. Headstones propped up twistersplit benches and confetti-like bits of glass and paper adorned the sunken vaults. Strangely, the church building itself was untouched.

Everyone was shocked at the violent severity of the storm, following such a calm, deceptively summer-like day. Three of Rufus Goldin's cows were killed. One had been impaled with a weather vane. John Evans' chicken house was shattered. People spoke of going into the woods later in the day to count their pigs.

It soon became evident that, incredibly, no one had actually witnessed the storm as it ripped through the community. Considering how destructive it had been, surely someone must have awakened during the night to seek shelter in a storm pit. But if someone did, no one admitted to it. Everyone claimed to have slept soundly through the night, blissfully unaware of the destruction just outside their bedrooms until waking up to sideways school buildings and chickens gone limp. God be praised, no one died. No one received so much as a scratch.

After a brief survey and exchange of remarks with his fellow onlookers, T.J. turned around to go back up the hill to his house, which appeared untouched. He saw his father on a ladder, inspecting the roof. He looked stunned.

"What is it?" asked T.J.

"The shingles are all gone. Every one of them," his father said. "It didn't hurt the roof, but it swept all the shingles away, just like someone had taken a shovel up there and pried them off one at the time."

T.J. glanced down to the woodpile and saw that his photographs were still safely concealed. He looked back in through the window to see if Grady was stirring yet. A glint in the windowsill caught his eye.

He moved in closer and saw what at first looked like a shiny rock. He picked it up and brushed off the dirt and mud and saw that it wasn't like any rock he'd ever seen before. It looked more like gold. A gold nugget. T.J. put it in his pocket without comment.

"Tom!" It was his mother's voice. He could see her through the window, sitting on the side of Gammy's new bed. They had stayed up late the night before making it for her.

"Tom!" she said again, putting her hand on Gammy's round, weatherbeaten face. T.J. opened the door. His mother looked sad and startled.

Gammy's eyes were open and empty. T.J. knew that look. He had seen it before. She had wrestled with the devil last night. She had lost.

CANTO VII

A sudden thirst overtakes me, so I stop by the well for a drink of water. I know it will be my last. I put my hammer down at the side of the well and peer down into its depths. The Poet is there with me.

"There is a place in Hell called Malebolge, wholly of stone and of an iron colour," he tells me, "as is the circle that around it turns. And right in the middle of the field Malign there yawns a well, exceedingly wide and deep."

As I fetch my water I listen to the well, and down there I can hear them all, in their torments and their anguish, suffering the lash. I will be there, soon enough. A part of me feels I should just go ahead and jump in now, and join with the naked sinners, the horned demons with their great scourges. It's not the first time I've felt the urge.

But I'm a coward. And maybe there's still a way out. It's not quite morning yet. There's still time.

The Poet laughs at me.

"Oh, what a royal aspect you still retain!" he tells me, mocking me. "So you still have your pride, do you? After everything that's happened? You think you're cunning enough to weasel your way out of this? Even now?"

The well is incrusted with a mold that sticks there from the exhalations coming from below. The bottom is so deep, no place suffices to give me sight of it. I feel smothered in filth, like the well. The water does not help. I will never be clean again. I am all encased

127

in a filth that reeks of the most foul privies. I have shit in my nails, caked in and dried.

I shake off the water and pick up the hammer.

"No," I tell the Poet. "I am committed. Watch and be satisfied. Taunt me no more."

Chapter Seven

1

Gammy died the day before Thanksgiving. Lois told T.J. to walk across the road to the church and toll the bell 75 times while she laid the body out. T.J. took Grady along to help him keep count and to aid with the tolling if his arms got tired. As they walked across the field the scene reminded T.J. of some pictures he had once seen of battlefields of the Civil War. The people barely noticed the two boys, or at least not until they got closer to the church doors. That's when they began to whisper and point. When the boys shut the doors behind them and the bell started to toll, that's when everyone knew for certain.

They assumed the worst for a moment, thinking that one of the Latham children must have been killed in the fury of the storm. Certainly a storm this devastating must have claimed a few victims. Everyone was pensive in anticipation and a silence fell over the churchyard. When the number of tolls passed the number two, Erlene's age, and the number eight, the age of Collier, a collective sigh ascended from the crowd. They had seen Grady and T.J. enter the church and Tom had been outside on the roof. That left Lois and Mrs. Taz Latham.

The tolls numbered 48, 49, and 50, and then they knew it was the matriarch of the family who was dead, and preparations began almost immediately. John Evans, the local carpenter, knew a coffin would be needed. Several of the men agreed to go home for shovels so that the grave could be dug. The women knew the Lathams would need several meals prepared.

When T.J. and Grady returned to the house their mother already had Gammy laid out on a board. Mother was massaging Gammy's cheeks and had laid quarters on her eyes to keep them closed. Lois met them at the door to keep them away from the body. She had a wet sponge in her hand.

"You boys go out to her house and get that dress she wore last Easter. You know the one I'm talking about? She looked real pretty in that dress. Get your father to drive you if he's up to it."

The boys went into the kitchen where their father sat, rubbing his temples as he had the other night. His eyes were closed.

"Dad?" asked T.J., but there was no answer.

"Dad?" he asked again. Still there was only silence as his father's hands continued to rub circle after circle. His eyes opened, but it was obvious that their father wasn't looking at them, but through them, into some private abyss. It was the cold, empty stare of death. The boys had seen it on their father's face once or twice before and knew it was best to avoid him for a while. Grady grabbed T.J.'s arm, nudging him toward the door. T.J. looked at his father for a second, hoping for some sign of recognition, and then, when none was forthcoming, he turned and followed Grady out the door, closing it softly behind him.

T.J. wondered how Gammy's death would affect the family's plans for Thanksgiving. He knew Eloise, his older sister, had already made plans to come home from her school in Powder Springs for the weekend. Uncles Taz and Edgar had also planned to come from Atlanta. So at least it wasn't a situation where last-minute arrangements would have to be made. But he supposed there would be no cakewalk this year.

130

"Do you think we'll still have a hog killing?" asked Grady. Their father rounded up several of their pigs three weeks ago and put them in the pen to be corn-fed to sweeten the meat.

"No, I don't guess we will," said T.J.

When they reached the Five Points Road they stopped and stared as the mass of water that had flooded the area and taken the bridge with it. The river wasn't as high as it had been just hours before, but they were still forced to take an alternate route up the hill to Gammy's place.

"Do you think the storm did it?" said Grady as they navigated the dripping wet woods.

"Did what?"

"Killed Gammy."

"She was old," T.J. said. "She was hurt. She was lonely."

"But she didn't seem like she was gonna *die*," said Grady.

T.J. shrugged.

"You can't always tell," he said.

When they reached the house they quickly realized that, for the first time they could remember, the door was locked. Gammy must have locked it when they stopped by to look at the fence, knowing that she would not return. They went around to the back, where she grew the cabbages, and found that door locked, as well. They frightened the rabbits, which quickly hopped through a new hole in the fence. T.J. saw that the cabbages were almost nibbled away. He guessed he wouldn't be fixing the fence, after all.

Grady circled the house and noticed that a window in the kitchen was slightly cracked. T.J. lifted Grady onto his shoulders and he squeezed himself inside, then went around to the back and opened the door.

It was unsettling to be in the house when it was empty. Gammy and Pappy had so many children and grandchildren that the home was always overflowing with the business of life. But now there was nothing but an overwhelming, reverent silence. Even Birdy had packed her things and returned to Uncle Victor's house after Gammy broke her hip. The creaks of the floorboard and echoes of the boys' footsteps seemed intrusive. T.J. felt like a rat sneaking aboard an empty vessel.

They went up the stairs to the bedroom and opened Gammy's closet. It was strange, he told Grady, to be rummaging through her closet when she had told them as small children so many times to stay out.

Even stranger is that they didn't have to search for the dress at all. T.J. was certain it would be buried in the back of the closet since it had been last spring since she had worn it. But Grady pointed to it immediately, hanging in the very front, as if Gammy had already gone through the closet herself and pulled it to the front to wear the next day.

"You get the dress, Grady," he said.

"I'm not getting it," he said. "You get it."

T.J. gulped and grabbed it, then tucked it under his arm, trying not to think too much about it.

The house was dark and every footstep seemed a thunderclap as they descended the stairs, groping for daylight.

2

When the boys returned home with the dress,
neighbors were already beginning to gather. The Summerville
boys were on the roof, nailing new shingles. It would be a
long night tonight and T.J. planned to stay out of the way as
much as possible.

"You boys are just in time," their mother said with a
sigh of relief. She was wet with sweat. "Your grandmother's
starting to stiffen up."

Their mother closed the door on the boys again as she
and Beryl prepared to dress the body. Grady and T.J. walked
out to the porch, where their father was sitting. He wasn't as
tightly wound now, and he acknowledged their presence
with a barely perceptible nod before stepping off into the
front yard. He tripped and missed the last step with a hard,
clumsy footfall into the wet dirt.

The familiar rumble of a Model A engine churned the
air. T.J.'s eyes lit up as he spun around to see Carl's car
coming up the drive. Only this time, Carl wasn't in it.

Hoke was driving the car with Abijah in the passenger
side. It was Abijah's car, after all. But he wondered what had
happened to Carl since that day they had played Mumbly
Peg. Had he returned his mother's whiskey as T.J. had asked
him to? He hadn't even thought to check.

In the back seat of the car was the girl who had so
brazenly worn flowers in her hair at Pappy's funeral. She had
a new hat and a new bruise on her face. Both were blue.

Tom tried to speak with Abijah but his brother
brushed past him, stomping into the house.

"Bije!"

Hoke shook his head as he pulled out a cigarette and lit it.

"He heard the bells," said Hoke. "Did she die in the storm? Hey, Slick."

"Hey, Hoke," said T.J., who smiled at the girl in the back.

"You like her? You can have her if you want her. How much you give me for her?" said Hoke.

"That's not funny, Hoke," said Tom, making no attempt to temper the words with a smile or a friendly laugh. The words fell like a rock. Hoke, after an awkward silence, grinned like a monkey.

"Oh, she don't mind, do you, honey?" said Hoke, reaching around to smack her leg. She recoiled instinctively before he could make contact. Hoke started to glower, then laughed it off.

"She's just a good ol' girl, Uncle Tom," said Hoke. "So what happened?"

Tom explained that Gammy had died sometime during the night. T.J.'s eyes kept flashing over at the girl, whose name he still did not know. She kept her arms tightly crossed across her chest as if she were cold. She stared out into the woods, not saying a word. T.J. wondered where she had met Hoke, where she was from, what she saw in him. It was hard for T.J. to understand what anyone saw in Hoke. He was handsome enough, to be sure, with his golden blonde hair and lean, muscular build. What was especially hard for T.J. to take was Hoke's easy-going relationship with his father. Tom was unusually forgiving of Hoke's faults and would often laugh off things Hoke said. T.J. knew that if he had said the same things in the same manner, his father would never forget or forgive it.

T.J. thought he knew why. Hoke's father, Henry, had died when he was only 32, of Bright's Disease, which had left his liver a yellow, bloody lump. T.J. remembered it as a slow, painful death. He remembered hearing screams come from the outhouse. Tom had been devastated. Henry was the closest to Tom in age. While growing up they had shared a room together. That meant they had also shared one another's secrets and dreams. Tom was close to Virgil, too, but his relationship with Henry had been an especially singular one. A part of T.J.'s father died that day, almost 10 years ago now.

Ironically, it was also through Henry's death that Tom's professional teaching career had begun, since Henry, who had taught at Philadelphia School ever since Edgar had left for Cedartown to start his law practice, had asked Tom to cover for his classes when he fell ill. Tom assumed the teaching position permanently upon his brother's death.

T.J. still remembered Uncle Henry's funeral. Hoke had been only a little older than Collier was now. Henry was buried just a few graves over from where Pappy had been laid to rest in the summer and where Gammy would be put to rest tomorrow.

Tom had tried to be a substitute father for Hoke, just as he substituted for his father at the school, and had even at one point tried to convince Hoke's mother, Elizabeth, to allow Hoke to live with him. But Bije lived on Henry's farm and tended it after Henry's death, and his close proximity and similar temperament helped him to forge a close bond with the boy. For a while, at least, before the moonshining operation kicked into high gear, Bije and Hoke ran one of the more prosperous farms in the county. T.J. always suspected his father was more than a little envious of the relationship Bije had formed with Hoke after Henry's death, and that this

135

is what had soured the two brothers' relationship with one another. The words Tom always used when describing his brother were "bad influence," but T.J. wasn't so sure about that. Hoke had always wanted to be bad, even without Bije's help. Even if Henry had lived, it wouldn't have made a difference, he thought. Hoke was the kind of boy who would pick legs off a Granddaddy longlegs to watch it flop around or hang a cat from a tree by one foot and laugh as it flailed around in a panic. He and Carl were always thinking of ways to trip people at school or steal something from their desks. But Carl had always at least been good-natured about his mischief. T.J. always suspected that Hoke actually enjoyed hurting things, even hurting other people, and sometimes even himself.

T.J. gradually became aware of hammerfalls. The cadence had lulled him away for a short time, and when he came out of it he realized he was staring into the eyes of Hoke's girlfriend. He smiled uncomfortably and looked away, hoping that no one had noticed. His father and Hoke were still engaged in friendly discussion, but he was certain the girl had seen him staring at her. He hadn't even meant to, and he hoped she wouldn't misinterpret it.

The *tink-tink-tink* of nailstrikes littered the air as the boys finished their shingling. But underneath these marched a new sound: slower, harsher, undeniable. *Plunk! ... Plunk! ... Plunk! ...*

T.J. knew that sound. John Evans was cobbling grandmother's coffin.

Someone was coming up the driveway. T.J. turned around and saw a group of about 15 marching slowly to the drone of the hammer, with color guards hoisting both

136

American and Confederate flags, along with a red cross of roses. The Klan.

T.J.'s father stepped out to meet them with a half-hearted handshake. He talked under his breath and pointed to the house. A door slammed and T.J. spun around to see Bije barreling out of his suspenders.

"Get the hell out of here!" he said, his eyes twice their normal size and his flesh twice as red. "Tom, you tell them to get the hell out. Get out!"

Bije rolled up his sleeves. T.J. turned to see their reaction and that's when he noticed, for the first time, that Virgil was the one holding the roses. His face emerged like the sun as he carefully set the flowers in the dirt.

"What the hell are you doing, Virgil?" said Bije.

Virgil stepped forward, taking off his jacket and folding it neatly over his arms.

"Same thing you are," he said. "Only I'm not screaming at the mournful and good-intentioned."

"Good intentioned?" was all Bije could spout before taking a wild swing at Virgil, who ducked, sending the stout Bije into the dirt.

"You son of a bitch," said Bije. "I knew you was one of 'em."

As Bije stood and dusted off his pants, Virgil relaxed, turned, and reached over to pick up the flowers. Just then, Bije slammed into him with his 300-lb. frame, sending Virgil reeling into the mud. The flower arrangement burst into a hundred loose petals.

Virgil flashed a look of bewildered anger as his fellow Klansmen began to laugh at him. Tom and T.J. watched as Virgil reached into his coat pocket.

"Virgil, no!" Tom said, rushing to intervene as Bije readied for another swing.

Tom smacked Virgil's hand and sent the gun flying into the air with a percussive pop as it discharged. Bije flailed at anyone in his way, striking Tom in the ear, sending him tumbling into the wet leaves.

Bije stood straight up, popping his suspenders back into place. He ambled to his car, patted Hoke on the arm and motioned for him to follow inside.

T.J. went to his father, who was clutching his ear. T.J. saw blood running out of it, streaming down his father's arm.

"Dad?" he said, but his father did not answer. He rocked back and forth in agonized silence, clutching his ear, like a silent wail in the center of a tempest.

"Dad? Are you all right?"

His father would not answer and would not look at him, veiling himself with his arm. He started whispering something to himself in a voice so small and still that T.J. couldn't understand any of it.

"Dad? Dad? Are you all right? Answer me, Dad. Answer me."

There was no answer. It was almost as if the father T.J. loved was no longer there at all.

3

By the following afternoon, everyone had arrived, even those who didn't know of Gammy's death. They thought they were simply coming home for Thanksgiving.

Eloise, T.J.'s older sister, was home from her school in Powder Springs. He was happy to see her as she had been gone since August. T.J. had always been close to his sister, closer than he was to his other siblings. He could remember a time when he and Eloise were the only two children in the house. They used to play hide-and-go-seek in the orchards. She had brought blank post cards back from school for T.J. to mail to friends and family. On the front was a picture of the campus. It was smaller than T.J. had imagined.

"When did Daddy go out and buy a car?" she asked him.

"Just a few days ago."

"Did he tell anyone he was going to do it or did it come on him all of a sudden? Can he afford it?"

T.J. shrugged.

"I guess so. He got it, didn't he?"

Eloise frowned with concern.

"Is Daddy all right?"

"He's just a little down, lately," said T.J. "Everything will be all right."

Uncle Victor and Aunt Lillie had come the night before and had stayed up all night with the body. Edgar arrived in the morning. For the first time T.J. could remember, Uncle Taz wasn't with him. Edgar explained that Taz hadn't felt well lately, and that his nose had been getting worse. But he was under the care of a different doctor now, he said, who assured him that there was a new remedy they could try and that things would soon turn around.

T.J. remembered the last time he had talked to Taz, at Pappy's funeral. He had been rubbing his nose nearly the whole time, nudging his glasses. T.J. had noted how red and raw it had looked.

"What's wrong with your nose, Uncle Taz?" T.J. had asked. He immediately regretted having spoken. He always

139

felt around Uncle Edgar and Uncle Taz that every utterance of his was horrifyingly clumsy and inadequate.

"My nose?" Taz said. "Jesus, T.J., is this the first time you noticed that? I dunno. Scales or something, I guess. Itches all the damn time."

"Scales?" said Tom.

"We don't know what it is," said Edgar. "I'm sure it's just a skin condition."

"The doctor said it's nothing to worry about," Taz said. "It started in my mouth, my upper mouth, along this ridge here. Damn cigars, you know. I'm gonna give 'em up, soon as I retire. Already had to give up spicy food."

Taz always presented quite the character, with his straw boater hat, his oversize cigar with its silver holder, and his Coke-bottle-thick glasses and red nose. T.J. always pictured Uncle Taz in the same way, creaking back and forth in Gammy's rocking chair, puffing on his cigar. To T.J. it seemed as if Uncle Taz creaked wherever he went, like his body was fashioned from old wooden planks and rusty nails. He had not aged as gracefully as his brothers and now even his face seemed to be splintering apart.

T.J. had felt a split-second of disappointment when he found out Taz wasn't coming today, since Uncle Taz was the one who always brought back gifts from Atlanta for all the children. But T.J. immediately realized this was a selfish reason for wanting his uncle to show up, and he chastised himself for even thinking that way. He wasn't a boy anymore. He didn't need fancy gifts. And why should he be thinking of gifts at all on such a solemn occasion as his grandmother's death? It was wholly inappropriate.

Hoke and Bije had gone home early the day before without saying much to anyone, and they had been the talk of the funeral since their departure. Everyone had an opinion on what should be done. The whiskey runs had to stop. Virgil suggested that the Klan could help, while most of the wives agreed that it might be time to call the law. Tom wanted to have at least one more chance to talk to Abijah before anything drastic was done. He had helped Bije when he was institutionalized in Milledgeville and he was sure he could still help him now, if he would just listen. Victor remained silent on the matter. Everyone knew why. It was Bije who was supplying Victor with his whiskey. It was Bije who was supplying half the county with whiskey, it seemed.

They had looked the other way as long as they could, but the purchase of the Model A was the last straw. The family couldn't pretend any longer. And now Gammy couldn't stand in their way. Bije was unprotected now.

"T.J., what do you know, young man?" said Uncle Edgar, leaving the circle of conversation in the living room for the relative quiet of the front porch.

"You know, Uncle Taz and me, we got you something," said Edgar.

"I don't need anything," said T.J.

"No, no, no. It's an early Christmas present," said Edgar, stepping off the porch and motioning for T.J. to follow him to his car.

T.J. tried to tame his excitement as his uncle reached into the glove compartment. He felt six years old again. Edgar and Taz never disappointed with their gifts.

Edgar pulled out a brown paper sack.

"Here you go," he said. T.J. smiled, tucking it under his arm.

"Thank you."

"Go ahead and open it," Edgar said.

141

T.J. gushed, shrugged and reached into the sack. He tried not to appear overly enthusiastic, but it was difficult.

What he pulled out was a magazine. He had seen it before. It was the magazine of the National Geographic Society.

"Whoo, man!" said T.J., leafing through the slick pages. "Thank you. This is great."

Just a casual flipping showed articles on the Hawaiian islands and the monkeys of South America, and other photographs of faraway places.

"It's not just a magazine," said Edgar. "You are now an official member of the National Geographic Society. You'll be sent one of these every month in the mail."

"Thank you," said T.J. "You didn't have to do that."

"Don't think about it," said Edgar. "It's nothing, T.J. I just want you to look at this. Like this, here, T.J. I don't have my glasses on. What does that say?"

"Mt. Kilimanjaro," T.J. said.

"It's beautiful, isn't it?"

"It sure is."

"I want you to go there, someday," said Edgar. "You do that for me, T.J. You look at these pictures in this magazine, here. And then you think up ways to go there. You don't need to be cooped up here the rest of your life. And then I want you to call me when you get to Mt. Kilimanjaro or Mt. Fuji or Mt. Vesuvius or wherever it is you're going, and then I want you to fetch me and take me with you. That's how you'll pay your uncle back, you hear?"

T.J. nodded and smiled. Then he had a thought.

"Wait a minute," said T.J., his face suddenly lit up. "Wait right here, all right? I'll be right back."

T.J. ran into the house and went into his dresser drawer. He rifled through his socks, feeling each one. When he found the appropriate sock he emptied it and raced back out to the porch, where his uncle was now sitting and staring across the street to the toppled school and the graveyard, where preparations were being made.

"Here," said T.J., extending a cupped hand. Edgar held out his hand in return and T.J. dropped his gift into his open palms with obvious pride.

"Well I'll be a — T.J., where did you find this?" he said. "It's gold, isn't it?"

"I don't know. I think so," said T.J. "I found it after the storm."

"Where?"

"In the window," said T.J.

"The window? Really?"

Edgar smiled, stared at the stone, then looked back out to the graveyard and closed his eyes.

"I knew it," he said. "I always told Tom there was gold here. No one believed me. It's one of the reasons I left."

T.J. remembered Old Man Wallace telling him something about it while he was playing checkers in front of the blacksmith's shop. A story about Edgar, as a young man, desperately tunneling into the local hillsides, looking for gold. Everyone thought he was nuts. T.J. had forgotten about it, as had everyone else. Edgar had since proven himself, going to Cedartown to become an attorney, even having his bright, shining moment as president of the Young Mens' Democratic League in Atlanta, introducing Democratic Presidential Candidate William Jennings Bryan in 1900.

"Did I ever tell you what happened? Why I thought there was gold out there?" he said. T.J. shook his head.

"When I was a boy, growing up out here on the Tallapoosa, we had some Indians come visit one day. There was a group of about 20 of them. I don't remember if they were Cherokee or Creek or what they were. But you could hear them out there dancing and singing at night. They'd start a fire and they'd camp out there by the water.

"One of them was an old Indian woman. She must have been about 80 years old, at least. She couldn't speak any English. But her granddaughter was there and she told me that the old woman used to live here, right here on this place, on the Tallapoosa, when she was a little girl.

"And I remember this like it was yesterday, T.J. It affected me that much. My dad, your grandfather, Taz, he wasn't going to let them pass. He didn't trust the Indians and he thought it was just going to be trouble. I'd have to say I agreed with him. We were scared of them. We didn't know them. But that old lady, she started to cry. She dropped down on her knees at my father's feet and clutched them, just wailing. She wouldn't let go. Her granddaughter was with her, interpreting her words, you might say, and she explained that the old woman's daughter was buried down there, by the river. She just wanted to find her grave and visit her one last time before she died.

"So Daddy, he finally relented. He said they could stay, but that they couldn't come up to the house and they couldn't ask for any food or anything. And so, like I said, I could hear them at night, from my bedroom window. I could hear them chanting and talking in their Indian whoopty-whoop. I tried to imagine what it must have been like when they had lived here. It was hard for me to imagine my home being their home, although I guess now that I think about it we used to find their arrowheads all over the place, nearly every time we'd plow up the ground. But they were so foreign. Not like the folks I knew at all. It was hard for me to believe that there was still an Indian living who used to live here.

"But I remember Daddy and me and Bije, we followed them to the river, just to make sure they weren't up to something funny, you know. And she looked confused for a while, like she didn't know where she was at all. But then we got down to the river, and she ... well, she just about lost it. We got to a turn there in the path and this look came over her face, a look I can't explain. She recognized it immediately, I could tell that. And she just started to cry. She got down on her knees, kissed the ground, and just sobbed. She started talking that Indian talk and her granddaughter explained that this was the place where she had lived. And, sure enough, there under an old chestnut tree was a pile of rocks. And you could tell someone had put them there, had stacked them on purpose as a marker, although I had never noticed it before. And so Daddy took me and Bije back to the house and he told us to just leave them alone. Leave them be, he said. And he didn't bother them any more. He let them stay as long as he wanted. I could tell he was moved by it.

"And T.J., as they were leaving, I could see that three of them were carrying something heavy, about the size of half a bale of cotton. They had waited until Daddy had gone to town - I think they had done that on purpose. It was about two weeks after they had arrived. And after they took off I went back down to the creek where they had camped, and I saw a big hole in the ground where those rocks had been. And it was about the size of their burden. So that's when I knew, you see."

T.J. thought about this for a moment as Edgar rolled the gold over and over in his palms, but he couldn't make sense of it.

"What did you know?" he finally asked.

"That was no baby buried there," he said. "It was their *gold*. When the white men told them they had to leave, the Indians had buried all their gold there, to come get later."

Edgar explained that he began digging from that day forward, hoping to find the vein of gold. But he never found a thing.

"I found a huge quartz ridge. I thought the gold had to be down below that," said Edgar. "I dynamited it. I did everything I could think of. I'd dig around in the rock, then bury the dynamite down in there and set it off. Nothing. We did manage to find a bit of copper. We set up a copper mine for a time, big enough to put a two-horse wagon in it. But we never found anything that looked like a piece of gold at all. Eventually I just gave up.

"But there was gold here," said Edgar, holding the nugget between his thumb and forefinger. "You've proven me right, T.J., after all these years. I was right. There was gold here, after all."

Edgar rose and put a large, warm hand on T.J.'s shoulder, squeezing slightly. He pocketed the gold nugget and went back into the house through the kitchen, slamming the screen door shut behind him.

T.J. saw the mule-drawn wagon coming up the drive for Gammy. It was getting dark, even though it was early afternoon. He wondered if it would rain today.

Just when Brother Griffith was about to give up on getting someone saved at Gammy's funeral, a strange thing happened.

A big, black, brand-new Ford A-model Roadster drove up to the Philadelphia Cemetery and lurched into a spot under a tree. A young girl shrieked as she narrowly missed hitting the trunk. T.J. almost didn't recognize his cousin, Effie Mae, as she caught her breath behind the wheel. Her mother tried to calm her by wiping her face with a tissue while Opal, Effie Mae's sister, quickly climbed up out of the back seat in protest, horrified that her sister was making such a spectacle out of herself.

Aunt Lizzy had always been late. Everyone knew to tell her a different time than all the others, if she were to have any hope of making it to a family event. They knew this would most likely be her last. T.J. had heard Uncle Virgil say that he would miss her prized sweet potatoes. She was known for growing the best in Haralson County. Elizabeth had recently remarried, to Jim Ledbetter, and she was seen at fewer and fewer family gatherings. It was to be expected. Uncle Henry had died a young man. Elizabeth was still lean, pink, and hungry, with plenty of life left in her. To stay here in Latham Town, for her, would be death.

So now she and her two daughters would be headed to Cedartown, to set up house with Mr. Ledbetter. But not Hoke. He would stay with Abijah on the family farm. She had already signed it over to Abijah and given him the keys to the "big house." He had found a way to come up with the money to pay her, probably from the same pot that he'd used to pay for his new Model A.

Hoke whispered something to Bije and sneered as his mother approached, adjusting her new high-heel shoes as she crunched awkwardly through the gravel. T.J. admired her smart outfit but wondered if his mother and aunts would think it too flashy for a funeral. It was black, but perhaps too stylish. Opal crossed her arms and scoured, keeping her distance, trying to appear as if she didn't belong to Lizzy at all, while Effie Mae smiled broadly, still marveling at her narrow scrape and thrilling at the fact that she was actually old enough to drive. But by the time she reached the gravesite she was appropriately somber enough.

T.J. barely listened as Brother Griffith intoned and admonished, praised and comforted the family. He felt numb. He wondered if everyone else felt the same way. It wasn't the same as Pappy's funeral. That had been a shock to everyone. This one was almost expected, as if everyone knew that Gammy wouldn't last long without Pappy. There hadn't been much crying, save for Uncle Abijah, who was inconsolable. T.J. wondered if, for the most part, the Lathams were becoming reconciled with the idea of death.

"Amen," he said, not because he was listening to the preacher, but rather because he sensed that everyone else was about to say it.

"Ashes to ashes," said Brother Griffith, "and dust to dust."

T.J. looked at Aunt Lizzy's new car and wondered if she had used the money Bije had paid her for the farm to buy it. Elizabeth was trying to talk to Hoke, but he was doing his best to look the other way. He had never approved of Mr. Ledbetter. It was one of the things that drew him out of the house and closer to Abijah. T.J. supposed that Hoke's

148

relationship with his mother was just about done. Not that he cared.

Everyone asked Lizzy if she would be staying for dinner after the funeral, since it was Thanksgiving, after all. But she said that Mr. Ledbetter was expecting her and the girls to have dinner with him at his mother's house in Cedartown, and that she would have to get going, but that she would try to stop by and visit as often as she could. She tried to kiss Hoke goodbye but he shook her off and turned away. T.J. hoped he would never show his mother such disrespect. Of course he couldn't imagine his mother marrying someone other than his father, either. He didn't know how he would react to that. Maybe he would act just like Hoke.

T.J. and Beryl lingered as everyone else wandered up to the house following the service. T.J. said he wanted to watch the men bury her. His mother kissed him on the head and left him.

"Don't linger too long," she said.

"You staying?" asked Beryl.

T.J. nodded.

"I just want to think," he said.

He gradually began to suspect that Beryl genuinely wanted him to go, which was strange, because Beryl never liked to be alone, and she absolutely hated graveyards. But her incessant pacing and sighing not only kept T.J. from making his own reflections, it also made him certain that she had none of her own.

"You can go on back if you want," T.J. said. "I'm all right."

"No, that's fine," she said. "I just want to be alone, too."

149

"Well," said T.J., "we can't *both* be alone."

Beryl furrowed her brows.

"Why not? You don't want me here?"

"It's not that," he said. "It's just that, if you and I sit here together, then neither one of us gets to be alone."

"Well," she said, dumbstruck, "what's so great about being alone, anyway? Being alone is boring."

"But I thought you just said you wanted to be alone," he said.

"Well, maybe I do," she said. "Just leave me alone."

T.J. stopped and considered this, then decided to press on.

"What's going on?" he asked.

She looked incredulous and offended. She began to blush.

"What do you mean?" Beryl said.

"I mean why are you acting so strange?" he said. "What do you have up your sleeve?"

"Nothing!" she said, crossing her arms in a huff. Now he knew he was onto something.

"You running away? Is that it?" he said.

"No!"

"You going to the circus?"

"No!"

"Going to see…"

Suddenly a thought struck him. He thought he might have an inkling of what her plans were.

"Going to see—"

He heard a rustling in the bushes behind him. T.J. wheeled around.

"Shit, she's a-goin' to see me, all right? Keep it down low, if you don't mind, T.J."

150

Carl was almost unrecognizable, his face painted black like a minstrel.

"What in God's creation are you doing, Carl?" said T.J.

"Shh! If yer Daddy sees me, he'll have my hide fer sure," said Carl. "Come on, if you want to. You can come, too."

"No, Carl. Not T.J.," said Beryl.

"Oh, why not?" he said. "He knows, anyhow. You want him to run up and squeal?"

"Where are we going?" said T.J., still unsure.

"T'the daints," said Carl.

"What?"

"The daints!"

T.J. blinked, unsure if Carl was actually using English. Carl sighed and rolled his eyes.

"You know!" he said. "With all the people a-sangin' and a-hollerin' and a-hoopin' it up!"

The tumblers slowly clicked into place.

"You mean a *dance*?" T.J. said.

"Well, ain't that what I said?" said Carl. "Now come on!"

CANTO VIII

Who ever could, even with untrammelled words, tell of the blood and of the wounds in full which now I see? Without the first swing of the hammer, even, I have seen them all, in my mind's eye. All my precious little children.

"Each tongue would for a certainty fall short, by reason of our speech and memory, that have small room to comprehend so much," the Poet assures me.

He places his cold hand against my cheek and tells me of horrors.

"A cask by losing centre-piece or cant was never shattered so, as I saw one rent from the chin to where one breaketh wind," he tells me.

"Between his legs were hanging down his entrails; his heart was visible, and the dismal sack that maketh excrement of what is eaten.

"While I was all absorbed in seeing him, he looked at me, and opened with his hands his bosom, saying: 'See now how I rend me? How mutilated, see, is Mahommed? In front of me doth Buddha weeping go, cleft in the face from forelock unto chin; and all the other disseminators of scandal and of schism. They were all cleft thus."

As we ascend the porch steps, the Poet leans in and whispers in my ear:

"A devil is behind here, who doth cleave us thus cruelly, unto the scimitar's edge, putting again each one of all this ream, when we have gone around the doleful road.

"But who art thou, that musest on the crag, perchance to postpone going to the pain that is adjudged upon thee?"

Chapter Eight

1

As they walked to Carl's house in the gathering fog Carl explained that he had tried to return the whiskey, as T.J. had told him to do, but that their father had caught him in the act.

"I didn't think no one was home," Carl said. "I just snuck into the pantry and put it back in there, and here comes yer daddy."

Carl was told, in no uncertain terms, to never set foot in the house again and to stay away from Beryl and T.J.

"Yer Daddy don't miss nothin'," said Carl. "I had a heck of a time jest cornerin' Beryl to get her t'come to the daints."

They could hear the music about a half-mile from the house. Carl launched into an impromptu jig, spinning Beryl around under the stars. She giggled and pushed him away playfully.

"You Lathams are a little different, aren't'ye?"

"Naw, I don't guess so," said T.J.

"You ever been to a daints before?" asked Carl.

"Sure, we've been to dances."

"I don't mean no church daints!" Carl said. "I don't mean no all-day sangin', neither. Come on!"

Carl began running to the house, motioning for T.J. and Beryl to follow. Walking up to the house they could see couples standing outside, by the barn and the corn crib, cradling one another in awkward, young embraces.

"Hey, Carl. Where you been?" asked one.

"We been waiting on you!" said another.

T.J. saw where all the furniture had been pushed out onto the front porch. The house was packed to overflowing with young folks who managed to tell their parents some lie or other to satisfy them.

T.J. dealt Beryl a wary glance.

"We can't stay long," he said. "You know your mama is going to be wondering where we've gone. They're going to start looking for us."

Beryl rolled her eyes.

"Go back home, then, if you're so worried about it," she said. "I'm going to dance!"

At that, she burst through the door, and the music lit up the place, punctuated by flat dancing of the *chig-a-chunk, chig-a-chunk* style.

On a makeshift stage by the fireplace were all of Carl's brothers, with Preston playing guitar, Nathan on mandolin, and Legs on banjo. All were in blackface and bow ties, with monstrous red lips encircling their mouths.

"Hold up, hold up, boys!" said Preston, holding up his hands to signal an abrupt halting of a spirited rendition of *Chinese Breakdown*.

"Here ol' Carl comes!" he said. Everyone in the room broke into spontaneous applause, cheering and hooting as Carl took the stage. He grabbed the whiskey bottle his brothers kept handy. Behind the band was what looked to T.J. like a makeshift still. He couldn't tell if it was just a prop for the show or the real deal.

"Whatcha see out there, boy?" asked Nathan.

"Boys!" said Carl, wiping his mouth clean after chugging down a few swallows of moonshine. "The law is on you *right now*!"

156

At that, a whistle blew in the back of the room –
rrrrrrrrt! -- and a boy in a homemade blue uniform, on cue,
pushed his way through the crowd.

"All right boys, simmer down now, we got you
covered!" said the boy, hoisting a rifle.

"Who's runnin' this place?"

"I'm runnin' it m'self," drawled Preston, patting the
still.

"Well, what kind of run you got started?" The
audience burst into laughter, raising their glasses and
shouting to the rafters.

"We got about five hunnerd gallons done run off, I
reckon. But quite a bit of it's drunk up b'now."

More laughter and foot-stomping. It seemed to T.J. that
the poor little house would collapse at any moment.

"I'm sorry, boys," the officer said. "We'll have to bust
up your still and take you back up to Rome."

A collective groan filled the room, with the people
booing and tossing their drinks on the boy, who set aside his
gun and pulled up his britches, which were a couple of sizes
too large.

"Now, now! Settle down, settle down," said the boy.

"Now, officer suh, we got about six hunnerd bushels of
corn out yonder in the crib that's goin' t'rurn if we don't do
somethin' with it," pleaded Preston.

"Hoo! I don't think there's no use tryin' to farm nohow so long as Prohibition's in effect," said Nathe. "Officer,
tell me what's the use to try to sell corn for two dollars a
bushel in the ear when you can get twenny dollars fer a can?"

"Well, I guess there's no way to git outta this mess,"
said Carl, extending his arm and showing his pearly whites,
offering the officer a swig from the bottle.

"No, no, no, fellers," said the boy in uniform, shaking his head with his homemade hat flopping around his ears. "I'm an officer of the law, now. That jest wutten do."

"Come on! Take a drink!" screamed a young woman from the crowd.

"Just a swaller!" said a young man. Gradually the whole room joined in, urging the "officer" to sample the run. T.J. couldn't help but smile.

The officer extended his hand to settle the crowd.

"All right, all right, now. Settle down," he said. "All right, son. Let's have a taste. Just a swaller, now."

The boy took a small sip, then stopped and bugged out his eyes, prompting a cheap laugh from the crowd.

"Hooo-ey!" he said. "I might have to jest' take me another swaller."

He chugged down a few more, wiped his mouth with his shirtsleeve and hooted again, eliciting a cheer from the crowd.

"Well, this is pretty fine liquor, boys. I'll grant you that," he said. "I guess I ain't no camel!"

"An' this ain't no desert, neither," said Preston. "How much you want, lawman? Drink on up!"

"What's all these instruments doin' around here?" the officer said. "Awright, boys, come on an play 'em a little tune! Come on, boys, hoop it on up! It's either play or go to jail!"

Another loud cheer from the crowd and clapping all around as Carl slung his guitar over his shoulder and let out a loud holler, launching the boys in a hellfire rendition of *Down Yonder*. The officer threw off his hat and grabbed a surprised Beryl, whipping her around and stomping in a fury.

T.J. began clapping to the beat along with the others, absorbed by the pulse of the dance and the tickle of the

158

mandolin. T.J. felt a tap on the shoulder. He spun around and there, with a mischievous smile, was the girl who was mysteriously absent at the funeral today. It was Hoke's girlfriend. Her bruise was gone but she still had on her new hat.

"Wanna dance?" she asked.

Before T.J. could think to answer, she grabbed his hand and dragged him to the dance floor. The music sounded primal and wild as she led T.J. through the moves, touching him in ways he'd never been touched before. T.J. thought his chest would burst open right there on the dance floor.

2

After the music stopped and the boys settled into another comic interlude, the girl led T.J. outside to the barn, where several other young couples were in some stage of embrace. T.J. barely had time to catch his breath before she draped her arms around his neck and kissed him.

"Whoa!" said T.J. "Wait, wait."

"What is it? What's wrong?" she asked. T.J. could smell the liquor on her breath.

"What's your ... I don't even know your name!"

She smiled. A howl of laughter came from the house as the Bishop boys continued their routine.

"Jo Ann," she said, drawing in closer for another kiss. T.J. reciprocated for a lost moment then pushed her away again in sudden guilt.

"I need to ... just a minute, Jo Ann," he said. "I thought you were Hoke's girl."

"Who told you that?" she asked with a devilish grin. "Did Hoke tell you that?"

"Well why are you always with him, then?"

She rolled her eyes and sighed.

"Just kiss me, T.J.," she said, grabbing his shirt and drawing him closer. "Let's don't talk about Hoke."

"You're drunk," he said.

"Naw, you think so?" she said, kissing him again, knocking him backwards into the barn.

Suddenly her hands were everywhere, like a slithery octopus, groping in the darkness. T.J. was excited and confused, ecstatic and guilty, all at once. He could feel a stirring below the waist and he wanted desperately, in his shame, to pull away, but she was having none of that. Instead, as her tongue explored the deep recesses of his mouth, her hands found their way to his place of shame, and she stopped for a moment, pulled back, and smiled.

"Whoo, you like me, don't you, T.J.?" she said with pride.

"Sure," he said. "I think you're nice."

She put on a pouty frown as she caressed his waist and cast her gaze downwards.

"Just nice? Is that all you think of me? Ain't I beautiful? Hoke says I'm beautiful. He says it all the time."

"No he doesn't," T.J. replied. She pulled back. He immediately realized he'd said the wrong thing.

"What?"

"I mean it just doesn't sound like something he would say, that's all."

The girl looked hurt and surprised. She hadn't expected to be hurt tonight, least of all by T.J.

"I'm sorry," he said. "I shouldn't have said that, should I?"

She shrugged.

160

"No, you're right," she said. "He don't say it. He don't never—"

BLAM! Just then a gunshot went off and everyone at the party began to scream and run.

"Oh my God. Oh my God, no," said Jo Ann, straightening her clothes.

"What's going on?" asked T.J., tucking in his shirt.

"It's Hoke."

T.J. peered outside and, sure enough, it was Hoke, yelling for Jo Ann to come out of the house. Everyone insisted she wasn't there, which just made him scream all the louder.

"Jo Ann!" he said. "Come out here, you whore! I know you're in there!"

He shot the gun again and the blast echoed through the dark, empty woods.

Then there was another scream as a second gun came into play. Someone in the homemade policeman's uniform stuck a muzzle out the window.

"Now you just settle down now, son," said the person in the uniform. It wasn't the boy, though. T.J. immediately recognized the voice. It was Carl.

"I want Jo Ann!" Hoke wailed.

"We told you. She ain't here," said Carl. "Now why don't you just get on home. If we see her, we'll send her on."

"Hoke!" Jo Ann screamed, darting out of the barn. Hoke dropped the gun to the ground and embraced her, then collapsed to his knees, in a sobbing fit. T.J. just watched, feeling like a voyeur as a weeping Hoke kissed Jo Ann on her neck and breasts and groped her. She wrapped her arms around him and kissed his golden hair.

T.J. sat there for a moment in the hay, trying to absorb everything that just happened. Then he stood, straightened

161

his clothes, wiped his face, and walked back up to the house, which had fallen suddenly quiet. T.J. listened to the crickets sing as he sloshed through the mud. It was getting colder, he thought.

3

When he entered the house, everyone was gathering up their things to go home. That had been enough excitement for one evening.

Beryl was helping Carl drag the furniture back into the house. T.J. suddenly wondered where Carl's father was. It turned out he had taken Carl's sisters to visit his old in-laws, the Shedds, for the Thanksgiving holiday. He wouldn't be back until Sunday night. As T.J. stepped inside to get out of the cold, someone fell into him with a shriek, spilling her drink onto his shirt.

"I'm so ... T.J.!"

He looked up to see his cousin, Birdy, who even more shocked to see T.J. there than he was to see her. Birdy could barely keep her footing, but she was helped along by a young man T.J. had never laid eyes on before.

"Oh my God. Don't tell Daddy," she said. "Please, T.J. Don't tell Daddy I was here. Promise me. Promise me, T.J."

"I promise," he said.

She breathed a sigh of relief. Then she pointed a finger in his face as she stumbled out the door.

"I'm gonna hold you to it, T.J.," she said. "And don't you tell your daddy, either."

"I won't if you won't," T.J. said as Birdy stumbled off the porch and into the strong arms of the unknown beau. T.J. had always heard stories about Birdy. Now he knew why.

Carl and Beryl dragged in the last stick of furniture and plopped down to rest. Beryl laid her head on Carl's shoulder and grasped his hand. Carl motioned for T.J. to join them.

"T.J., you know Birdy, she took your grandma's death real hard," said Carl.

"I'm not gonna say anything," he said.

"She needed to bust loose, you know," he said. "And she never did get over Woodrow."

Woodrow. That's a name that had gone unspoken for a long, long time. T.J.'s cousin, Woodrow Wilson Latham, had been hit by a train while out hoboing across the country. His father, Victor, never got over it. No one doubted it's what led to his drinking binges. For a long time everyone in the family ignored Uncle Victor's drinking because they felt so sorry for him. He and Woodrow had always been close, even closer than Woodrow had been to Birdy. Woodrow, too, had been a heavy drinker. He had spent the night in many ditches, slept under many houses, and been driven home many times by kind neighbors. It was a wonder that he lived as long as he did, T.J. thought.

Beryl suddenly let go of Carl's hand and shot straight up, like a scared rabbit.

"What is it?" said T.J. But he thought he already knew. His stomach sank to his knees as he stepped out to the front porch and squinted his eyes at the approaching headlights. He immediately recognized the churning sound of the engine, more of a freight train than a car. It was his father's Maxwell. He had found them.

Of all times to have Birdy spill a drink on him. He had absolutely no idea what he would say.

163

T.J. and Beryl walked out to the car and got in without offering a word of explanation. Their father, too, was silent. The quiet was much worse than any tongue-lashing he could have given.

Hoke and Jo Ann were also in the car. Good, T.J. thought. Maybe his father would assume the alcohol smell was coming from them and not him.

"I'm just glad your grandma wasn't here to see this," was all T.J.'s father could manage to say.

"Yes sir," said Hoke. "I don't understand it, myself. Why they would want to off and--"

"Oh, hush," said Jo Ann, smiling at T.J.'s father in a flirtatious manner. "It wasn't anything, Mr. Latham. I hope you aren't gonna be too hard on them kids. It was all my fault."

She laid her hand on Tom's right arm reassuringly. T.J. saw his father's stern face soften a bit. It was an expression he hadn't seen before. His father looked almost embarrassed.

"I understand," was all he could manage to say as he gripped the steering wheel a little tighter.

"I know you do," she said, smiling and rubbing his arm. Hoke was getting noticeably uncomfortable, almost as uncomfortable as Tom. "That's what I always liked about you, Mr. Latham. Your understanding nature. You aren't like the rest of them."

"What's your name?" he asked.

She never got a chance to answer the question. In a flash, something darted across the road. It scurried by too fast for T.J. to see what it was, but it must have been an animal, maybe a dog. Tom jerked the steering wheel, sending the car careening off into the ditch. When the Maxwell finally came to a stop, everyone lay frozen in the icy grip of fear. Jo Ann stumbled out of the car, leaned up against a tree, and threw up.

"Everyone get out," said Tom.

They all walked around to the front and saw the extent of the damage. The front end had skidded across the dirt and slid into a tree. T.J. didn't know that much about cars, but he could see that it was bad. His father bent over and tried to open the hood. Hoke walked across the road to see if Jo Ann was all right.

T.J. held onto the hood as his father bent over and inspected the damage.

"Shit."

He watched as his father felt his way in the greasy darkness, trying to navigate through the tangle of wires and metal. Then he just stopped and shook his head.

"That's ... that's," he said, shaking his head again. Then he cried out, grabbed his ear, and fell to the ground.

"What is it, Dad?" T.J. said as his father curled into a fetal position, clutching his ear.

"Jesus!" was all he said.

T.J. felt helpless as his father writhed in the mud by the side of the road. He glanced at Beryl, who looked frightened, and then yelled out to Hoke, but no one knew what to do to help him.

T.J. kept his hands tight on his father as he clawed at his ear like an injured animal.

5

There were times when Tom would crawl into his cave and stay there for weeks. He could not -- or would not -- get out of the bed. He kept the windows clamped shut because the light, he said, hurt his head. He wouldn't eat for days, wouldn't change his clothes, wouldn't even take a bath. Everything was too much effort. It was all hopeless, Tom said. Nothing seemed worth doing. And even if it were worth doing, he felt unqualified or unable or unmotivated. The bedroom would begin to smell, and Lois would be forced to set up a pallet in the living room, by the fireplace, for her and the smaller children to sleep.

"Your father is sick," she said, "but he'll feel better soon. Just pray for him."

And so they did. Within a week or two, Tom would usually crawl back out into the sun. He would get up, walk out to the creek to wash himself, put on his farming clothes and get back to work, as if the preceding two weeks had never happened.

It was getting worse. Even when he had been teaching, Tom would have periods where he would fall into the abyss, crawl into his hole for a time -- but usually for just a few days, and never this severely. More than half of the time, Tom was a man of exuberance and energy, "like a cricket," Lois said -- a man of enthusiasm, with a passion for learning. More and more, Tom was like a spinning planet, screaming through the void, with alternating periods of light and darkness. Now the days were getting shorter and the nights longer. It was even worse in the winter months. As the days shortened and Christmas approached, a cloud would envelop Tom. He began to spend money in strange ways, often on patent medicines advertised in newspapers and magazines for headaches and ear ailments. T.J. would hear his father's heavy footsteps echo through the house at night, sometimes pacing all the way 'till morning. Other times the footsteps would venture outside, into the chilly dark, and T.J. could hear his father's boots crunch the icy grass outside his window.

It seemed as if the footsteps were walking farther and farther from the house, a little farther each night, until T.J. resolved one night to follow them, wherever they might lead.

T.J. quietly exited the house, careful not to swing the screen door too widely. He began shivering almost as soon as he hit the porch, and found that he had to step back in for a moment to don an extra layer of clothing.

The sky was a cold, perfect black, with no stars or moon whatsoever to light the way. But T.J. thought he could see his father's silhouette out by the main road. So he followed, as quietly as he could manage.

As he approached Eaves Bridge Road, he caught sight of some pale reflections on his periphery. The realization suddenly hit him: those were gravestones. He was very near the cemetery.

T.J. lost sight of his father for a moment and he stopped by a huge oak, which provided a kind of safe harbor. He learned against the tree and listened. He heard nothing for a moment, not even an insect. It was all deathly silent.

Then he thought he heard something coming from the graveyard. Something like labored, heavy breaths.

He peered out into the cemetery but could see nothing. Looking closer, he kept his eye on the white stones, and thought, for a moment, that he saw a shadow pass in front of one of them.

T.J. felt like his heart had been jabbed with a stick of ice. Every instinct told him to run back to the house. But he had to find his father. What was he doing out here?

He heard a loud rattle of wood to his left, opposite the graveyard. It was coming from the old, toppled schoolhouse.

T.J. squinted and saw a faint, flickering light within. He snuck up to one of the windows and peered inside. His father was crouched down in the rubble, leafing through a book. He watched as Tom waved the coal oil lamp, searching under boards and shattered desks – looking for what, T.J. did not know. His father appeared intent, almost frantic, as if he were searching for something specific. T.J. thought of a rat in a maze he had read about in the *National Geographic*, looking for a bit of cheese.

As T.J. leaned in closer, pressing against the window, a board fell out from under him.

"Who's there!" Tom said, shining the lamp into the window.

"It's me."

"T.J.? What are you doing out here at this time of night?"

T.J. slid his thin frame through the broken window frame.

"Be careful, now. There's shattered glass all through here," said Tom. He offered T.J. his arm.

"You should go back home," Tom said, pulling his son through the window. "It's not safe."

"Then why are *you* here?" asked T.J., brushing himself off. It was odd to see the schoolhouse on its side, with all the desks and shelves piled onto what had been the eastern wall.

"Don't worry about me. I'm an adult. You need to be in the bed, now. Get on back to the house."

168

T.J. sat on the floor and glanced around the room, bathed in ghostly yellow lamplight. It was like an ancient cave. Former students of the school had snuck in and painted hunting scenes on the walls, and the splintered desks were piled up on the floor like old bones.

"Can't I just go back home when you do?" asked T.J.

"I just need to have some time by myself," said Tom.

"Dad, *all* your time is time by yourself," said T.J. "Even when you're with us." T.J. immediately regretted saying it.

Tom looked angry for a moment. Then a wave of sad recognition came over him, followed by a knowing laugh.

"I'm sorry, T.J.," he said. "I just thought—"

He sat down on the floor opposite T.J. and reached for a book lying among the scrapheap.

"T.S. Eliot," muttered Tom.

"I remember him," said T.J. "You taught us about him. *The Waste Land.*"

"That's right. That's him. You remembered," said Tom, leafing through the pages. He smiled as he ran his fingers over the annotations he had penciled into the margins through the years.

"Most people won't teach him, you know," said Tom. "They say he's not Christian. But he was. He was a devout Christian. Of course, then again, he was Catholic."

He came to a page with a bookmark and clipping and he stopped.

"*A cold coming we had of it,*" he said, reading from the clipping. "*Just the worst time of year ... the very dead of winter...*"

He trailed off and seemed lost in his thoughts. T.J. waited patiently for the rest of the poem.

"I don't remember that one," said T.J.

169

"That's because I didn't teach it to you," said Tom, closing the book. "It wasn't even published until just a few years ago. Besides, that one's for me."

"What's it about?"

"Were we led all this way for birth or death?" said Tom.

"Is that from the poem or are you asking me a question?"

"Both," he answered. "But don't answer the question until you've read the poem. And don't read the poem. Not yet."

"Why not?" said T.J.

"You're not old enough."

His father continued to rummage through the rubble. He crouched down and sifted through a stack of torn papers and emerged with another book.

"Found another one?" asked T.J.

He could tell from his father's expression that this wasn't just another book. This one was special. Maybe this is what he had come here searching for.

"T.J., have you ever read Dante?"

T.J. thought for a moment.

"The Inferno?" he said. *"'Abandon all hope, all ye who enter here,'* or something like that?"

"Hello! I didn't know you were such a reader," said Tom.

"I pick stuff up. Somtimes."

"La Divina Commedia, by Dante Allighieri," said Tom, reading from the title page. *"'The writer, having lost his way in a gloomy forest, and being hindered by certain wild beasts from ascending a mountain, is met by Virgil, who promises to show him the punishments of Hell, and afterwards of Purgatory; and that he shall then be conducted by Beatrice into Paradise."*

170

Tom stopped and coughed.

"Are you all right?" T.J. asked. Tom nodded.

"You know," he said, "her name wasn't pronounced Beatrice. It was much more beautiful. The Italians, they said, 'Bee-ah-tree-chay.'"

"Bee-ah-tree-chay,'" repeated T.J.

"Do you know that she was a real woman? I mean girl. Dante met her when she was only nine. He fell in love with her right then."

"That sounds kind of sick," said T.J.

"Well, he was young, too," said Tom. "Age didn't matter. He knew. They both knew."

"So he married her?"

"Oh, no. No. That's not how courtly love worked. They hardly even spoke," said Tom. "I believe he only spoke to her twice in her whole life. She died when she was only 24, or something like that. They both married other people. But he never wrote about his wife. He didn't immortalize her, like he did *Bee-ah-tree-chay*."

"Sounds like someone got the sh — the short end of the stick," said T.J.

Tom smiled.

"Well, I'm sure he would have liked to have consummated the relationship," he said.

"No," said T.J. "I mean his wife."

"Oh," he said. "Oh, yes. But you have to understand, T.J. This girl, she showed him the *Celestial City*. All the joys of Heaven. Here was a man, *'Midway of this our mortal life, in a gloomy wood, astray,'* and this girl, she takes him by the hand to that place where *love impells all*, and *'moves the sun in Heaven and all the stars.'"*

T.J. fiddled with his shoelaces.

171

"Yes, but," he said, "but isn't it possible ... isn't it possible that he just imagined her to be this perfect, heavenly being? I mean, he didn't even know her, if he only spoke to her twice. No one is that perfect. Don't you think he kind of put her on a pedestal and kind of -- kind of idealized her?"

"Maybe," said Tom. "But he didn't have to know her, T.J. You see, he loved her. He absolutely *loved* her."

Tom stood up, closed the book, and motioned for T.J. to follow him back through the window. He took one last look around the old school building before helping his son back onto the cold ground.

"Some things you just can't understand when you're 16, T.J.," he said. "You'll understand when you're a man. And then you'll read this book and it will all make sense to you."

As they ascended the dark path to the house, T.J. could see a lamp in the window. Either it was morning or his mother was up searching for them. By now, she was accustomed to searching for Tom in the dark.

CANTO IX

*"I am dead, and so it behooves me to conduct you
down here through Hell, from circle unto circle. So it shall soon be
with you."*

Thus the Poet tells me.

*I open my front door. The warmth of the fire envelops me.
Soon I will stop shivering. Then it will be time to get to work.*

Winter

Chapter Nine

1

Dec. 17 came and dumped 14 inches of snow on the ground. Collier was more excited than anyone, begging his mother to suit him up so he could go play in the drifts. Erlene, too, squawked gleefully when she saw how beautiful everything was, with the ice-coated trees glistening in the sun and an unsullied layer of white coating everything for miles around. Lois had to keep haranguing the children to step back inside until they were fully dressed in the appropriate number of layers.

T.J., of course, had seen snows like this before, although usually not this early in the season. Grady told him he'd been saving an old board under the house just for this occasion.

T.J. and Beryl wanted to stay indoors, but the smaller children pleaded until they were persuaded to come help them build a snowman.

Grady climbed to the top of the hill above the house with his board and waved to everyone as he went down flat on his stomach and pushed off.

"Watch out for those trees!" their mother warned, but he was already barreling towards the apple orchard full-tilt, screaming as he zipped across the ice.

Their father, who'd had more trouble sleeping, lately, was out in the shop, working on the Maxwell, which hadn't run since that night of the party, when he'd smacked it into a tree. It seemed to T.J. that the more his father tinkered with the car, the worse off the problem became. The last time he'd stepped into his father's shop the poor car lay there in at least

20 different pieces. He hadn't the proper tools to wrench its innards back into submission, anyway. The automobile was something new, something Tom just didn't know how to deal with, something that lay outside his field of reference.

T.J. saw a car approaching, a car he immediately recognized. It was Carl, driving Uncle Abijah's Model A Ford again. He honked the horn a few times in a friendly manner and waved.

After he pulled into the driveway he stopped the car and stood up in his seat.

"Howdy, there, Miss Latham!" he said to T.J.'s mother.

"Hello, Carl," she answered. "You get by all right in this storm?"

"Oh, I get by jest fine, I reckon," he said. "But I could do with a little help. I was wonderin' if I might work out a trade."

He explained to Lois that he needed a first mate to help him get to Buchanan through the snow and ice. His father wanted him to pick up a few things and he would be glad to get anything the Lathams needed, free of charge, so long as T.J. could accompany him to town.

"You won't make it, Carl," said Lois. "I measured over a foot of snow. You should take a horse."

He shook his head and waved her off.

"Naw, naw," he said. "I know how to do this. We'll be fine. I got through storms worse'n thissun."

Lois cocked an eyebrow suspiciously, but she'd already decided to let her son go. He'd been grounded for two weeks already for going to the party on Thanksgiving and he'd earned a trip to town. She gave him a list of things to fetch and sent him off.

"What about Dad?" T.J. asked.

177

"Oh, you let me worry about your daddy," she said. "I'll set him straight."

That was all T.J. needed to hear. He smiled and jumped into the car with Carl, who cranked up the engine.

It was only after the car began sliding down the driveway that T.J. started to have his doubts.

"You sure you know how to do this?" he asked.

Carl smiled, reached into the back, and threw a pile of burlap sacks into T.J.'s lap.

"What's this for?" asked T.J.

"You'll see," he said. "Let's stop and get us some gas, and then we'll be on our way."

"Won't all the gas stations be closed?" asked T.J.

"Not the one I use!" he answered.

2

At the bottom of the hill was a blacksmith's shop maintained by old Mr. Ivey. Carl explained that he kept a big drum of burnt motor oil that could be used for gasoline. Carl could get it for free most of the time. Mr. Ivey, it turned out, was a regular customer of Bije's.

"Won't that old oil ruin your car?" asked T.J.

"Well, first off, it ain't my car," said Carl.

"And second?" T.J. said, after the requisite pause.

"Second?" said Carl. "Well, second, it ain't my car."

They skidded across an ice patch into the front lot of the shop, which looked closed. Carl puffed a few warm breaths into his hands and hopped out.

"You wait here," he said.

"They won't be able to see us from the house if we park here, will they? Shouldn't we honk the horn?"

"Naw, naw. Let's don't bother him. I know where it's at," Carl said.

T.J. watched as Carl legged his way into the shop. Carl peeked around the corner and then shuffled inside. Just a few seconds later, T.J. spotted a hunched-over figure trotting down the hill in a housecoat and long underwear. Old Man Ivey.

"Hey!" he said, waving a large wrench in T.J.'s direction. "Can I help you boys?"

T.J. looked to the shop and saw Carl in the window, shaking his head and putting his finger to his mouth in a shushing gesture. T.J. quickly averted his glance and slid over to the driver's side.

"Got any gas?" he asked.

"Naw, I'm closed," said Ivey. "You fellers don't need to be headed out anywhere in all this mess, no how. Is Carl with you? I thought I saw two of you pull up in here. Ain't this Bije Latham's car?"

"It's just me," said T.J. as Carl popped back up in the window, shaking his head again.

"Carl asked me to find a place to fill her up and take her on back," T.J. said. "He said you had some burnt up motor oil we could get cheap."

The old man nodded his head, coughed, and spat something thick and yellow into the snow.

"Naw, we're clear outta that," he said. "You tell Carl not to fool with coming around for that stuff no more. It'll tear up the engine on your uncle's car, for one thing. Carl needs to just put up the money and buy some regular gasoline like ever-body else. I can't keep showing preference. Other folks might get the wrong idea. You tell him that. You boys don't need to be out in this storm, no how."

179

"All right, sir," said T.J. "Thank you."

The man stood there for a moment as T.J. sat in the driver's seat, not knowing what to do. T.J. looked back to the window and saw Carl making some kind of gesture he couldn't understand, flicking his wrist with his fingers pinched together. He began mouthing something. T.J. studied his lips but couldn't make it out.

He slowly came to the realization that the old man was waiting for him to start up the car and leave, which presented a problem, since T.J. had never driven before.

"Well, guess I'll be going," T.J. said to buy himself some time.

He had never paid much attention to Carl's machinations while driving. He was always too busy being a passenger. But T.J. supposed it must have something to do with a lever. That's how most machines get started, after all, he reasoned. So he reached down and pulled the only lever to be seen, and the car started to move.

"Good evening, Mr. Ivey!" T.J. said, waving and steering as best he could.

"Ain't you gonna start her up?" said Ivey.

"No, this is fine," said T.J., waving again and trying to remain calm.

What did Ivey mean? Wasn't the car already started? Then he noticed that the engine wasn't making any noise.

The car was rolling faster and faster now. T.J. looked behind him for help. The doors of the blacksmith's shop burst open and a huge barrel came rolling out of it, with Carl running close behind.

"Hey!" said the man, holding the wrench aloft. "Hey, now! Stop it right there! Hey!"

180

The old man couldn't run, though, especially on this ice. Even as he slipped and slid, Carl kept pace with the rolling barrel, which was trailing just behind T.J. as he careened down the icy slope.

"Carl!" he said. "I can't stop! I can't stop!"

"Don't worry about stoppin'! Just keep a-goin'!" Carl said, kicking the rolling barrel back on the path.

"Steer it like you'd steer a mule!" shouted Carl.

T.J. didn't know exactly what Carl meant since mules didn't have steering wheels. And no mule he'd ever come across went this fast, ever.

The icy trees whipped by at a quickening pace as T.J. maintained a frosty grip on the wheel, and the whole car began to shake. He decided he'd push a pedal, any pedal. Carl often pushed the pedals. It seemed to work for him. The car was moving so fast, he knew that whatever pedal he pushed, he'd have to push it hard.

The first pedal did nothing. So T.J. braced and shoved his foot down on the second pedal as the oil drum barreled along closer and closer behind him.

He was jarred about a foot out of his seat as the wheels locked and the car spun backward. T.J. screamed as the barrel tumbled closer and closer, coming off the ground like a bouncing cannonball, ready to smash into the windshield.

"Not the brakes!" Carl screamed. But it was too late.

The car slid across the icy road and took to the air as it was whisked off the shoulder. As the rear of the car caught the snowbank, it shot ice through the air like a confetti cannon. The oil barrel tumbled to a resting place just inches from T.J.'s head.

His heart palpitations got the better of him as Carl crested the hill.

181

"Good night!" he said, and he winked out.

3

"T.J, are you all right?"

Carl's raucous laughter rustled T.J. from his stupor. He performed a quick self-examination, then looked up to see Carl bent over, hands on his knees, catching air.

"That fixed us pretty good, didn't it?" Carl said, pumping his fist against his chest and clearing his throat. T.J. lifted himself up, brushing the snow from his clothing, trying to mentally piece together what had just happened.

"We need to—" said Carl, beginning to wheeze. "We should -"

He shook his head and leaned over the hood of the car.

"Carl? Carl? You all right?" asked T.J.

Carl nodded, leaning in on his rolled knuckles.

"I'll be—" he said, then stopped and shook his head again.

"Carl!" said T.J., standing up in the car and jumping out the side. Carl collapsed in front of the grill, bumping his head on the fender on the way down. T.J. leaned over Carl, unsure of what to do. Something told him he should remove Carl's shirt, but he worried that the cold of the snow would make matters worse.

Carl motioned for T.J. to come closer. He then whispered to him in a ghostly, faint voice:

"Look in the back seat."

T.J. stood and raced back around to the rear of the vehicle. A few blankets were piled up on the floorboards. He grabbed one and brought it back to Carl, covering him. Carl shook his head and tossed the blanket to the side.

"Look *under* it, you nincompoop," he whispered.

T.J. nodded and returned to the back seat, lifting up the blankets. Underneath were about 10 clay jugs. T.J. grabbed one of them and popped it open.

Carl propped himself up against the fender and downed the whiskey. He put a hand on T.J.'s shoulder.

"I'll be all right in a bit," he said. "We gotta get this thing outta here."

He asked T.J. to rummage through the back a bit more to find his honey jar. T.J. found it without much trouble and brought it back to Carl, who dabbed some in his mouth, chasing it with another few swallows of whiskey.

"Help me up, now," he said.

T.J. crouched over to aid Carl but stopped short as the low rumble of an engine approached. T.J. turned around to see a sheriff's car up on the shoulder. An officer tumbled out, leaving the car door open.

"Shit," said Carl, under his breath.

"What should we do?" asked T.J., still cradling Carl.

"Nothing," Carl said. "We cain't do nothing."

T.J. watched the man, a deputy, slide down the ice slope on the shoulder. He and Carl were still as deer as the lawman trudged his way across the white blanket of snow, leaving four-inch-deep imprints in his path. When he finally crunched his way to the car the man shook his head.

"Looks like you boys could do with a little help," said the man, extending his hand.

"What's that?" asked T.J., staring blankly.

"I said it looks like y'all could use some help!"

"Oh, yes. Yessir," said T.J., taking the man's thick, rough hand.

"My friend here, he has asthma," said T.J. The deputy nodded and pointed to the barrel.

"Is that yours?" he asked.

"Naw," said Carl.

"Yessir," said T.J., simultaneously. "That is, it was our barrel, but we were trying to put that gas in the car and the barrel rolled off, so we lost it. But now we found it so I reckon it's ours again."

"Well, here," said the deputy, bracing himself. "You boys pick up that other end."

T.J. and Carl tried not to stare at the deputy, but they were unsure of what kind of game he might be playing.

"Come on and just lift it on up," he said.

T.J. and Carl walked around to the opposite side of the barrel and grabbed hold.

"You all right?" T.J. asked. Carl nodded.

"Ready? Let's just take it on over to the car and set it down."

The deputy brushed the snow off his hands.

"You boys got a hose?"

Carl thought for a moment.

"Yeah, I believe I got a hose," he said, stepping over to the back seat of the car. T.J. watched him as he threw the blankets back on top of the whiskey jugs.

"I know it's back here somewheres," Carl said, straightening out the blankets.

"Well, here. I'll help you look," said the officer.

T.J. looked to Carl in a sudden panic. But the deputy stopped before he ever got to the back seat and looked up at his fellow officer, still sitting in the car on the shoulder of the road.

"Wait a second," he said. "We got one in the car. Hey, Lewis!"

The other officer rolled down the window. He had a half-finished sandwich in one hand and mayonnaise drippings on his face.

"What?" he said.

"Toss me down that hose," he said.

The man squinted his eyes and wiped his mouth.

"What?" he asked again.

The deputy turned around and rolled his eyes at T.J.

"I'm sorry, boys. Lewis is a tad on the slow side."

Carl and T.J. smiled and exchanged glances as a hose fell into the snow. The officer scooped it up and walked back to the car.

"Open up the tank there, son," he said. The officer opened the drum and placed one end of the hose into it.

"I hate this shit," he said, putting the other end of the hose into his mouth. He sucked on it for a few seconds, then grimaced and spit the black sludge into the snow, quickly shoving the hose into the tank.

"Good Lord!" he said, wiping his mouth and spitting once more. "What is that shit, boys? That ain't regular gasoline, is it?"

He wiped his mouth and patted T.J. on the back.

"You boys got yourselves in a real fix, didn't you?" he said. "There are people stranded all over this country because of the storm."

"At least folks won't be running no whiskey," said Carl with a toothy grin. T.J. glared at him. The officer smiled and looked back at the car.

"Looks like you boys are gonna need some help getting outta that snowbank."

185

"That's all right, officer," said T.J. "I think we can get it on out."

"It's not a problem, son," he said, gripping T.J.'s shoulder and giving it a squeeze.

The officer moved around to the back of the car, motioning for T.J. to step to the opposite side.

"Lewis! Lewis, get your ass on down here and help these boys!"

"That's all right, sir. I think we can get it," said T.J.

"Aw, he needs to do some work, anyhow. There ain't a sorrier man alive."

Lewis put aside his sandwich, opened the door and came sliding down the bank. He had thin, gangly legs, large hands and a crooked nose. As he stood he wiped the ice from his hands and pulled his coat in closer.

"Shoot, it's freezing!" the man said.

"Well, it is a snowstorm, Lewis," said the larger officer, pointing Lewis around to the rear.

"Y'all ready?" asked Carl, turning the ignition key. The officer nodded and Carl eased onto the gas pedal. The car lurched forward about six inches, then slid back about a foot as the tires slipped over the ice.

"Hold up, hold up!" shouted the deputy, glancing into the car. "You boys mind if we use these blankets here to get us some traction?"

"I got something even better," said Carl, reaching into the passenger side.

"Throw one of these up under there, officer," he said, tossing him a burlap sack.

"Well I'll be damned," said the officer. "You boys come prepared."

"You know, we got a lot of these in the trunk," said Lewis as he placed the sack under the rear tire. Carl tossed a second bag back to T.J. on the opposite side.

"Remember when we broke up that still down the river near the old Pollard place?" Lewis said. "They was using these same types of burlap sacks for the corn mash and for sieving. We broke up the still, but I kept all them bags."

"Right smart of you, Lewis," said the deputy. "They might come in handy today."

Slowly, steadily, the two deputies and T.J. worked the car through the snow in fits and starts, gradually working their way up the embankment. Lewis lost his grip and tumbled back into the snowdrift. As he came back up he spotted something in the snow.

"Hey Sheriff!" he said. T.J. and Carl exchanged glances once again. *Sheriff?*

"Sheriff, take a look at this!"

T.J. knew what it was, even without looking. It was the whiskey jug he had handed to Carl just before the officers arrived on the scene.

"I'll be damned," said the sheriff, brushing the snow and ice off the jug and taking a whiff.

"You boys wouldn't tell on me, now would you?" he said, winking at Carl.

The sheriff chugged down the jug without so much as coming up for air and wiped his mouth across his sleeve.

"Now that's some mighty fine whiskey," he said. "You boys want a swaller?"

"No, thank you, sir," said T.J. "I don't drink."

"I guess I might have me a swaller or two," said Carl, reaching out for the jug. Carl coughed a few times then took a sip, handing the bottle back to the sheriff.

"Looks like you boys get around," said the sheriff.

"I want you to do me a favor, now," he said. "I want you tell everybody you know, vote for Buford Richards for sheriff. We got a primary coming up in the spring. You'll remember that, won't you, boys?"

T.J. and Carl both nodded their heads.

"You boys are old enough to vote, ain't you?" the sheriff asked. Carl and T.J. looked at one another then nodded again.

"Well," he said, "even if you ain't, we can fix that. You just show up and we'll take care of you. See you on election day. And you boys be careful out there."

Carl looked down the road and saw a hunched-over Mr. Ivey plodding his way through the snow. He motioned for T.J. to get into the car as he gunned the engine.

"We'll do it, Sheriff Richards!" said Carl, kicking up ice as his tires spun in the snow.

"Hey!" he heard Mr. Ivey call from down the road. "Hey! Sheriff! Stop them boys!"

But Carl and T.J. were already gone. And, besides, everybody knew that Mr. Ivey was a Republican.

4

Carl told T.J. he had to make a stop before they headed into town. Every half-mile or so, the car would get stuck in the snow and ice, and T.J. had to jump out of the car and toss a burlap sack under a wheel to get them going again. Carl assured him that they had enough sacks to make it to town, although he wasn't sure if they were going to have enough to get back, so he might have to stock up again.

Carl pulled up to Bije's new house, the one he had purchased from Aunt Lizzie. When he drove into the yard, Jo Ann walked outside, accompanied by an older woman T.J. didn't recognize. They both carried two suitcases. Carl kept the car running as he hopped out and opened up the rumble seat. He took the luggage from the older woman and threw the bags in, then helped the ladies ascend the high rear wheel. Jo Ann wore white gloves. As she got into the car, she took one of them off to wipe her face. She had been crying.

"Here, ma'am. You can sit up front," said T.J.

"No, that's all right. I'll just sit in the rumble seat," she said. The woman, who looked like an older version of Jo Ann, climbed in and closed the rear door. Carl followed.

"Don't worry about them blankets, ma'am," said Carl. "Y'all can put yer feet on 'em. It won't make no differnce in the world, to me."

T.J. wondered what was going on – why was Jo Ann going to Buchanan? Who was the woman accompanying her? Her mother? How had Carl gotten involved? And why was Jo Ann crying? But there were some questions you just could not ask.

"So where's Hoke today?" he asked instead, hoping this would lead to some type of inoffensive conversation. He also suspected that Hoke might be the cause of the trouble.

"We don't know and we don't care," said the older woman. T.J. glanced at the rear-view mirror and saw Jo Ann now had tears streaming freely down her beautiful, pale cheeks.

Carl took a turn too quickly and the Model A was suddenly thrust into the air on the passenger side, balanced precariously on two wheels. The older lady grabbed her hat and everyone gripped their seats.

189

"Hold 'em, Simon!" T.J. yelled as his side of the vehicle landed back in the snow and skidded a few yards into the bank.

The by-now-familiar sound of wheels sliding against ice sent T.J. hopping out of the car once more, and he was grateful, this time. Sitting in tense silence was hard to take.

When they finally arrived in town, nearly two hours later, Carl hopped out like a chauffeur, opening the doors for both Jo Ann and the older woman, then scooted around to the rear to pull their suitcases out and plop them on the sidewalk.

"We'll catch the bus from here, Carl. Bless you," said the woman, reaching into her purse and pulling out a 10 cent piece.

"Oh, no ma'am," Carl said, pushing it away politely. "It weren't no trouble a'tall. I was a-comin' to Buchanan, anyhow."

"Well," she said, nodding appreciatively.

"Thank you," said Jo Ann, picking up her luggage and following the woman.

When they walked across the street, past the court house, out of earshot, T.J. prodded Carl for more information.

"What's their story?" he said.

Carl pulled open the rumble seat to reveal a compartment underneath. He yanked aside an old oil cloth, revealing rows of neatly-stacked jugs of whiskey.

"Go fetch one a' them blankets," said Carl. T.J. whisked one out and handed it to Carl, who began expertly wrapping up the jugs.

"Where are we going?" T.J. asked.

"Wallace's store," Carl said. "And don't you ever say a word about this, you understand? Can I trust ya?"

"Yes, Carl," T.J. said. "You can trust me."

190

Carl patted him on the shoulder and handed him the blanket, loaded down with whiskey jugs.

"That's good," he said. "Cause you're a whiskey runner, now, son."

T.J. didn't know that he liked the sound of that, but he took the blanket and headed into the store with it, like Carl instructed. Carl went into the back seat and gathered up the remaining jugs, wrapping them in one of the other blankets, then followed T.J. into the store.

T.J. didn't want to know too much about the business end of things. He was more interested in what was going on with Jo Ann. So as Carl settled up with the man behind the counter, T.J. wandered back outside and watched as the two women waited at the bus stop. It appeared that the older woman was lecturing Jo Ann, waving her finger harshly in several different directions while Jo Ann continued to wipe her tears.

T.J. supposed that Hoke had broken her heart in some way, which he had expected to happen. He wished he could walk across the street and say something to comfort her. But he knew there was nothing he could possibly say.

As he was looking at the two ladies, he noticed a familiar gait behind them. Uncle Victor?

T.J. squinted his eyes to focus and he was sure he was right. Victor was coming out of a diner with what looked like two young women. He could hear him laughing from all the way across the square.

T.J. looked back into Wallace's store and saw Carl still talking with the man, inspecting the goods behind the counter. T.J. decided to walk up the square a bit to get a closer look.

191

He tried to lay low, like the detectives he'd seen in the picture shows, moving from awning to awning. He could clearly see now that it was his uncle. The two women were definitely not Aunt Lillian, Birdy, or any of Victor's other daughters. They were wearing too much make-up and flapper-type clothes that had gone out of style years ago. Why would Victor be associating with girls like those? This was the kind of thing his mother must have been talking about.

T.J. watched as some man he didn't know drove up in a Model T. Victor and the two girls got in, but not before one of the girls put her arm around Victor's waist and nuzzled him.

T.J. walked back to Wallace's store and found Carl already in the car, waiting for him.

"Follow that T model," said T.J.

"Which?" asked Carl. "You mean that one with the curtain top?"

"That's the one," said T.J. "Follow it."

Carl smiled as he started up the car.

"There ain't no need to foller that car," said Carl.

"Why not?" said T.J. "I asked you, please, to follow it!"

Carl laughed as he headed back home, across the bridge, ignoring T.J.'s request.

"Because I already know where that car goes. It goes to Gobbler's Knob."

Gobbler's Knob! T.J. had heard the young men speak of that place. When you wanted *something to screw*, and had a few extra dollars to pay for it, that was the place to go, they all said. He had heard some of the older men at church vilify the place, calling it a den of sin. On the other hand, he had heard Hoke rate the place rather highly.

"Whatsa matter?" asked Carl.

192

"Nothing," said T.J. "Just get me home, Carl. I want to go home."

CANTO X

When we were now right over the last cloister of Malebolge, so that my little ones could manifest themselves unto my sight, diverse lamentings pierced me through and through, which with compassion had their arrows barbed...

Whereat mine ears I covered with my hands.

195

Chapter Ten

1

T.J.'s mother was washing the dishes when he came in the door. He tossed the bag of items she had requested on the kitchen table. Erlene pushed an old spool across the floor, squealing every time her tormentor, Collier, grabbed it.

"Well, I guess y'all made it all right," she said, placing a clean dish in the stack. "Did you get everything I asked?"

T.J. nodded and sat at the table. The family Bible sat there. He opened the book and began to leaf through it.

"I was afraid I told you the wrong thing," his mother said. "I began to think that maybe I shouldn't have let you go out in this weather in that open-top car. What if y'all got stuck and couldn't get out?"

T.J. nodded as he leafed through the pages of II Kings.

"I saved you some supper," she said. "You want it?"

T.J. shrugged his shoulders.

"Yes, ma'am. That sounds good," he said.

"It'll just be a minute," she said, moving two pots over to the wood stove and leaning down to open the vent.

Lois looked at T.J. and noted his sullen expression. She walked over to him and straightened his shirt.

"You sure you're all right?" she asked. He nodded and began to trace passages with his index finger.

"You know," she said, bending down playfully and whispering in his ear, "I can always tell when something's bothering you."

T.J. took off his glasses and wiped them with his shirt.

"Mama," he said, "what does the Bible say about tattling?"

Lois pulled out a chair and took a seat beside T.J. at the table.

"Well, I'm sure it says it's wrong," she said. T.J. seemed comforted by that answer. A little too comforted for Lois' liking.

"On the other hand," she said, "I do know this. The Bible says thou shall not bear false witness. And keeping quiet, in some cases, is just the same thing."

"*EEEEEEiiiieeeeeaaahh!*"

The awful noise roared into the kitchen from the back bedroom, followed by a mad rush of footsteps.

"*The devil!*" screamed Collier, racing back into the kitchen. "Mama! Mama! I seen the devil!"

Collier hugged his mother's leg and Erlene followed suit, not because she saw the devil, but because she didn't want Collier to get all the attention. It would have been funny, had Collier not looked genuinely frightened. He was shivering and panting.

"Collier, there's no devil in this house."

"Uh-huh, there is a devil, I saw him!" said Collier. "I saw him in the bedroom! It had skin white as death and just growled at me!"

"Whose bedroom?"

"In Grady's bedroom!"

Lois shot a glance at T.J. that said, basically, "Well, that explains it."

She marched into Grady and T.J.'s room and pushed the door open. Grady was sitting on the bed with T.J.'s Bible, leafing casually through the pages.

"I suppose you don't know anything about this, right?" said Lois.

"What?" said Grady, innocently. Lois nodded.

197

"So where is it?"

Collier pointed to a hole in the floor.

"In there! In there! We saw it, didn't we, Grady! We saw the devil!"

A knot had fallen out of the wood plank in the floor, leaving a hole about two inches wide.

"Collier," said Grady, sitting up and putting the Bible aside. "I told you there ain't no devil in there. I was just joking."

"But we saw it! We saw it!"

"Here, look," said T.J. "Wait a minute."

T.J. whispered something in Grady's ear and his brother sprinted out of the room toward the kitchen.

Collier and Erlene clung to their mother as they stared down into the menacing, empty hole. T.J. bent over the put his ear to it. He thought he heard something. *Panting. Sharp, labored breaths.* Was there a dog up under the house?

Grady returned with a piece of cork. He handed it to T.J., who pulled out the knife he'd won from Carl and carved into it.

"Look, Collier," said T.J. "That's a cross I'm putting in this cork. That's the mark of the Lord Jesus Christ. No devil can break through it."

He knelt down and plugged the cork into the hole.

"See?" he said. "You're safe, now. It's the hedge in the gap. You understand? You'll be all right."

"Where'd you get that knife?" Grady asked admiringly. T.J. shrugged his shoulders and pocketed it.

Grady smiled at his mother, who rolled her eyes. He pounced back onto the bed and opened the Bible once again. T.J. followed his mother back into the kitchen to get a drink for the little ones.

"So, I suppose, then," said Lois as she scooped out the water, "it becomes a matter of individual conscience."

At first T.J. didn't know what she meant by that. But then he realized she had circled back around to their previous conversation about tattling.

It wasn't the answer T.J. had hoped for. But his mother aimed to make it a little easier for him.

"What is it?" she asked. "Is it something to do with your father? Grady?"

He shook his head.

"Your uncles, then?"

T.J. stared at the open pages of the Bible for a moment, then nodded.

"Uncle Virgil?" she asked. T.J. shook his head.

"Uncle Bije?"

He shook his head again. Lois thought more intently.

"You're not talking about my two brothers, are you?" she said.

"Uncle Paul? No, no, no," he said. "Of course not. No, it's ... it's Uncle Victor."

She thought for a moment, searching through the memories of the past few weeks.

"We all know he drinks, T.J.," she said. "Your Daddy is trying to get him straightened out. And I have to believe that your Uncle Victor is trying real hard, too. It's just that ever since Woodrow died—"

"This isn't about that," said T.J.

A screen door opened and suddenly T.J.'s father was there. He could sense that he had walked into the middle of a serious conversation.

"What is it?" he asked.

Lois exchanged glances with T.J.

"T.J. was wanting to tell me something. Something about Victor."

"What?" asked Tom, wiping sweat from his brow and putting a part of the car engine on the table with a thud. He had been in the shop for weeks now, trying to repair the Maxwell. The first payment to the bank would come due when the crops came in, in the spring. T.J. had heard his father say that he was determined to fix it by then because he couldn't stand the thought of paying for something he couldn't even use.

"When I was in town this afternoon..." said T.J., trailing off.

"He saw Victor," said Lois.

"Victor was in town today?" Tom asked. "That's strange."

"What?" asked Lois.

"Well, he was out chopping wood at his place and loading it up with his girls all yesterday and then again this morning," said Tom. "I felt kind of sorry for those girls. I saw Birdy and Dora out there. But I figured it was because of this cold snap, and the storm..."

"You don't think he *sold* the wood, do you?" Lois said.

"What was he doing there, T.J.? Who was he with?"

T.J. shook his head.

"I'm not sure, Dad," he said.

"Now don't lie to me, son," said Tom. "Who was he with?"

"I didn't recognize them. Just two girls."

Tom slammed his fist on the table. He looked at T.J. and Lois and bit his upper lip in frustration. He grabbed a chair from the table and tossed it into the wall, shattering it to bits.

"Tom!" said Lois.

But he was already out the door.

"Tom, wait!" She motioned for T.J. to get up and follow them.

"Where are you going?" she said, pacing after him through the front yard.

"To Virgil's. To get the car."

"Wait, Tom. What are you going to do?"

"I'm going to go get my brother," he said. "And then I'm going to take him back home."

"You're not going to hurt him, are you, Tom?" she said.

"You're worried about me hurting him? What about the hurt he's caused? What about his family?"

Lois looked desperately at T.J.

"Take T.J. with you," she said.

"What? No. He can't go. It's Gobbler's Knob, Lois."

"But I want to come. I won't be any trouble."

Tom looked at T.J. and shook his head.

"All right. Come on," he said. "But don't say anything, and don't do anything, unless I tell you to do it, you hear?"

T.J. nodded. His mother kissed him and whispered in his ear.

"Don't take your eyes off your father," she said. "You hear me? Don't take your eyes off your father."

She kissed him again, tears welling up in her eyes, and spun around to walk back into the house. All the kids were on the front porch, staring.

"What did she say?" Tom asked T.J. as soon as Lois herded the children back into the house.

"She said to do what you say," said T.J. His father nodded.

It wasn't long before they made their way to Virgil's house. He was already asleep but Tom woke him up and they began rummaging through the house, looking for guns and ammunition.

"Should we give the boys a call?" asked Virgil. Tom furrowed his brows and shook his head.

"This is a family matter," he said.

They handed two rifles to T.J. as they headed out the door. He took a seat in the back and soon they were racing through the ice to Gobbler's Knob.

2

Enough of the snow and ice had melted and run off during the day that the trip, by evening, was far less treacherous. The three of them only had to get out of the car four times to push it clear of ice.

By the time they arrived at Gobbler's Knob the sun was low on the horizon. The place wasn't much to look at. There were two small, dilapidated hovels, abandoned sharecropper houses. T.J. expected to hear the cackle of laughter from inside but there was nothing, just dead silence. A lamp shone dimly in one of the windows.

"Hand me that rifle, T.J.," said Tom.

"Do I take the other one?" asked T.J.

"Yeah. You take that one. You know how to use it, don't you?"

Tom and Virgil stepped out of the car and T.J. followed. Tom looked back and shook his head emphatically.

"Where are you going? You're staying here."

"But I want to come with you."

"You stay," he said. "We'll be right back. It'll be all right. Give us two minutes. If we're not back by then, you come on in. But take a peek in the window first, all right? Assess. Otherwise, stay here."

T.J. slumped into the car seat as his father and Virgil walked up the dirt path to the old house. T.J. lost sight of them when they crept around to the back door.

The wait was interminable. T.J. wondered what they were seeing. Naked girls? He had to admit that rushing into a cathouse with guns blazing was an exciting proposition, a welcome break from the monotony of school and farming. *So this was the infamous Gobbler's Knob?* It looked somewhat less exotic than the place described by Carl. Places just like this one dotted the backroads all over the county.

A girl's scream pierced the silence, followed by a gunshot.

T.J. gripped the shotgun tightly as he watched the house for any sign of movement. He heard some more voices. Men's voices, he thought. Harsh words, shouting. Maybe it was his father?

Then the front door burst open and his father and Virgil galloped through, lugging Victor between them. He was too drunk to put up much of a struggle.

They opened up the back door and tossed Uncle Victor in, then slammed it shut and hustled into the front seat.

"Come on, let's go," said Tom. "Make sure he's all right, T.J."

The smell was awful. His uncle stank like liquor and something else T.J. couldn't quite peg. Something earthy. All his clothes were undone, hanging loosely around him, even his pants. He was crying and burying his face in his hands.

"I'm so sorry, I'm so sorry," he said. "T.J. don't look at me. *I am of the flesh, Tom. I try so hard, but I am of the flesh.* Please don't tell Lillian and the girls. Please don't tell them. I swear…"

"Shut up, Victor," said Virgil. "You know it's the same shit every goddamn time."

"I know," said Victor. "I know, you're right. But please don't tell them. It would hurt them. I don't mean to hurt them."

"Then why do you do it, Victor?" asked Tom.

"I don't know. There's something wrong with me, Tom," said Victor, sobbing. "I need … I need some … I'm dying, Tom."

"What are you waiting for?" Tom asked, realizing that Virgil still hadn't started the engine.

"I'm dying," Victor said again.

"What?" said Tom as Virgil revved up the engine and put the car into first gear.

"I said I'm dying. It's cirrhosis of the liver, Tom. It's the truth. I ain't got more than a year or two. It's all over for me. I need your help. I need God's help."

"Then God help you," said Virgil, spitting out the window. "He ain't dying, Tom. It's the same old shit."

"I'm dying, T.J.," said Victor, burying his fat, sweaty head into the boy's lap. "I'm dying and it hurts. *I'm dying.*"

T.J., not knowing what else to do, put down his gun and stroked Victor's large, wet head.

"Shhh," he said. "It's all right. It's going to be all right."

He looked out the back window and caught the silhouette of a slender young woman standing in the front door. She was completely naked.

"You sons of bitches!" she screamed. It sounded like she was ripping her vocal chords right out of her throat and tossing them at the car.

"Goddamn you to hell, you Latham sons of bitches! *Goddamn you to hell!"*

T.J. kept his eyes on her until they turned the corner. He could still hear her shouting even when he couldn't see her anymore. She sounded, T.J. thought, like some wild animal.

3

When they arrived at Victor's house, he had already fallen unconscious. They tried to wake him up but he was in such a stupor that it was hopeless.

Birdy was the first one out the door. When Tom opened the back of the car Victor tumbled into the dirt like a sack of potatoes. He curled up into a ball at Tom's feet.

Birdy flew into a protective rage.

"Daddy!" she said, running to his side.

"What did you do to him?" she asked. "T.J.! What happened?"

T.J. sat silently, looking to his father for some instruction. His father shook his head.

Birdy shouted into the house.

"Dora! Eurinee!" she said.

She put her father's arm over her shoulder and whispered to him.

"Come on, Daddy," she said.

"You stay away from my father, you hear, you son of a bitch?" she said. "I'll kill you, I swear. You're killing him! You

205

goddamn bastards are killing him! You stay away from my father!"

T.J. saw Aunt Lillian step out onto the porch. She screamed.

"Victor!"

Tom walked up to the porch but Birdy pushed him away.

"You stay right there!" she said.

"Go!" screamed Aunt Lillian, helping Victor into the house.

"Lillian, it's not—"

"*Go!*" she screamed again. The sound was even more frightening than the cry of the young prostitute, which still rang in T.J.'s ears.

T.J. watched his father try to prop a comforting arm on Lillian's shoulder as he muttered something in a calm, authoritative voice, but she pushed him away. Birdy shoved Tom three times until he tumbled off the porch steps.

"Forget it, Tom," said Virgil, balancing his brother. "Let's go."

"Lillian!" Tom shouted, but she slammed the door shut. Tom then slowly turned and walked back to the car. He slammed the car door shut as he got in.

"Goddamn it!" he shouted, hitting the side of the car.

"Hey, now, watch it," said Virgil. "I just fixed that door handle."

It was only the sixth time T.J. had ever heard his father take the Lord's name in vain.

He felt something brush up against his leg. T.J. looked down. It was a purple hair pin, with lace edges. T.J. sniffed it. It smelled like flowers. He tucked it into his pocket.

"Now, T.J., don't tell your mama anything about what you saw today, and don't tell Grady or Beryl or any of them, either," Tom said. T.J. nodded in agreement.

"So you think he's dying?" asked Virgil as they headed back home.

"Shit, we're all dying, Virgil," he answered. "And there's not a goddamn thing we can do."

4

In church that Sunday, Victor, who was a deacon, came up to the altar, confessed his sins, and begged forgiveness from the church. He began to sob, which didn't help his case as much as it might someone else's, someone younger and not as apt to weep all the time. But then he said those magic words, as he knelt there at the altar: "Oh God, I miss my son. I miss my son so much." Griffith urged the congregation to forgive him, after running him through the usual round of questions about whether he was truly penitent, whether he truly understood the wrongs he had committed, and whether he was now committed to changing forever. It was all affecting, seeing Victor cry as his wife and daughters hugged him and supported him. But T.J. had seen this too many times before. He remembered two years ago when someone from the congregation had pulled him out of a ditch, drunk. And then a year before that when he swore at the preacher. He had promised to change, each time. T.J. knew better. He wondered if the cirrhosis might make things different this time. And then he wondered, again, if he really had cirrhosis of the liver or if it was just a card he was playing to get sympathy. It was hard to tell.

Birdy did not repent for her harsh use of language. She just sat there in her proud, silent way. She didn't come to the altar to atone for her night of drinking, either, but then again neither did T.J.

After the service, Mrs. McConnell cornered T.J. again. She had a look of pity, which T.J. did not understand.

"T.J.," she sighed. "You simply must come over to the house. We'll fix you supper. When can you come? I'll put it on my calendar immediately."

Irene smiled at him, but it wasn't a shy smile, or even a flirtatious one. It was an opening in the doorway.

Mrs. McConnell hugged T.J. and grabbed him by the hands, squeezing.

"So when's it gonna be, T.J.? Friday night?"

"I'll need to see if my parents..." he said. "I don't know if--"

She leaned in closer, although such a thing didn't seem possible. Her puffy face smelled of perfume; her cheeks were swollen hams.

"The Lord is *calling you*, T.J. Latham," she said, in all earnestness. "Don't you know that? You're being *called*."

T.J. laughed. He knew this wasn't the correct response, and certainly not the one Mrs. McConnell had been expecting. He felt compelled to explain.

"Called? Called to preach, you mean? Me?"

Mrs. McConnell warmed to his awkwardness. She rubbed his arm again.

"You think about what I said and then you come over for supper, you hear?" she said. "I'll talk to Tom and Lois if you want me to."

She hugged his neck and lingered for a second as if she wished to console him, but she couldn't find the words. So she turned and waddled away. Irene paused for a moment and whispered in T.J.'s ear before she turned to follow.

"You'd better help that uncle of yours, and your cousin, too, if you can, T.J.," she said. "Everyone around here says they're *goin' to hell.*"

When T.J. went to his room later that evening, he opened his Bible and resolved to read it fresh from Chapter One, Verse One, as he had wanted to do for some time. He had begun the task several times, under the tutelage of his grandmother, but had never finished it. He wanted to be able to say that he had read the Bible from cover to cover. Since his parents had him busy with school or chores during the day, the only time to sneak some time would be at night.

So, after Grady dozed off, T.J. lit a candle and read, from "In the Beginning."

He wondered at the fact that he hadn't noticed how much sex and debauchery was in the Bible before. Everything seemed to revolve around it. It started with Adam and Eve eating the fruit. It didn't specifically say it was an apple, he noted. God killed everyone in the flood, and then Noah paraded around naked and drunk, to the shame of his son. Sarah apparently slept with Pharaoh, as did Rachel, with their husbands' full consent and even their encouragement. Lot slept with his own daughters, who got him drunk so he wouldn't know what he was doing. Abraham had a whore named Tamar, with whom he had fathered a child, before his wife chased her into the desert. God seemed overly interested in Abraham's seed, which he kept promising over and over again to multiply and "spread upon the earth" to "make a great nation," although for some reason he withheld the promise until Abraham and Sarah were both in their nineties. Then there was the rape of Dinah that T.J.'s father had

209

mentioned a few weeks ago, when he talked about Leo Frank, and the whole circumcision thing. Why didn't anyone ever talk about these things in Sunday School? It would have no doubt made it a hell of a lot more interesting.

He was so swept away by it that before long he had finished Genesis and was all the way into Exodus. And that's when he came across a most curious passage, more strange and more difficult to understand than any that had preceded it.

It was just after Moses had been told to lead his people out of Egypt, at the burning bush, just after the Lord tells Moses, "I am that I am." It was Exodus, Chapter 4, verse 24. Moses had stopped at an inn for the night on his way back to Egypt to liberate his people.

"And it came to pass by the way in the inn, that the Lord met him, and sought to kill him.

"Then Zipporah took a sharp stone, and cut off the foreskin of her son, and cast it at his feet, and said, Surely a bloody bridgegroom art thou to me.

"So he let him go: then she said, A bloody bridegroom thou art, because of the circumcision."

What?

This was the passage Grady had been referring to. Why hadn't it struck him before? Why had no one ever spoken of it? It didn't seem that people were even aware of it. Certainly his mother had never mentioned it, and she was a great student of the Bible.

Why would God want to kill Moses, his most faithful servant? What if he had succeeded? Would the whole Bible story have turned out differently? The whole history of the world, even? Would the Jews have remained in Egypt? Would there even have been an Israel? A Christ? A Bible?

210

What was God thinking? What could have provoked such anger, provoke him to do something apparently so destructive to his cause? What had Moses done to offend God? On this, the Bible was silent.

Perhaps it was a test. But a test of whom? Moses was asleep and never even knew what happened. If Zipporah ever told him, the Bible didn't say so. Then it must have been Zipporah who was being tested. But why? She had no major part to play in the story. But, for this brief moment, the entire fate of Judaism and Christianity lay in her hands, in that inn.

If it was a test, T.J. reasoned, she must have passed. But by doing what? By cutting her son's foreskin and casting it at the Lord's feet and accusing the Lord? Who was she speaking to, anyway, when she talked about the "bloody bridegroom"? Was the bloody bridegroom Moses? Or was it God?

What if she had been asleep, T.J. thought? What if she had slept right through everything?

How are we ever to know when that defining moment will come?

T.J. heard a noise outside his window. It sounded like hail falling.

He went to the window and peered out into the darkness. His breath fogged the window. He traced a line through the fog on the cold glass.

T.J. jumped back when a face appeared on the other side.

"T.J.!"

He recognized the voice, of course.

"Carl?" he said. "What are you doing? It must be midnight!"

211

"Aw, it's only 11 o'clock," said Carl. "Come on out. I got somethin' to show ya."

CANTO XI

"So may your memory not steal away in the first world from out the minds of men, but so may it survive 'neath many suns, say to me who ye are, and of what people; let not your foul and loathsome punishment make you afraid to show yourself to me."

So the Poet whispers to me as I stare into the fire and kick at the embers.

"I have nothing I wish to preserve. Not even the memory of my existence," I say. And though I do not tell him this, the truth is that I have never shown myself to anyone. Why start now?

"I just want to wash all the pain away," I say. And for once, it's the truth.

Chapter Eleven

1

T.J. tiptoed past his parents' room. He knew his father wasn't there, which made this expedition easier to pull off. His mother had told T.J. that his father was out with Uncle Edgar, who had come back from Atlanta to share some kind of news. They probably wouldn't return to the house until very late.

T.J. knew the screen door would be the tricky part. He basically had a choice between a long, drawn out *srrrrraaaannnk* or a short, loud *screenk*, depending on how quickly he opened the rusty-hinged door. So T.J. grabbed the icy metal handle, looked once more to the back bedroom, then yanked it and stepped outside. He cringed when the door slammed unexpectedly behind him. During the day it certainly never was that loud.

It was chilly outside, to be sure, but not "cold enough to freeze water on the fireplace," as it had been a few days earlier. He saw his father was already prepared for the hog killing that was to come tomorrow. T.J. had helped his father chop and stack wood during the day, before Edgar arrived. They were a little late this year, due to his grandmother's funeral and other setbacks.

"Hey!" whispered Carl.

"Where's your car?"

"My car? I keep tellin' you it ain't my car, T.J.," said Carl. "It's over at yer Uncle Bije's, which is where we're headed, too. You think he actually pays me good enough to go buy myself a car?"

They would have to cross through the woods to get there, but Carl had a lantern and knew the trails well. T.J. wondered what was on his mind that would keep him up so late at night.

"What's Beryl been up to?" Carl asked as they slogged through the wet, dead grass.

"She's been her usual, red-headed self, I guess," said T.J. "Why don't you ask her yourself?"

"Yer Daddy won't let me go near," said Carl. "I don't blame him, I reckon. If I had a daughter like that, I don't reckon I'd let someone like me around."

"He just doesn't know you, Carl," said T.J. "Where are we headed? What did you want to show me?"

"We're gonna catch us a Hoover Hog, s'first thing," said Carl.

"A Hoover Hog? What's a Hoover Hog?"

"You ain't never heard of a Hoover Hog? You'll see," said Carl.

They trudged along, keeping the conversation to a minimum, in respect of the darkness. Plus there was no sense in rousing anyone's suspicions at such a late hour. Everyone in this part of the world had a shotgun sitting near the window.

Finally Carl stopped, about a half-mile into the woods.

"Wait here," he said. "Hold this. Hold it up high, so's I can see."

T.J. took the lantern and held it aloft while Carl crept into the woods, about five yards off the trail.

"I said to hold it high!" he said.

"Well, hurry it up. My arms are getting tired," said T.J. "What you got over there?"

Carl knelt down, and T.J. couldn't see him for a moment. Then he stood and walked back toward the trail, taking the lantern.

"Looks like I got nothin'. But that's all right. I got a few more."

"A few more what?"

"Traps," said Carl. "I got'em all in here."

"Hoover Hog traps?"

Carl smiled as he headed back down the path. T.J. didn't know of a Mr. Hoover who lived around here, but he was certain they shouldn't be taking his hogs. Most everyone in the country put special markings on their hogs so everyone would know whose was whose. It kept angry confrontations and shootings to a minimum.

"So, Carl," said T.J. "Tell me the story with that girl. The one we took to town with her mother. That was her mother, wasn't it?"

"Yeah, I reckon that was her mama," said Carl. "Actually, that's one of the reasons I decided to come fetch you tonight, T.J. Hoke's gone. He's been gone for two days."

T.J. didn't see why that should be cause for concern. Hoke had been known to disappear before.

"Yer Uncle Abijah is real tore up about it," said Carl. "He got a letter in the mail. He put it in the trash but I fished it out when he wasn't looking. He was a-cryin' and a-cussin' over it, but he won't tell me nothin'."

Carl reached into his pocket and handed the letter to T.J.

"Shine that lamp over here," he told Carl.

The letter wasn't from Hoke, that much was certain. It was a girl's handwriting. The spelling was atrocious – that's the first thing that caught T.J.'s attention. But the handwriting

216

featured some of the neatest, most pleasing script T.J. had ever laid his eyes on, like it was written in strawberry juice dipped in honey.

The letter seemed to T.J. to be something like a ransom note. He couldn't understand all the things she referred to in the letter, but she kept alluding to the fact that Bije "knew what had happened" and didn't do anything to stop it, making him "responsible." There were thinly veiled threats, demands for money, and a brief mention of law enforcement authorities.

It wasn't signed, but T.J. thought he knew who it was from.

"This is from Jo Ann?" he asked Carl.

"I don't know. I was hoping you could tell me. I kind of assumed it was."

"She didn't sign it," said T.J. "Was there a return address on the envelope?"

"I didn't get the envelope," said Carl. "What did it say?"

"You need to read it," said T.J., handing it to Carl. Carl took the letter and looked at it for a moment, then shook his head and handed it back to T.J.

"What's the matter?" T.J. asked. "You need to read it. I think you'd underst—"

"I cain't read, T.J.," said Carl. "Never could. I can sign my name all right, and I can read some of that Bible. But that's about it. I had to leave school, T.J., and I never was much count to start with. Daddy never could afford no books, and I was out with sickness so much. You remember."

T.J. thought back and recalled that Carl had always had problems of that sort. He had just forgotten over the years.

"She wants money. Jo Ann wants money," said T.J. "She thinks that Bije has it now, since he got that farm from Aunt Lizzie. She keeps referring to some awful night. She says that she's willing to go to the sheriff about it."

Carl nodded.

"I kinda thought that's what it was," said Carl. "You know yer uncle bought that farm from your aint, T.J. He didn't inherit it. And he just bought that car, too. He don't have a lot of money right now. It ain't like she thinks."

"Well, what happened?" T.J. said.

Carl took a moment to gather his thoughts as they continued to crunch through the pine straw forest.

"Well, I'll tell you. Hoke and his buddies ... you remember that party you was at, over at the house?"

"Yeah, of course."

"This was about two or three days after that, I reckon. Hoke was up at Bije's house with some a' his buddies. And they got to a-drankin' and a-cuttin' up. And she was there. And one of them boys was a fiddler, so he was a-playin' that fiddle, an' ol' Jo Ann, she had a couple a drinks, I reckon, so she commenced t'daintsin. An' them fellers, they was about six a'them. And, like I say, they was drunk."

T.J. could quickly see where this was heading.

"Oh no, Carl. Were you there? Tell me you weren't there."

"I was there," said Carl. "But I left. I didn't like where things was headin', so I got out a there. But I shoulda stayed, T.J. I shoulda stayed."

They walked a few more paces. T.J. could see the moon shining through the treetops. He knew he couldn't let the story end there.

"So what happened?"

"Well, they took turns with that girl, the way I hear it," said Carl. "One a the boys was braggin' about it when I saw him the next day. Said I shoulda stayed. Said they had a big ol' time. And I reckon them boys did, but she--"

Carl stopped.

"I seen her a few times, but she wutten talk t'me or tell me nuthin', 'cept to ask me if I would carry her to town. I figgered it's the least I could do. Wait, now. Here we are."

Carl handed T.J. the lantern and told him to hold it up. Carl trudged about 10 yards out into the woods.

"Ah! We got us some vittles!" said Carl. He stood and walked over the ground until he found a large stick, then crouched and hefted it, raining blows on some unseen, squealing animal – *Whump! Whump! Whump!*

When he emerged from the trees he was carrying a limp rabbit, still twitching, by the ears. It was a thin varmint, with patchy fur.

"That's no hog," said T.J.

What're you talking about, son?" said Carl. "This here is straight from President Hoover, to you. Let's have ourselves a Republican-style feast!"

2

They walked to the site of the still, right off the river. T.J. had seen stills before, but never an operation this large. He was surprised the revenuers hadn't found it and chopped it up, but then Abijah must have had certain law enforcement officers on his payroll.

There was a campfire site already there, but everything, including the still, was covered in a large net, cloaked in leaves. Carl pulled off the net and they started a

219

fire to cook the rabbit. Slowly the conversation turned back to
Beryl, which seemed to be Carl's main concern. Carl broke
out a run of whiskey that had been stored there and opened a
jug. He passed it to T.J.

"Oh, what the hey," said T.J., taking a sip. *"Whooo-
ooo!"* he said, laughing as he capped it off and wiped his
mouth on his sleeve. "That ain't the same stuff my mother
has, no sir!"

"Naw, you're right, it ain't," said Carl. "You like yer
hog well done, I take it?"

"Please," said T.J. "I don't care for pink rabbit."

T.J. leaned back and looked up at the stars. He
watched lazily as his puffs of breath ascended.

"When I wake up in the morning, you know what I'm
gonna do, Carl? I'm gonna have my mama fix me up a
heaping pile of pancakes, Carl. This high."

Carl smiled wistfully.

"My mama useter make pancakes, too," he said.

T.J. quickly realized he may have said the wrong thing.
Just like always.

"I'm sorry, Carl."

"Naw, naw, it's all right. She died when I was jest a
little feller. I couldna been more'n seven'r eight years old."

"What do you remember about her?"

"I remember she swatted me good one time. I heard
one'a my older brothers say 'dammit,' so I runned around
ther house sayin' *'dammit! dammit!'* like 'at. And, boy, she
really let me have it. An' I remember her gettin' sick. She
turned all yaller. The doctor said it was pellagra. She was sick
a long, long time. And then I remember Poppa cryin' when
she died. 'Mind yer daddy,' she said. Those were her last
words, I reckon.

"That was right aroundt Christmas," he said. "I guess you could say I ain't one to git into the Christmas spirit. None a'us are."

T.J. propped himself up on one elbow.

"Hey, Carl, why don't you come on over to our house in the morning for the hog killing? People from all over the neighborhood will be there. You could just kind of slip in and see Beryl."

"I don't think yer daddy would much like that, T.J. Plus, I cain't eat pancakes no more, noway."

"Can't eat pancakes!" said T.J. "What in the world are you talking about? I thought everybody liked pancakes. Come on, now. I'll tell Beryl you're coming and we'll go fishing after we eat. My dad won't mind."

Carl took a container out of his pocket and opened it.

"What's that? Pomade?" asked T.J.

Carl laughed.

"Naw, I never was one for no style," said Carl. "It's that Vicks vapor rub. It helps my smotherin'. The whiskey helps some, and this helps a little, too. That's something else I remember about my mama. I remember her stayin' up with me all night, putting candles on me and this Vicks. Some nights I thought I like ta died. But she was there fer me, pullin' me through."

T.J. thought back to Zipporah, and then his own mother, and the nights she had let him sleep in her bed when he was sick as a small boy.

Carl smeared some of the rub under his nose and placed some more in a small tin he pulled from his pocket. He placed the tin in the fire to heat it. He sat back down, taking off his coat and wadding it up on a rock to use as a pillow.

221

"You know, I didn't leave school for the reasons you think, T.J. For the reasons everyone says I did."

"I don't really know what you mean, Carl. I don't remember anyone saying anything."

"Well, that's nice a' you," said Carl. "But I know how people talk."

Carl leaned over to breathe in the vapors, then settled back down to stare at the starry canvas above him.

"You and the others thought me and Clarence left school on accounta the other kids calling us names and such. That weren't it."

T.J. took another sip of whiskey and waited on Carl as he struggled to get his breath.

"You know them textbooks, they cost money, T.J. I knowed the Lathams always had money, or more'n most people did around here. Plus yer daddy was a teacher an' ever-thang. But me and Clarence, we had to buy ours. And we had to buy our school clothes. Mama usedter dress us in clothes she made out of guano sacks before she died. But Daddy wouldn't send us to school in that. And he couldn't afford storebought clothes. It got real tough, for a while there, after Mama died."

Carl took another drink of whiskey and leaned over to breathe in the vapors.

"My Poppa, he's a good man, despite what yer daddy might think a'him," said Carl. "He's a good man who worked fer ever-thing he got. Nobody ever gave him nuthin'. He was swindled outta his inheritance by some folks in Texas and forced to sharecrop for his living. He's a broken man, now, an' he's sick. But I never knowed a better man."

"He's a good man," T.J. agreed.

222

"We worked for those books and school clothes, T.J. It liked t'killt us, but we did it. And Poppa was right there with us while we did it. After we finished up our own fields, we'd go on over to the Goldins, the Summervilles, the Browns, the Whittens. We'd pick cotton, corn, sorghum – whatever needed doing that they didn't want to do theirselves. Or maybe they just felt sorry for us, I don't know. And that would pay fer our school clothes.

"But that fall of what was to be my seventh grade year, we'd finished up a job at the Summervilles, old 'White Charley' Summerville. Took us six weeks to pick that cotton, but it would be enough to see us through. I had to get new shoes, T.J. It was gettin' cold, like now, even as early as October that partic-lar year. And I had two pieces a'cardboard and a strang holding my shoes together. But we made that crop.

"Well, old Summerville, God bless 'im, he went and spent that $30 from his cotton crop on fertilizer. I don't blame him fer doin' it. He had t'have it. That's just how thangs are, T.J. But, anyway, he didn't have enough money left t'pay us. Not a cent. So we waited. My Poppa didn't say a word to the man for weeks, other than 'hi' and 'how are you.' But he knew that cold was gettin' t'me. He could see how sick I was.

"The winter set in, you know. That was a terrible winter, like this one's shapin' up t'be. We managed to pay fer the books, but I had to have them shoes. So my daddy goes to Mr. Summerville and says we got t'work somethin' out. Well, Summerville's sorghum crop had come in during that time, and he hired a colored boy to cook it up for him. He figgered he had about 30 barrels worth, and at a dollar a barrel that would take care of what he owed us. Okay, then.

223

"But then that nigger went and scorched that syrup. I mean scorched it. He tried to sell it, anyway. But nobody wanted it. So do you know what he done, T.J.? After a couple of weeks, that man drove his wagon on up to our house and he and his boys stacked up those 30 barrels of syrup on our front porch. That was our pay. And we had scorched molasses to eat all that winter. And you know what? We ate ever bit of it, T.J. Ever last bit of it. And I quit school. But I don't eat pancakes no more, T.J."

T.J. threw his cleaned rabbit bones into a nearby bush and stood up. Carl leaned over to breathe in some more vapors.

"We could fry up some eggs, instead," T.J. said.

Carl smiled and placed his arm over his eyes.

"I'll be right back," said T.J., taking the lamp and heading to the river.

3

T.J. felt his way to the riverbank. There was a distinct, sharp chill in the air, here close to the river. He could hear the rush of the waters in the cold darkness and he seemed like the only person in the world. T.J. suddenly realized he had wandered off the path, somehow. He shined the light all around and could not see either the path or the fire. But he could still hear the river, and so he followed the churning sound, stepping over branches and through briars that tore at his pants. Thankfully, the early cold snap had eaten away with much of the undergrowth.

When T.J. tore through the last of the briars, he found that he was on a steep precipice, with the waters surging about 20 feet below. He shined the lamp down the cliff and saw the tangle of roots beneath his feet. He hoped it would be enough to support him as he teetered along the edge.

The river looked deep, black, intent, and unforgiving, rushing forward like a mass of bodies, all of a single purpose. The waters had receded from their highs during the storm that washed away the local bridges. The waters were shallow now, rippling through the rough, razored rocks. Mangled branches and even whole trees had washed downriver. He could see one lying down there, buffeted by the waters, a twisted oak.

As he undid his trousers to relieve himself, T.J. lost his footing and tumbled down the steep mudbank and into the frigid waters. The lamp and his glasses cascaded down with him. T.J. flailed about in the deep wintry rush, blind and beaconless.

He fought the current and grabbed what was closest, which happened to be the once-mighty oak tree. There he found a moment's shelter, latching on tenuously as he was buffeted by the frigid waters.

He thought he could see a flickering through the trees on his left side. Maybe it was Carl or maybe it wasn't. He couldn't make out much of anything.

As he braced to push off, T.J. caught a glint, just above him. He squinted, wiping the water from his eyes. Sitting there on the tree was something that struck him dumb with awe. Perched on the oak, as if it were resting, was a fish. But it was unlike any fish T.J. had seen before. The fish must have been at least six feet long. It looked ancient, fearless, and proud. Rather than scales, the fish had leathery, spiked skin, like that of a lizard, or like one of the ancient creatures he had read about in the *National Geographic* magazine, the dinosaurs. The fish looked like something out of the past, displaced and lost. It apparently intended to stay there, perched on the oak. T.J. wondered if the fish were even alive. He reached up, tentatively, to touch it, and the fish permitted it, if only for a moment. Then it pushed its snout into the air, flinging T.J.'s hand aside, like a king unable to withstand the touch of a commoner. T.J. tried to push the fish back into the water, but it was too large and heavy; T.J. didn't have solid footing. This ancient fish would die here, and there was nothing T.J. could do. T.J. reached out and touched its lizard-like skin once more before pushing off to shore.

When he emerged he was shivering like a Chihuahua, his testicles drawn up tightly in his crotch. He turned to see if the marvelous fish were still visible but, without his glasses, he couldn't even see the oak tree.

He realized, then, that he still had to go to the bathroom. So he tried once again to relieve himself. Maybe, he thought, that would at least warm him up a bit.

And that's when he heard the gunshots.

4

T.J. raced through the woods in the direction of the fire, oblivious to whatever branches and briars blocked his way. When he got back to the still site, Carl was putting out the flames with dirt from a nearby tin.

"Did you hear that?" Carl asked. "Shit, T.J., what happened to you? Don't you know it's too cold for a swim?"

"I heard the gunshots, too," said T.J. "I fell in. I lost the lamp. Sorry. Is it revenuers? The sheriff?"

"I don't think so," said Carl. "But it sounds like it's coming from your Uncle Bije's place. Let's go. Here, take off your shirt and take my coat."

T.J. took the coat gratefully and pulled it close around him as he followed Carl up the path to his uncle's house. When they had walked about 100 yards up a shallow hillside they could see the lights from the house and could hear voices pierce through the cold night wind.

"I recognize that voice," said T.J. "That's Daddy's voice."

"Let's go in a little closer, then," said Carl.

They crept up, quiet as possums, and hid behind a fallen log. From the new vantage point they could see that the combatants were Edgar, Tom, and Abijah, who was screaming at his brothers from the safety of his house, pausing every few words to punctuate his remarks with a gunshot. Tom and Edgar were crouched behind Edgar's shiny new Koln, which now had several bullet holes in it. Edgar winced as a new round of bullets plinked and rattled his door. T.J. winced right along with him. It was like seeing a beautiful girl get knifed in the face.

"Not the fucking car!" Edgar shouted.

"Get the hell off my property!" screamed Bije as he paused to load another round.

"Not until you promise to shut down the still!" shouted Tom.

Two more gunshots rang out, forcing Tom and Edgar to duck behind the car again.

"Let's go," said Edgar. "That asshole's turning my car to Swiss cheese."

"Not yet," said Tom, reaching into the back seat, much to Edgar's dismay.

227

"Aw, no, Tom! *No, no no! Goddamn it, I'm an Atlanta attorney!* It ain't legal to go popping off shots on someone else's property! You want me to get disbarred?"

"You want Victor to die?" asked Tom, cocking the rifle.

Then he stood, squinted, and took aim at Bije's windows, knocking them out one by one.

"Tom! Please!" Edgar pleaded, reaching for the gun.

"Take down the still!" Tom shouted again.

"I'm gonna send you a bill for them winders, you son of a bitch!" screamed Abijah.

"Yeah? We'll send you a bill for my fucking car!" screamed Edgar.

"I ain't payin' for your car, Mr. Bigshot Atlanta Attorney!" said Abijah. "Go cry about it to your Atlanta friends. You're on my property! Now git!"

"Tom, please," said Edgar, begging him now. "If my car takes another hit I won't even be able to drive her back home. Let's go. We'll talk to him again in the morning."

Tom nodded and put the gun back in the car. He climbed into the passenger side, but not without first cupping his hands and shouting:

"You're killing Victor, you son of a bitch! Your liquor's killing him!"

"Go to hell!" shouted Bije. "He's a grown man, Tom! You and Mr. Bigshot Attorney both can just get your fancy-ass Atlanta car outta here, you sons of bitches!"

T.J. leaned back against the log and looked at Carl.

"And you thought your family had problems," he said. Carl arched his eyebrows.

"They'd better come to some kinda understanding or somebody's gonna get shot," he said, reaching for his

228

whiskey jug, which was empty. He tossed the jug to the ground and looked at T.J., who was still shivering.

"Let's get you back home, son," he said, patting him on the back and helping him to his feet.

5

When they reached the Philadelphia Church, Carl said goodbye to T.J. and headed home through the woods, so no one would see him. T.J. thought it would be smart to do the same thing, so he decided to cross through the cemetery.

He still couldn't see well without his glasses, but the stars shined brightly enough here where he could see the head markers well enough not to trip over them, or at least he thought so, until he stumbled and hit his head against a low tombstone.

As he pulled himself up to a sitting position, holding his hands to his wet head, he realized that he couldn't tell how long he had been lying there. It seemed more like early morning than night, as the air was thin and damp. He was shivering from the cold. He rubbed his head again and didn't like what he felt. A semi-dry, thick goo matted his hair. In the darkness, he couldn't tell whether or not it was blood. Had he been unconscious?

He looked up to get his bearings. The first thing he saw was a lamb. He knew this headstone. He'd even memorized the inscription, even though he couldn't make it out for lack of glasses and light. *"He dies not, but sleepeth..."* It was the grave of little Charley Latham. He had heard the story many times. This was the smallest Latham brother, T.J.'s uncle, although he never knew him. Charley had died as a small boy, only 10 years old. He had been bitten by a mad dog, within sight of this cemetery, just off the Eaves Bridge Road. It had taken about a week for him to succumb to the rabies. T.J. remembered someone telling him that Charley had an unquenchable thirst, and that they had given the boy water out of a black hat. The dog was never captured.

The wind was whipping the bare trees, rattling the limbs with a *click-click-click*. T.J. looked behind him, to the hill across the road. The lights at his house were all off. T.J. wondered how late it was. He wondered if anyone even knew he was gone. He hoped not.

He stood and almost toppled over immediately from the dizziness. Now he knew how his father had felt lately, with his ear problems. He steadied himself on a rock wall that enclosed the graves of his great-grandparents. As he sat on the wall and felt his head again, he looked to the rustling branches above him, and then to the sky. The stars were all out this evening but the moon was nowhere to be seen.

Below the whistle of the wind, T.J. thought he heard a strange sound, like panting. As the wind subsided, the panting labored on. T.J. turned around but saw nothing.

"Time to go home, time to go home," he whispered, as he stood. Something dark darted behind a tombstone. He had always been told to beware of mad dogs and had especially been warned to stay away from cemeteries after nightfall, when haints and 'ghost dogs' came out. But he never believed such stories.

Still, there was the mind, which told him to calm down and think rationally, and then there were his emotions, which caused his heart to thud in his chest and his bones to quiver as he took one tentative step, then another, and then another, holding onto his gooey head for fear that it would tumble from his neck. It didn't help that he couldn't see a damn thing without his glasses, which were now at the bottom of the Tallapoosa River.

A mad dog, a ghost dog, her fur and skin white as death...

Something rattled in the bushes and T.J. broke into a run, making for his driveway as fast as he could manage. He fell once more in the attempt and scrambled quickly back to his feet as he swore he could feel the hot breath of a dog just behind him.

...all tooth, jaws snapping, head up, ravenous...

When T.J. finally reached the safety of the front porch he turned and stared back defiantly into the darkness, but there was nothing. Just a cold, still emptiness.

His breath was still ragged --- too loud for the confines of the house. He was scared that he might wake his parents, especially his father, who would wonder where he had been all night and demand some kind of an explanation. He stood on the porch for a moment and tried to regain his breath and composure.

T.J. opened the squeaky screen door quickly, wincing as he did so. Then he walked into the cold house and down the hallway to his bedroom.

Grady was asleep, snoring as he often did, much to T.J.'s chagrin. But tonight it was kind of comforting to hear that snore, he thought as he changed out of his wet clothes and got into bed.

No sooner had he done so than the glow of yellow lamplight came down the hallway, then spilled into the room. The footsteps of his father were measured, slow, and heavy. He didn't say a word, but loomed over the bed menacingly. T.J. pretended to be asleep for a moment. What time was it, anyway? Three in the morning?

231

"T.J.," his father finally whispered. "I know you're awake."

T.J. rubbed his eyes and propped himself up on his elbows, squinting into the light. His father was nothing but a shadow. T.J. couldn't make out his facial features at all.

Suddenly something flew into his face. T.J. shook his head, then saw what it was. It was his collection of Louise Brooks pictures.

"I found those out in the woodpile yesterday. They yours?"

T.J. thumbed through them. One was missing. The blue nude. What could have happened to it? He didn't know what to say to his father, so he said nothing.

"Your Uncle Taz shot himself Saturday night," his father said. "I guess that sickness went from his nose on up into his brain. Get your clothes on. It's time to kill those hogs."

CANTO XII

'Tis no enterprise to take in jest, to sketch the bottom of all the universe, nor for a tongue that cries "Mama" and "Dada."

But here I am, of the ill-begotten rabble, speaking of that which is so hard.

It were better I had been born a pig or a goat.

Chapter Twelve

1

T.J. was able to glean from the early morning conversations that Taz had been suffering from a steadily worsening pain as the flesh of his nose and nasal cavity deteriorated. He had lost all hope for a cure as early as the fall, and the sad state of his face had forced him to leave work at the railroad and miss Thanksgiving. Taz kept telling his brother Edgar that he felt like a burden. Edgar said he tried to reassure Taz. As bad as it was, he hadn't imagined that Taz would think of taking his own life. Edgar found him Saturday night, dead from a gunshot wound at their shared Atlanta apartment on Luckie Street. He first tried to hang himself, but achieved nothing more than a red scuff on his neck and a broken pipe in the bathroom, which flooded the apartment. When the water began to drip into the other flats below, Edgar received a frenetic phone call from the landlord to come home quickly. That's when they found the body.

Edgar returned home to Haralson County to talk with Tom and his other brothers about how to handle the death. Should there be a proper burial with a funeral or should it be a hushed affair? Should the body be brought back from Atlanta to be buried in the family plot at Philadelphia Church? Who was going to pay for all of this?

T.J. tried to talk with his father about it, but Tom was in no mood.

"We all die, there's no helping it," he told T.J. "Look at what we spend all our time doing. Killing things. That's what we do here. I mean the plants, the animals ... everything dies,

234

everybody dies. On this earth. All over. The ground we plow, I mean look at it, it's just rot."

"But new things are sprouting up all the time, out of—" T.J. countered.

"Yes, until we plow it back under or kill it and eat it," said Tom. "Don't you remember? *'Earth, that nourished thee, shall claim thy growth, to be resolved to earth again; And, lost each human trace, surrend'ring up thine individual being, shalt thou go to mix forever with the elements, to be a brother th' insensible rock and to the sluggish clod, which the rude swain turns with his share, and treads upon.'* Don't you ever hear it just crying out to you, T.J.? The world just aches with it. Even the world itself it dying, sure as you're standing here."

Tom spat into the earth and looked at T.J.

"But you and I know that there's another world, don't we?"

He patted his son on the back, smiled, and led him back into the house. Mother was already stirring and the air smelled of coffee, sage, and cayenne pepper. Lois was still upset that Tom had stayed up all night. She complained that he had re-stacked and alphabetized the goods in her kitchen cabinets again. She griped that she couldn't find anything, anymore. T.J. tried to enjoy the humor in the situation, but couldn't shake the feeling that his father was deeply troubled, and he didn't know what he or anyone else could do about it.

T.J. pulled his coat tight around his collar as he followed the lamp light to the barn, the frozen mud crunching under his soles. His father hung the hissing lamp on the wall of the barn and grabbed one end of the small cart near the entrance.

"You grab that other end down there, T.J."

235

T.J. moved around to the opposite side, shooing a chicken out of his path.

"All right, you ready? Lift it up."

The two hoisted the cart and pulled. T.J. noticed that his end was lagging down and he tried to lift it a bit higher.

"I know it's heavy. It's just a little ways."

T.J. nodded and continued to pull. It was difficult since the lantern was still in the barn. He wanted to rub his nose, which was beginning to run from the cold, but he couldn't let go of his end. Not this time.

"All right, set her down," said Tom.

He brushed off his hands and turned to the pig pen.

"*Wark! Wark!*" Tom said, cupping his hands together near his mouth. "*Wark! Wark!* Here, T.J., you call to 'em while I go fetch that lantern." T.J. nodded as he wiped his nose on his sleeve.

T.J. moved over to the edge of the pig pen. No smell, he noticed. Not much of one, anyway. That's what a good freeze will do.

"*Wark!*" he said. He noticed Hank approaching. Hank was the biggest pig, originally feral. His dad had found him in the woods out behind the house and he was no trouble to feed, since he foraged most of it on his own. He had tusks and was the more aggressive of the Latham pigs.

"*Wark! Wark!*" T.J. said, putting out his hand in a friendly gesture.

He heard Dad approaching behind him and the steady hiss of the lamp. He wanted to hold it because it was warm.

"Dang it!" Tom said, stomping the mud.

"What?"

"I left the dad-blamed hammer," he said. "Go out there to the shop and fetch it for me, would you T.J.? The ballpeen hammer."

Tom hung the lamp on the side of the pig pen and reached out to scratch Hank behind the ears. Hank had always liked Tom the best of anyone in the family. He knew who brought the food.

"Hurry, now," he told T.J.

T.J. nodded, cupped his hands and blew into them as he reached for the lamp and plodded through the 4 a.m. darkness to the shop.

T.J. had only been back outside for 10 minutes or so and the cold was already numbing. His cheeks and ears were red with cold and he could no longer feel his fingers. T.J. even had trouble opening the shop door. He struggled with the latch so much it slipped and ripped a chunk out of his index finger. The blood oozed out at the door swing open. The smell of sawdust permeated the air as he hoisted the lamp to scout out the shop interior.

The shadows covered everything like a blanket. T.J. hated when his father asked him to fetch something. Not only was it dark and dusty in the shop but he could never find anything there. He didn't dare ask where the ballpeen hammer was because his father would only roll his eyes, sigh, and say, "You know good and well where the hammer is. It's in the same place it was hanging last time I sent you after it."

T.J. shined the lamp across the wall and, failing to see it, he scanned the table top, then he began rummaging through the drawers.

His father startled him as he appeared noiselessly in the darkness of the doorway.

"Got it?" he said.

"I can't find it," said T.J. "I lost my glasses last night."

"Lost your glasses? Do you have any idea how expensive those glasses are?"

Tom stepped inside, grabbed the hammer off the wall, where it had been hanging in plain sight, and he exited without looking at T.J., shaking his head and muttering to himself.

T.J. followed his father, hopping over the fence into the frozen mud.

"Wark! Wark!" he said affectionately to the pig, scratching it on the ears with his left hand as he gripped the hammer handle firmly in his right hand. Then, in a sudden flash the hammer rained down, pummeling Hank squarely between the eyes. Hank fell down into the mud, squealing, legs flailing.

"Quick, T.J.! Hand me that knife!" Tom said.

T.J. fumbled around for it, forgetting that his father had handed it to him. Then he remembered it was in his overalls pocket.

"T.J.! Throw it on over!"

T.J. quickly grabbed the handle and clumsily tossed it into the pen. It landed in the mud with a slight splatter.

"Don't throw it in the mud!" said Tom, gripping the blade and deftly slicing it into the chest of the pig, twisting his wrist.

With that, the pig unexpectedly jumped to its feet and began to chase Tom around the pen.

Tom managed to jump out of the pen just as his leg was getting gorged by a tusk. Not knowing his father was injured, T.J. watched as Hank circled the pen, first quickly and then slowing to a jog, then a trot, leaving a swath of blood. Then Hank stopped for a moment as if having a

238

sudden revelation, sank to two knees, breathing heavily. The creature fell onto his side, his breathing even more labored. Within 10 seconds T.J. couldn't tell that he was breathing at all.

"How many are we doing today?" T.J. asked as his father examined his wound.

"We'll do another one, I reckon. No more with tusks, though."

It wasn't a slight injury. T.J. thought he spotted a bit of leg muscle through the blood and denim. With his eyesight the way it was, though, he couldn't be sure.

"Dad!" was all T.J. could manage to say. His father put up a hand.

"It's all right," he said. "But I'll need you to finish this."

He tossed T.J. the hammer.

"I've got to tend to this," he said. "It's time you learned how, anyway."

T.J. nodded and grasped the hammer.

"What do I do?" he asked.

"No use trying to calm them down. Pigs are smart, T.J. They know what's going on here. They're gonna be scared from here on out. Real scared. You gotta just get in there and do it. Just hit 'em hard. Don't think about it too much. Just hit."

The pigs scattered to the other side of the pen as T.J. jumped in.

He saw the girl, Maybelle. She would probably be the easiest of the bunch. Not much question. She was the smallest of the adults.

"Go ahead, T.J.," said Tom. "Go on."

"Wark! Wark!" said T.J., tentatively, letting the hammer fall to his side.

As he approached Maybelle in her corner, she charged him slightly and snorted. She let him know she wasn't going down without a fight. She would fight for her life.

"Just jump her, T.J."

T.J. looked into Maybelle's eyes. He had been the one who named her. He remembered when she was born to Hildegard. T.J. remembered when she was still small that she had been a favorite of Beryl's, fearless and friendly. Even house trained. Mama had let Beryl bring Maybelle indoors on several occasions. T.J. remembered Beryl chasing Maybelle around the yard, giggling. He remembered how proud Maybelle had been when she'd had her first litter of her own. She had been a good mother. It wasn't her fault that she'd lost her sucklings to cold like this. The winters had been brutal.

"Come on, son. It's cold out here. We got six more after this one. Let's get this over with."

T.J. nodded to his father and grasped the hammer. He came down on the pig and missed, falling into the mud. His dad laughed.

T.J. swung again in anger and missed.

"We can't be here all morning," Dad said. "We're gonna freeze to death."

T.J. wiped the mud out of his eye and looked around in the dark for the hammer.

It lay there at Maybelle's feet, as if she were daring him to come after it. She looked ready to pounce.

T.J. got to his feet and took a step. Then another. Then a third.

"Maybelle!" he whispered. "Maybelle! Remember me? It's T.J. We used to play together. I dressed you up in one of my ties. You remember that, girl? Sure you do. I wouldn't hurt you. It's all right."

T.J. held out an open hand to the pig.

"It's all right," he said, scratching the pig's snout. "*Shhh!*"

Then, in one swift motion, he struck her in the skull. She fell down in the mud and did not move again.

"Good, son," said T.J., tossing him the knife, which landed in the mud. "Proud of you, son," said Tom. "Now let's finish the job."

T.J. nodded and picked up the knife just as her legs began to twitch. He thrust the knife into her pink chest flesh. As the blade did its work, T.J. washed his frigid hands in Maybelle's warm blood.

CANTO XIII

I hold the hammer in my hand as I stare down at my wife and child asleep in the bed. So peaceful. I hate to wake them. And despite what they must think of me in just a few moments, I do love them.

Almost Spring

Chapter Thirteen

1

It was more funeral than birthday party, with the celebrant stalking the floors like some haint. Tom had frozen all the color out of the room. It was like his pacing had kicked up a thin layer of ash, contaminating everything.

T.J. didn't recall celebrating his father's birthday with a party in years, if ever. But his mother had insisted on it. He had not been himself for the past year, since he had taken over the farm. Now that Gammy was gone the family was free to sell the farm, divvy up the assets and tell the sharecroppers to find work elsewhere, but that didn't solve much for Tom. There was no longer any school for him to return to -- the local children were now attending school at Mt. Zion. And many of the parents (and children) there were scared of Tom now, or at least a little wary, due to his recent behavior. He would never be asked to fill a teaching position. Of this he was certain.

T.J.'s mother had hoped that a party to celebrate his 47th birthday would rejuvenate Tom's spirits. It was a valiant effort. She had even baked a cake and put up streamers.

It hadn't helped that none of Tom's brothers could attend, or wouldn't. There were still hard feelings between Tom, Abijah, and Victor. Edgar lived in Atlanta and couldn't make it since he had an important case coming up. Something about an old woman's cow getting killed by a rail car, T.J. had heard. That left Virgil, who was in Cedartown on some kind of business. "I can't tell you what it is," he had told Lois, "but I can't miss it, either." Charlie, Henry, and now Taz, were all dead.

So Lois had resorted to inviting her brother, Paul. Paul was not exactly a party-type personality. In fact, T.J. thought Paul the shyest person he had ever met. He hadn't always been such a loner, his mother had assured him.

"Oh, my brother's always been *shy,* I suppose," she had told T.J. "But he used to be more like you, T.J. -- not a hermit, at least not until Miss Casey died." Miss Casey had been Uncle Paul's fiancée, many years ago. She was only 16 when, just before the wedding, she "up and died," T.J.'s mother had said. No one could figure out why. "She just woke up dead," Lois explained. Paul was never the same after that. His thin, tall frame became even leaner, and he never wanted anything to do with another woman.

"Oh, we tried, believe me," said Lois. "Actually, Paul was quite handsome as a young man. There were plenty of interested women. But he wouldn't go near them."

He became more and more of a recluse, living with Grandma Cora just up the road. Any time company came over – even family members – Paul tended to shut himself in his room. He rarely expressed an opinion on anything but seemed to have a smile for every occasion. He was pleasant enough, T.J. observed, but not a whole lot of fun. Lois' other brother, Carl, was more gregarious, but he and his wife and children lived in Virginia and T.J. rarely saw them.

Erlene was covered in a half-inch thick layer of chocolate cake. Tom told T.J.'s mother to hurry and undress her.

"Why?" she asked him. "It's just one of Beryl's old dresses."

"It's store bought," he said. "Easter's coming."

"Tom," she said, trying to contain a rising tide of frustration. "You said I could take the money I've been earning from Peacock Alley and use it however I want to. You know I always buy the children new clothes for Easter."

"Well, this year is different, Lois. I told you that," said Tom. "How much did you spend on this party?"

She glared at him, setting aside the baby. Erlene stumbled over to Beryl, who took her into the back room.

"Tom, I did this for *you*."

"I know. And I appreciate it. I do. But money is tight right now. For everybody. I'm not getting my regular teaching pay. We just bought T.J. new glasses. The crops won't come in for a while yet. We still haven't sold Mama's farm."

"We'd have plenty of money," said Lois in careful, measured phrases, "if you hadn't — "

She stopped herself and marched into the kitchen.

"If I hadn't what?" asked Tom.

"Nothing," she said.

"What?" Tom said, standing. "Excuse me, Paul," he said, scooting around his chair. Paul moved aside without saying a word. T.J. smiled at him apologetically, a little embarrassed that his parents had decided to take up this issue at this particular time.

"*If I hadn't what?*" Tom insisted. Lois shook her head almost imperceptibly. She always does this, T.J. thought. When she's ready to explode, she just shuts down and doesn't say a word. It was her defense against saying something she might later regret.

"Fine," Tom said. "Buy the Easter clothes. I just won't make the car payment."

Lois stopped and put the child down, throwing the rag into the basin.

"Go play with Collier, now," she said, pushing her along.

"No, I want you to make the car payment," she said. "We have to make the car payment. The children just won't have Easter clothes."

She stopped again and stormed to the table. She began furiously scraping the plates. She grabbed T.J.'s plate and scraped it clean even though he wasn't even finished, but he dared not protest.

"Do you want to starve us to death?" Tom asked.

She slammed down the dishes on the table.

"Tom! We may have a lot of things happen, but we ain't gonna starve. What are you talking about? We got plenty of food stored up, not even counting the food at your mother's. That's not it."

"Then what?" he said. "I don't understand you, anymore."

"You don't understand me? I think I'm fairly simple," she said. "It's you I don't understand. Why did you go off and buy that car, Tom, if we aren't even going to get to use it? How long have you had it out there in the shop? It's March, now, Tom. When did you get it? November? We haven't driven it but six times. Six! When do you plan on putting it back together, Tom? Why are we making payments on something we can't even use? Tell me why.

"And what's this I'm finding, all over the house? What are these?" She marched over to one of the cabinets, yanked out a stack of boxes and bottles and threw them across the kitchen table like a prosecutor presenting incriminating evidence to the accused.

"*Dr. Kinsman's Heart Tablets?*" she said. "I thought you said it was your ear."

249

Tom stared at her blankly, but there was a deep layer of pain, buried just beneath the smooth emptiness.

"It started in my head and now it's in my heart," he said. "Read what it says there, Lois. About the thickening of the valves, and then they don't close properly, and the impure bloods flows in and – and, uh – "

Lois looked like she was about to either hit him or burst out sobbing. Tom stopped talking, shook his head and stared into the fire.

"I'm doing the best I can," he said. "I'll get the car fixed soon."

"No you won't," she said, gathering up the dishes again as she wiped away the tears. "I keep telling you to get Virgil in there to help, but you're too proud! You don't know what you're doing in there, Tom. That car is in a million different pieces."

"No, it's not."

"Tom, I've seen it! I don't think you're ever going to get that thing back together! It doesn't even look like a car, anymore! What are you doing in that shop? It looks like you're not even trying to fix it. It's like you're, you're ... like you're just tearing up its insides."

"I have to take it apart to figure out what's the matter with it, Lois," he said.

"Will you please just get Virgil to help you? Why can't you ask Virgil to help?"

He looked up and stared at her viciously.

"You'd like that, wouldn't you?" he said.

She furrowed her brows.

"I'd like that? What's that supposed to mean?"

"You know what it means," he said, putting on his boater hat and bursting out of the house.

Grady slid his cake over to T.J.

"I don't want it," he said.

"Well, Lois," said Paul, getting his coat, "thank you for inviting me to your, uh .... I guess I need to be heading on back home."

Lois nodded and gathered up more dishes.

"Bye, Paul," she said, giving him a limp hug and wiping her nose.

"I'll walk with you, Paul," said T.J. He stood up standing adjusted his new glasses and slid Grady's cake over to Collier, who had been eyeing it for the past five minutes. He greedily smacked his lips and sunk his hands into the icing.

2

T.J. followed Paul to the end of the driveway then patted him on his shoulder and sent him on his way. Such a nice, quiet man, T.J. thought. He had never heard anyone say a bad word about Uncle Paul. If only uncles on the Latham side had been so fortunate.

T.J. wasn't up for working with his father in the shop, and he certainly didn't want to go home. The first place of refuge that came to mind was Willie and Nattie's house, so he headed through the corn field and was more than a little surprised when he arrived and saw the two of them packing up the back of a wagon.

"Well, I'll be. T.J. Latham! Where you been, son?" said Willie, giving T.J. a warm hug. "You say you love us but then you never come around! We're just across the yard, son. Why don't you visit us sometime?"

251

T.J. smiled and peered into the nearly empty house. Nattie was inside, crying, as she shoved some plates into a wood crate.

"What's going on, Willie?" T.J. asked. "Did something happen?"

"You mean were we asked to leave?" Willie said. "No, no. Although it's not the same without your grandma here, T.J. Things have changed. Things don't look so good. You remember old Black Charlie Summerville, don't you? He's offered to put us up, up there in Chicago. We thought we might give it a try. Things sounds good up there for black folks, T.J."

Willie picked up his guitar and looked lost in thought for a moment.

"You know I was borned in this house, T.J.? Thought I'd die here, too. Almost did, a couple of times. Yes sir. Almost did."

"What do you mean, Willie?" T.J. said.

"Well, I don't like to talk about it, but I guess since we're goin' north now there ain't too much anybody can do. So, T.J., I always liked you, and so I'm going to tell things the way they are. I'm gonna lay it plain. You wouldn't tell on me no ways, would you, son?"

"You know I wouldn't, Willie," said T.J., leaning against a post on the porch. It creaked even under his modest weight. T.J. wondered how many more years this home would be habitable, anyway. Maybe they had to move, regardless.

"Take a seat, T.J. I'm gonna tell you what really happened to Briscoe. To my boy, Briscoe. What they done to him. You ready for that?"

T.J. didn't understand.

252

"I thought Briscoe got sick," he said.

"I know that's what everybody told you, me included," said Willie. "But that ain't how it was. No sir."

T.J. took Willie's invitation and sat down. Willie's yellow eyes hung like greasy eggs in a black iron skillet.

"You know about the Klan. You know they started that thing up after the War. I mean the War Between the States. You know the War I'm talkin' about. They started it up to keep folks like me in line. They didn't much like the way the North had said black folks could vote and go to the gub'ment and the capitol and things like that. They didn't like that. So they started up that Klan and scared a bunch of folks, including my daddy. It was bad, T.J. If you voted Republican, they burned your house down. They had folks hidin' in the woods, they was so scared. But the gub'ment did away with it. They held hearin's and all. Folks got arrested. And that was that, you know. There was no mo' Klan.

"In fact, T.J., I know you don't remember this, but that may have been the best times we had, after they got that Klan out," he said. "For a while when I was growing up, things was really all right between white folks and black folks, least around here. Even ol' Tom Watson seem like he was on our side, there for a bit. It's like all that Klan stuff had got the devil out of 'em, and it was exorcised, you know. And we could live from then on. But that wasn't meant to be.

"You know they had that picture show, that *Birth of a Nation*. T.J., I can tell you right now, I ain't never seen it, wouldn't want to, but that picture show is the worst thing ever happened to black folks. It got all them old feelings just all stirred up again. And people had forgot about the bad things the Klan did. What that movie showed was making it out so that we was the bad folks, actin' like monkeys at the

253

capitol an' such, and the Klan was the heroes. They twisted it, you see. And folks don't know no different. Folks forget.

"It woulda been all right, T.J., but then that little girl, that Mary Phagan got killed by the Jew in Atlanta. And that set it off. They called themselves the Knights of Mary Phagan. And that right there was the start-up a' this new Klan, the Klan we've got today. And I don't know but maybe it's even worse than the first one, T.J.

"The first I knew of them was when ol' boy Snyder got strung up for talking haughty to some white woman. I remember seeing him because they left him hanging for a week. There was birds and flies all around and it stank to high heaven. But they wanted us to see, T.J. They wanted us to know what would happen if we didn't keep our place. And that's when they put that sign up. You know the one I'm talkin' about? I can't read much, but they tell me it says, *'Black man, do not let the sun set on you in Haralson County.'* That's addressed not to me, you understand, but to folks that don't live here. And to me, too, I suppose, if you count the fact that we ain't supposed to be out after dark.

"But, like I say, T.J., folks forget. They forget about what all this stuff leads to. They find a way to keep black folks and Catholics and Jews in line, and it works, for a while. But then they slip up. And then there's trouble, you see. And a day of judgment shall come. I truly believe that, T.J. A day of judgment shall come.

"But, anyway, your daddy, he was one of 'em. He was in that thing, that Knights of Mary Phagan, right from the start. You know, he's the one that let that mob in that jail to string that Jew up. He handed them the keys, T.J. He handed them the keys. And do you know he didn't even kill that girl? That's right. The gub'nor was gonna commute his sentence.

254

But your daddy let 'em in there and they took him and they strung him up out there in Marietta. And that's how this new Klan got started.

"But, T.J., you know how your daddy got out? You know why? He ever tell you that?"

T.J. cleared his throat.

"I ... I didn't even know he was ever in it," he said. Willie grunted.

"I'm sure now he wished he never was," he said. "But that's neither here nor there, because he was, T.J. Oh, yes, he was."

"Don't you bad mouth his daddy too much, now, Willie," Nattie said as she stepped out on the porch with the crate of dishes. "Tom Latham is a good man."

"Well, just let me finish, woman. Just let me finish," said Willie, sitting back on the rocker while he stroked the strings of his guitar.

"Well, you remember Briscoe, T.J. He was a sweet, sweet boy. Y'all used to play together right out here. You remember that, don't you? You'd get so covered in mud we couldn't tell you was even a white boy. You looked just like him, playing out there. And to you two, there weren't no difference, much.

"Well, you see, the Klan never much approved of me and Nattie, you see, because, you may not know this, but Nattie is my half-sister. But you see, T.J., you have to understand that on the plantation there was a lot of that going on because there wasn't nobody on the plantation that you wasn't somehow related to, and they wouldn't let you off. And most of the Negroes around here got run off, anyhow. And we thought, well, it's only half, you know, and we wasn't even raised up in the same house. So we got

255

together and she got pregnant. Well, the white folks didn't like this one bit, but I guess they wasn't much they could do. They said a few harsh words, but once she was pregnant, that was that, an' they let us get married.

"But that didn't matter, you see, because they took it all out on Briscoe. The white folks never treated that boy right. Your daddy, neither. They was downright mean to him sometimes, T.J. He couldn't understand it. To him, we was just family. He didn't know anything about us being brother and sister. All he knew was folks was mad at him and spitting at him and doing stuff like that and making him do things the other boys didn't have to do. So after a while he started to develop this, I guess you'd call it a hostile attitude. A defiance, they call it. Well, the white folks called it 'uppity.' He's a 'uppity negro.' 'You'd better watch that nigger. He thinks he's as good as white folks. He's uppity.' You know what I mean.

"Anyway, Briscoe said something to old Mr. White that he shouldn't have said. I don't even recall exactly what it was, to tell the truth, and I only heard it second hand. But, anyway, he came runnin' home. And the worst thing was that he had stolen something from the house. Something from Mr. White's wife. It was a little white scarf. He was gonna give it to his mama. Well, I can't say for sure, but I feel that's what he was gonna do. He was always—"

At that, Willie had to stop for a moment. His eyes watered up and he clutched his chest and shook his head.

"Well, anyway," he said, clearing his throat again, "they caught him before he got home. They was Klan members. And they found that scarf on him, I guess. And they beat him up pretty bad, T.J. I mean bad. When they brought him here, he was ... he was..."

256

Tears were flowing freely down the old man's face now as he paused again and wiped his eyes.

"Well, that set me off, you know. Here was my boy, and he was dead to the world, maybe already dead, I didn't know. But he was beat and here was the boys who'd done it. And they was young boys, in their teens and 20's at that time. And I felt like I could take 'em. And I didn't much care what happened to me then.

"Well, T.J., well," he said, stopping again. He cursed silently. "Well, they ... they ripped me up pretty bad, T.J. There was five of them and one of me. And they got me pretty good. And one of them had a knife. And they cut me, T.J. And when I say they cut me ... Well, I didn't have no more kids after that."

That seemed to be as much as he could say, but after another moment he continued on.

"Nattie nursed me and the boy as best she could, T.J. But I lived and Briscoe ... "

He trailed off again.

"Nattie, would you mind bringing me some water?" he said. She put a reassuring hand on his shoulder and went around back.

"That's when your daddy quit the Klan," said Willie. "He didn't approve of what they did to me and my boy and he said so. At least that's what he told me. And he quit the Klan that very day. And that's why me and Nattie respect your Daddy, T.J., and always will. But, if the truth be told, he was as much to blame as anybody. But that's not for us to judge, ain't that right?"

T.J. thought for a long moment.

"That's right," he finally said. Willie nodded.

257

"That's right. It's not for us to judge. Because we don't know what's in a man's heart. Only God knows that, the mysteries of the heart and soul. Only God knows.

"But, T.J.," he said, standing up and handing T.J. the guitar, "it's time for us to go. And I want you to have this, to remember me by."

"I can't take that, Willie," said T.J. "You never even learned to play it."

"I learned enough to know that I shouldn't be fooling with it," said Willie. "And I hear they got black folks with guitars in every street corner in Chicago. So you take it because Nattie would break it, anyhow, before we even got to town. You take it and you do me a favor. You learn that guitar. You learn it and play it well, son. Play it well. Write a song about Briscoe. Because now you's gonna be the only man here that remembers him. And if you don't remember him, then he really is dead and gone. So learn that guitar and play that song."

"I'll try," said T.J., taking the guitar. Willie nodded as Nattie brought him his glass of water.

"Your grandmama was a good woman," said Nattie. "You favor her, T.J. You remember that. You do favor her."

T.J. gave Nattie and Willie a hug, then slung the guitar over his shoulder and walked back to the house. His father had drug out the wagon and was calling to him. T.J. felt, for a fleeting moment, that he should turn and walk down the driveway to the Eaves Bridge Road and never look back.

3

The preparation for dinner at the McConnell residence had been an all-day affair. T.J. had been nearly frantic when he discovered he was out of pomade, but his mother provided him with an adequate substitute on the condition that he not ask from whence it came or what its constituents might be. It smelled like something from the kitchen, but it served its purpose. His mother attempted to disguise the odor by mixing in a touch of her perfume, but T.J. stopped her, saying that he would rather smell like a potato than flowers.

T.J. arrived 10 minutes early and he worried that he might appear too anxious. But those fears were quickly put to rest when he saw Irene on the front porch waiting for him.

"Hello," said T.J. as he stepped onto the porch and offered Irene some flowers that his mother had so graciously allowed him to pull from her garden.

"Thank you," she said perfunctorily. Irene rocked the porch swing back and forth in an irritatingly precise manner. The creaking sounds of the rusty chain sounded to T.J. like a maimed frog. But when Irene would kick her feet up to spur the momentum, T.J. would sneak a glance of her calf, which appeared pale and soft under the porch lights. Her face, on the other hand, didn't fare so well. She looked jaundiced.

"How are you, Irene?" said T.J. "Where's your Mama?"

"She's in the kitchen. She's been in there all day. She's really made a fuss over you."

T.J. groaned and shook his head with a natural modesty, but it went unnoticed by Irene, who busied herself arranging her new flowers.

"It's too bad I'm allergic," she said. "I love flowers. Love to look at them. Love their colors. They're so soft."

"I never notice them much," said T.J., thrusting his hands deep into his pockets.

259

Suddenly the screen door screeched open and Mrs. McConnell poured out of it. She seemed all bosom as she grabbed T.J. and clenched him tightly with her quivering arms, draped in blue-veined flab.

"T.J.!" she squealed and snorted, wrapping a meaty arm around his thin frame. "Are these flowers for me? I'm just joshing you, T.J., you can relax. Irene, go run those inside and put them in that big Mason jar on the window sill. I hope Irene has been hospitable, Terry. I didn't even know you were out here."

"I only just arrived, Ms. McConnell," he said.

"Come on in. It's not often we have a man in this house, T.J. You'll have to forgive us."

T.J. wondered just what he should forgive them for, but he knew better than to ask. Mrs. McConnell showed him to the big green sofa in the parlor. T.J.'s house didn't have a parlor, but Mr. McConnell had worked for the railroad before he died in the Spanish flu epidemic of 1918. Irene had hardly even known her father, but he had left her and her mother in good stead. Mrs. McConnell was much too conservative to join the speculators in the market frenzy of the Twenties, so when that bubble burst and other people were having their margins called in or were jumping out of windows, Mrs. McConnell sat securely in the knowledge that nearly all of her money was tucked away in real estate. The McConnells were one of the few families in town with any assets to speak of. T.J. had heard it said that Mrs. McConnell had never worked a day in her life, and wouldn't ever have to. She looked it.

He took his seat squarely in the middle of the sofa. T.J. was a little surprised when Irene and Mrs. McConnell sat on either side of him. When Mrs. McConnell sat down, the wooden frame creaked in protest and the whole couch seemed to tilt at an angle, or maybe it was just his rude imagination at work. Irene appeared uncomfortable but well rehearsed as she folded her hands in her lap and smiled.

"So," said Mrs. McConnell, slapping her weighty hand upon T.J.'s bony knee. "I hear you're planning on going off to the university, like your father."

"Where did you hear that, Mrs. McConnell?"

"I have my sources," she said, patting him on the knee again, but more playfully this time.

"I suppose I will, Mrs. McConnell," T.J. said. "But I..."

She arched an eyebrow and waited for his response. "Yes?"

"But I would like to travel some. Maybe go to Europe. Go hitchhiking."

"Hitchhiking? Oh, my dear boy, no, no, no," she said, shaking her head. "Who ever put that thought into your head? That's much too dangerous. *'The stranger did not lodge in the street.'* That's Job 31, verse 32, T.J. You don't know any of those people over there. Don't you know they all hate Americans? They're jealous, that's what it is. *'A sound heart is the life of the flesh: but envy the rottenness of the bones.'* Proverbs 15: 30. Everyone wants to live here in America."

T.J. thought that might have been true five years ago, but America was now a much different place than it had been. No one had much of anything, anymore. No one but the McConnells. T.J. glanced around the room. He had never seen so much lace and silver in one place at one time. Even the picture frames were fringed with lace. He wondered if she might have an indoor toilet.

"Anyway," she said, "we won't have you taking rides with strangers in some strange place with those kinds of people. You just go to the university like your father and be a

261

lawyer like your Uncle Edgar. You follow his example. *'That which is altogether just shalt thou follow.'* That's in Deuteronomy, somewhere. Chapter 16. Or ..."

She trailed off and bit her lower lip as she squeezed T.J.'s thigh.

"Or have you considered what I said? About being called to the service of the Lord? What do you think, Terry?"

T.J. hated it when people called him Terry. He hated it even more than when Hoke called him "Slick." The moniker just didn't seem to fit him.

"I've thought about it Mrs. McConnell. I've thought about it real hard," he said. "I guess, the way I see it, I've got plenty of time, still. I can see Mt. Kilimanjaro or the pyramids or what have you, then go finish school, and still come back and preach, you see. My daddy always wanted to see the pyramids. He never got the chance."

"Well, if you ask me, Terry, Moses led the people out of that land and out of their bondage so as to never, ever go back. But that's just me and I'm just an old woman, so I'm certain I would not know. Would you like some dinner? Irene, tell Jermena to bring out the chicken."

"Yes'm," Irene said, curtsying in a practiced manner that T.J. knew was meant to be endearing but that he personally found demeaning.

Mrs. McConnell leaned in and whispered conspiratorially into T.J.'s ear.

"Bless her heart, no one would give that poor Negro any work, so I had to give her something, but I have to get onto her every minute of the blessed day. She has a good, Christian heart, T.J., but she is who she is, and her mind wanders, so I do apologize."

"There's no need, Ms. McConnell," T.J. said. She smiled and squeezed his thigh again.

"Well, then," she said, slowly hoisting her girth from the couch, which seemed to sigh in relief as she splayed over it, "let's have a bit of supper. I'll follow you, young man."

As T.J. made his way into the kitchen, he couldn't help but notice the scores of pictures littering the hallway. She supposed most of them were of Mr. and Mrs. McConnell, and Irene as a child. There was a seriousness about them, and a quiet sadness.

Jermena was nowhere to be seen when T.J. crossed into the kitchen. Irene dutifully stood by the head of the table, waiting for T.J. to sit. The table was covered in a feast that would have been enough for 50 people. T.J. wondered how he could possibly eat enough of a percentage so as not to appear rude. He motioned for Irene and Mrs. McConnell to take their seats. Irene looked a little disappointed, as if she had expected him to do something rather different, but he couldn't fathom what he may have done wrong, and she did not say.

"Would you do us the honor of saying the blessing, T.J.?" Mrs. McConnell said. T.J. nodded and bowed his head.

"Thank you, Lord, for this food. This food which sits before us, ready to be consumed. We thank you for it, and hope you bless it for the nourishment of our bodies, and our bodies for thy service. And thank you for Mrs. McConnell and to Irene McConnell for preparing it. We thank you. And we thank you for all the blessings of this life. In your son Jesus Christ's name we pray. Amen."

The chicken was dry and lean, T.J. thought, but the butterbeans and corn were awfully good. The sweet potatoes weren't as tasty as Aunt Beatrice's, but nobody's were.

Jermena did come out of the kitchen from time to time with more fresh dishes, and she would take the dirty plates back with her. She said not a word. T.J. ate so much that he was bloated and immobile by the end of it.

The normally outspoken Irene was unusually reserved throughout the meal. T.J. attributed that to the fact that her mother was closely scrutinizing her every comment and gesture. He supposed there would be a critique and notes following his departure.

While Jermena gathered up everyone else's dessert dishes after they finished their cobbler, Irene, at the prompting of Mrs. McConnell, took T.J.'s.

"Are you finished?" she asked first. T.J. thought he detected a hint of nervousness, which was unlike her.

"Thank you. It was very good."

"Not really," said Mrs. McConnell. "But you're very kind to say so. Jermena used too much butter. I've warned her so many times about using too much butter. But you know how those people are, T.J. Once they become habituated to doing something one way, it's nearly impossible to get them to learn something new."

He wanted to say something, say anything, but he felt paralyzed. He knew better than to respond to such remarks. It was useless and would only get him into trouble. So he nodded politely without saying anything. Jermena, who had heard every word, also said nothing.

"So, young man," said Mrs. McConnell, reclining in her chair, "so tell me ... just what are your plans for the future? I mean, other than this business about seeing Europe."

T.J. took a sip of his glass of sweet tea, which was nearly empty.

264

"Well," he said, "I know I'd like to meet people, ma'am."

"Meet people? What kinds of people?"

"All kinds, I guess," he said.

"No," she said. "Not all kinds."

"Ma'am?"

"T.J., you're young. There are a lot of things about this world that you just don't know. And there are certain kinds of people -- In fact, that's one of the reasons I wanted to invite you here tonight, T.J. I've heard some talk, and I hope it's not true, that you've been associating with ... well, I'll just state it plainly, since that's just my way, you'll have to forgive me. You were seen in town, T.J. On that day when your uncle was involved in all that business. You were seen in town, at a certain establishment, with a certain young man known to frequent that establishment. I won't say who saw you, because that's neither here nor there. But this person you were seen with, it is well known, was not there to purchase groceries. Now, I don't even want to know what you were doing there. I'm sure it was innocent. It was snowing that day and most likely your mother wanted you to pick up a few things at the store and you got there any way you could. But people are talking, T.J., and I just wanted you to know that. Of course I know what kind of young man you are and I let everyone know that, in no uncertain terms, when they try to spread such malicious gossip in my presence. I won't hear it. T.J. Latham is one of our county's finest young men, I say. But, T.J., darling, you can't be seen with that boy anymore. Do you understand what I'm saying? *'Wine is a mocker, strong drink is raging: and whosoever is deceived thereby is not wise.'* That's the twentieth Proverb. I worry about you, T.J., like a mother. You're like a son to me, you really are. And I

265

certainly don't want to embarrass Irene, but I know she thinks the world of you, too. So please just consider this, Terry."

T.J. tried to take another sip of his tea, but the glass was completely empty now, so he let his tongue lather an ice cube. His family couldn't afford ice. Most people couldn't. He'd only had ice on a few other occasions, mostly at ice cream socials they would have periodically at the church. And when it snowed, like that day Mrs. McConnell had mentioned. He remembered hearing one of his uncles say that some years ago two men had been expelled from the church as liars when they came back from New England with tales of machines that made ice.

T.J. set the glass back on the table. Mrs. McConnell gave him a look of pious concern. T.J. hated that expression. He wanted to smack it right off her face. It made him feel inferior. He didn't think that he deserved to be made to feel that way.

"Mrs. McConnell," he said, "are you talking about the Bishops? About Carl?"

"Yes, I believe that's the name," she said. "I was trying to be polite. I didn't want to single anyone out."

But that's exactly what you were doing, T.J. thought. *You were singling out Carl. You're trying to say that Carl Bishop is a bad influence on me.*

"T.J., those people ... God bless them, they don't have anything at all, and we have to make allowances. I know they're poor. But, T.J., there are lots of poor people in this country, as you well know. But that doesn't give one a license to steal. You remember what happened with your father and his hens. And it doesn't give one license to become a drunkard and to ... to fornicate ... and that girl, T.J., that girl

266

from Carrollton or wherever she came from. What was her business here in the first place? She was a known harlot, T.J., and if you ask me, in the end, she got what was coming to her. Exactly that. And you don't want to be mixed up with any of that business, T.J. Latham. That isn't you. That isn't your people at all. The Bishops are another kind of people, T.J. They're sharecroppers. My word, T.J., that boy doesn't even know how to spell his own name!"

With that, she let out a titter and glanced over to Irene, who snorted right along with her. T.J. felt like he was going to be sick. He wiped his mouth with the fringed, white napkin and stood up.

"I'm certain I don't know what you're talking about, Mrs. McConnell. My uncle is -- one of my uncles, that is to say, is the biggest producer of liquor in this county, as you well know, and he thinks so well of Carl Bishop that he allows him to distribute his whiskey to all who are in need of it in these hard times, and keep a cut of that money for hisself. Himself. My Uncle Victor, I'm sure you remember, is not only one of the country's most prolific drunks, but he also finds association with harlots a most rewarding and enlightening experience. So when you say my family and Carl Bishop's family are of two different kinds, Mrs. McConnell, I'm not sure what you mean by that statement. It seems to me that we're all pretty much on the same page. And if it's all the whispering that you're concerned about, I think you should know that one of the best-known and most often repeated rumors in this town involves the questionable parentage of your daughter here, as your deceased husband, God rest his soul, was well-known to have been rendered impotent in the Spanish-American War, where he distinguished himself most nobly in the service of my uncle, Col. Edgar Latham, as his

267

personal secretary and his horse keeper. My understanding is that it was while tending to one of those horses that your good husband suffered his battle scar, the result of a sudden, swift kick!"

For perhaps the only time in her life, Mrs. McConnell was utterly speechless.

"Jermena," T.J. said, taking her stiff hand and lifting it gracefully to his lips for a gentle kiss, "thank you for a most memorable dinner."

T.J. spun around and showed himself out of the door. His heart pounded a rhythm so fast and overbearing that his soggy legs couldn't possibly keep up. T.J. immediately began to doubt, as usual, if he had done the right thing. He was certain he wouldn't be seeing Irene any longer, or at least not in the way he had hoped to see her. But, ultimately, he felt good about himself, for the first time in a long, long while. He felt peacock-proud and full of the seething blood of life, and not dirty and restrained and belittled, as he was so accustomed to feeling. And, no matter the consequences, he was satisfied.

As he walked down the wide-open road, he thought of Mrs. McConnell's wide-open mouth and her tiny, ugly, yellow teeth.

4

That night T.J. took up reading the Bible again. If the Bible was to be the weapon of choice in public and private discourse, he wanted to ensure that from this point forward he was well-armed. T.J. had tried this before, but had been derailed by a few pages of genealogies and had put the Book aside; but now he committed himself to sticking it out to the bitter end.

He had only made it to Deuteronomy before and, since he couldn't remember the exact point at which he left off, he just started over again from the first chapter.

"These be the words which Moses spake unto all Israel on this side Jordan in the wilderness," the book began. What followed was at times tedious, basically a long list of laws and ordinances for the Israelites to follow. Rules like, *"Ye are the children of the Lord your God: ye shall not cut yourselves, nor make any baldness between your eyes for the dead,"* and *"Thou shalt take of the first of all the fruit of the earth, which thou shalt bring of thy land that the Lord thy God giveth thee, and shalt put it in a basket, and shalt go unto the place which the Lord thy God shall choose to place his name there."*

When he came to passages like Chapter 13, verses six through nine, he had to stop and ponder them for a while. He trusted that his limited understanding is what stood in the way.

"If your very own brother, or your son or daughter, or the wife you love, or your closest friend, secretly entices you, saying, 'Let us go and worship other gods...' Show him no pity. Do not spare him or shield him. Your hand must be the first in putting him to death..."

T.J. wondered if God meant this literally. He had never personally met someone who worshipped other gods, but there were pictures of people in the *National Geographics* that he had been sent by Uncle Edgar where people had never even heard of Jesus Christ. What of them? They looked like such nice people in the pictures. And they had children. Surely the children who worshipped other gods would not be put to death?

He kept reading, coming to Deuteronomy 21, verse 18:
"If a man have a stubborn and rebellious son, which will not obey the voice of his father, or the voice of his mother, and that, when they have chastened him, will not hearken unto them;

"Then shall his father and his mother lay hold of him, and bring him out unto the elders of his city, and unto the gate of his place;

"And they shall say unto the elders of his city, This our son is stubborn and rebellious, he will not obey our voice; he is a glutton; and a drunkard.

"And all the men of his city shall stone him with stones, that he die; so shalt thou put evil away from among you; and all Israel shall hear, and fear.

"And if a man have committed a sin worthy of death, and he put to death, and thou hang him on a tree;

"His body shall not remain all night upon the tree, but thou shalt in any wise bury him that day; (for he that is hanged is accursed of God); that the land be not defiled, which the Lord thy God giveth thee for an inheritance."

T.J. thought back to what Willie had told him that afternoon, about the hanging of the black man who had been "uppity" with a white woman. They had kept the body up all week, for everyone to see. So what would become of this land, which was defiled? Was there a day of judgment coming? Or was the black man to be considered a man, like a white man? Or was he just an animal, like a circus ape, like Uncle Virgil had so often said?

T.J. wondered what the Bible meant by "a sin worthy of death." Then he thought back to a passage he had read before he had put the Bible aside. He still remembered the passage vividly. A man had been found out collecting sticks on the Sabbath day. The Lord said to Moses that the man

270

should be put to death, and the people obediently stoned him, unto death.

Grady entered the room and T.J. put the Bible aside.

"You still aren't finished with that?" he said, taking off his clothes and throwing them on the floor.

"I can't wait to get to the New Testament," said T.J.

"You can skip ahead, you know," said Grady. "I'm sure God wouldn't get too mad."

"I don't know, Grady," said T.J., rolling onto his side and drawing up the covers. "From what I'm reading, I don't think it takes too much to set Him off."

As T.J. fluffed his pillow once more, he felt something hard in the middle of it, like a rock. He reached in and felt around, rolling the feathers between his fingers until he came across the stone, then pulled it out.

He held it up in the light of the window. It was the gold piece he had given to Uncle Edgar. How had that wound up in his pillow? Had Uncle Edgar put it there on one of his return visits?

He admired the nugget for a moment and smiled, then tucked it back into the pillow. He would keep it there, safe, for another day.

5

The next morning there was a knock on the door, about an hour after Tom had left for town with Uncle Virgil to get some parts for the Maxwell. T.J. looked out the window as Beryl crossed the kitchen to answer.

"Wait," said T.J.

"What is it? Someone's at the door."

"It's that girl. That girl that came by here a few months ago. I think she came by a couple of other times, too. Mama said not to talk to her."

"No, I remember her. That's Beatrice," said Beryl. "She's all right. What? What is it?"

"Nothing. It's just that ... she's looking for Uncle Victor."

"Then why is she coming *here*?" said Beryl. "Forget it, I'm answering the door."

Before T.J, could protest, the door swung open. Beatrice had the little boy with her once again. Even though it had only been a few months, he appeared noticeably older. *He even looks like a Latham*, T.J. thought.

"Well, Beatrice!" said Beryl, hugging her neck. "Is that your little brother? Isn't he the cutest thing!"

Just as T.J. had feared, his mother rounded the corner. But her expression, surprisingly, was not of dread or disapproval.

"Beatrice, your timing is just right," she said. "I was just going through the kids' old things and I was thinking of that little brother of yours. Come on back here."

Beatrice looked hesitant. Beryl tugged at her arm, insistent.

"Come on, we don't bite," she said.

"Is your daddy coming back soon?" she asked.

"I don't know," said Beryl. "But we're gonna get you and this youngin' some clothes, all right?"

"I need to speak with your daddy," she said. "It's real important. I've been trying for a while but he don't come to the school no more and I can't go to the church."

"Why not?" said Beryl.

Beatrice only shrugged and shook her head. She followed Beryl and T.J. to their mother's room. Beatrice looked around as if she were in the king's palace.

"This place is real, real nice, ma'am," she said. She picked up an old photo of Tom and Lois, sitting on the end table beside the bed.

"Is this you?" she asked.

"Mm-hm. Many, many years ago, I'm afraid."

"And that's Professor Latham?" she asked. "He was kind of scrawny, wasn't he?"

Lois admired the picture briefly before setting it back on the end table.

"I suppose he was, wasn't he?" she said.

Lois brought out armful after armful of clothes from the closet.

"I'm so glad you're here, Beatrice. We just don't have any use for these, anymore. But don't worry. They're good clothes. They just don't fit any of us, anymore."

Beatrice appeared taken aback. She grabbed the boy by the hand and covered her mouth in a half-gasp.

"Oh, no, ma'am. We can't. We just can't!" she said. "This is too much. Look at this dress! Is this store bought? How much did this cost you? I'm sorry, ma'am. I shouldn't ask that. It's rude. Did Tom -- did your husband buy this for you?"

"I don't remember, Beatrice. Probably not," she said. "He doesn't buy me things like that. I usually have to go buy them myself. When we have the money. But that's so out of style, now. Would you even want it?"

"Oh, yes ma'am. I would love it. But I really couldn't. I really..."

With that, Beatrice, put her hands to her face and started to cry. Beryl and Lois exchanged a look of concern.

"Beatrice, darling, are you all right?"

Beatrice wiped her eyes on her sleeve and nodded quickly.

"Yes, ma'am. I'm sorry. I'm sorry. I just don't deserve this. I didn't expect you to be so nice to me. I just don't deserve any of this."

Lois knelt down at Beatrice and combed back her hair. She gazed at her with a kind of motherly love.

"Beatrice, sweetie," she said. "I shouldn't say this. But I know. I know what happened."

Beatrice froze. She looked like a frightened cat.

"You ... you do?"

Lois nodded and continued to stroke her.

"Yes, I do. I know that you've been hurt very badly by men. By a man in this family. And I'm very sorry for that. And I don't blame you. And I don't judge you for it. I'm truly sorry for what happened. And these clothes ... they can't even begin to make up for the hurt you must have been through. But I want you to take them. It's the least I could do."

Beatrice looked confused but nodded anyway.

"I just ... I just can't believe it, ma'am. Thank you. Thank you so much."

She reached out and hugged Lois' neck. T.J. watched as his mother, trying to disguise her slight discomfort, embraced Beatrice and patted her on the back.

"All right, then," Lois said, breaking off the huddle a bit suddenly. "Here's what I wanted to show you. Do you see this pink romper? This was T.J.'s. He wore this on the very first day of school. I bet you don't even remember that, do you, T.J.?"

274

T.J. smiled.

"Professor Latham, could you use a new student?" he said.

"You do remember!" Lois said gleefully.

"I always thought this was the cutest thing in the world. I was so distraught when T.J. outgrew it. I even made him wear it after it was too little for him and you can see the little tears on the seams there where he stretched it. But it's in the crotch, so I don't think it will be noticed."

Lois called the little boy up onto the bed and she started to dress him, like she would a doll. He was shy and reticent but Beatrice prodded him on and assured him that everything would be all right.

Within seconds he was all dressed up in the pink and white striped romper. Lois froze for a moment after she finished.

"My word," she said. "He looks ... he looks just like T.J. did when he wore this. Doesn't he? I mean he is just the spitting image."

Beryl and T.J both nodded as Lois combed the boy's hair. Beatrice started to look nervous again. A quiet suddenly fell over the room.

"What did you say his name is?" said Lois, staring into the boy's angelic eyes.

"Ma'am?" said Beatrice.

"What's your name?" Lois asked him, cradling his cheeks.

And he answered her.

275

6

When Tom and Virgil arrived home from town later that afternoon, Lois sent all the children to their rooms and sent Virgil out to the shop. The children didn't know what it was all about, but they knew it had something to do with the girl who had been there that morning. Lois had turned violent, suddenly throwing Beatrice and the child out the door with a fury they had never seen in their mother before. Beatrice covered the boy's ears and cradled him in her arms to protect him as Lois hurled equal portions of clothes, dishes, and insults in her direction as she ran down the driveway, in tears.

But that fury was nothing compared to what the children heard that night.

T.J. couldn't make out a lot of the specifics. But he caught enough to know that there were other reasons besides farming for his father to resign from his teaching position.

Because the little boy's name was not Victor.

The boy's name was Thomas.

7

When Carl showed up that evening with a baseball bat -- after Lois had slammed the door to her bedroom and collapsed on the bed in tears and his father had retired to the shop -- T.J. was about ready to send him back home.

"I don't really feel like playing baseball, Carl," T.J. said.

"Baseball?" Carl said. "Who said we were gonna play baseball? Come on and help me find a few choice sticks."

T.J. followed Carl outside, mainly because he was too fatigued to fight him. Carl seemed a little tipsy, which wasn't unusual. His good mood was infectious. T.J. liked the breath of fresh air Carl brought into his life. He wondered if Beryl felt the same way. He thought it was a shame that his parents disapproved of her seeing Carl. The only time they had together were stolen glances here and there when Carl stopped by to see T.J. Of course T.J. knew he wouldn't be afforded so many visits from Carl if it weren't for his interest in his sister.

"Where are we going?" asked T.J.

"To pick up sticks," Carl said.

"It ain't Sunday, is it?"

"Sunday? Naw, it ain't Sunday. Why you askin' that?"

"I've just been reading the Bible and it gets me to thinking, sometimes."

"Thankin's a bad thing, if ya ast me," Carl said. "Evertime I set out t'thank, seems like I wind up getting' m'ass whupped."

T.J. followed Carl as he went into the back yard and began to inspect the sticks lying on the ground. Between the two of them they gathered up about 15.

"Make sure they're good and straight and sturdy," said Carl.

Carl knelt down on an old stump and took a knife out of his pocket. He began whittling the end of one of the sticks.

"I don't have two knives with me, or else you could help," said Carl. "Seems like some feller took my best ones." T.J. smiled and wondered what he had ever done with them.

"What are we doing, anyhow?" T.J. asked, taking a seat on the wet grass.

"What do you thank we're doin'? We're goin' frog-giggin'!" said Carl.

That sounded great to T.J. He hadn't eaten frog legs in ages. When made with a little egg yolk and butter, nothing could be tastier. On a good day, one could hope to catch frogs so big that their legs took up the whole length of the frying pan.

Carl felt the end of the stick.

"Feel that. Sharp enough?"

T.J. put his finger against the end and was surprised at just how sharp it was.

"That'll serve," he said.

Carl put aside the first stick and picked up a second one.

"You know that girl, T.J.? That girl Hoke was seeing back in the winter?"

T.J. nodded.

"Jo Ann," he said. "Did she write another letter?"

"Lots of 'em," said Carl. "And no one's seen Hoke since then. Abijah's real worried that something's happened to him."

"I'm sure nothing's happened to him," said T.J. "He's just trying to avoid trouble."

"That's what I thought, at first," said Carl. "But---"

"But what?"

"Well ... How well would you say you know Hoke?"

T.J. thought for a moment. They'd grown up together, but had stayed out of one another's way, for the most part. They had been cousins, but not friends.

"I don't know," said T.J. "About like most folks, I guess."

Carl put aside the second sharpened stick and reached for a third.

"Well, it's like this," he said. "It turns out the girl got herself in trouble. And you know what I mean by trouble."

T.J. had to think about this for a moment because Jo Ann had seemed to him like the kind of girl that invited all sorts of trouble. But he thought he knew what Carl meant.

"You mean she's pregnant?"

"That's exactly what I mean," said Carl. "And she says it's Hoke's. Now how she knows that fer sure, I don't know, considering what happened that night. But she stands by it. And of course Hoke is nowhere to be found. So she's writing to Abijah, near about ever day now."

"Has he sent her anything?" T.J. asked.

"He's sent her a lot more than he should have," said Carl. "She keeps hintin' at maybe goin' to the police or comin' back to town to look for Hoke herself. Bije is trying to keep this quiet, for the sake of the family, I guess. I dunno."

"Well that's mighty big of him," said T.J. "I know this family is something he's always shown a lot of respect for."

Carl was quick to pick up on the sarcasm.

"Y'all don't think too much of Bije, do you?" said Carl, finishing his third stick. He tested the sharpness of the point with his finger.

"I can't really say," said T.J. "I know Gammy sure loved him. It got kind of difficult when he shot Uncle Simon, you know, and threw him into the river. But she stuck by him."

"Well, he don't have his mama standing by him no more, and I think he misses her more than anything," said Carl. "I know he's had his problems with his brothers, particularly concernin' the liquor. But he sure has been good

279

to me, T.J. I cain't say a thing in the world against Abijah Latham."

"I know you feel that way, and I'm glad," said T.J. "I guess I never knew how to take him. He just seemed so mad all the time."

"Maybe he's mellerin' with age," said Carl. T.J. thought back to that night where gunshots rang out of Abijah's home as his father and Edgar cowered behind the car. He could think of a lot of words to describe Uncle Bije, but 'mellow' would definitely not be one of them.

T.J. wondered what all of this was leading up to.

"I'm starting to worry about him," Carl said. "He ain't been the same since Hoke left. We got to find him, T.J. And we got to find a way to get Abijah some money in the short term. That girl's takin' yer uncle for ever-thin' he's got. He cain't even hardly feed hisself. That car and that new house done took all his money. Until his crop comes in, he ain't got a cent to his name, T.J., except what he makes on his whiskey. And now yer daddy is pushin' him to get ridda all that. You tell me, what's he gonna do? Don't a man gotta eat?"

T.J. stared at Carl and thought.

"Did he send you here?" he asked, finally. "Did Abijah send you to tell me all of this so I could tell my father to lay off? Because I'm not going to tell my father to do any such thing, Carl. I've seen what liquor can do to people. I've seen what it did to Woodrow, my cousin. I see what it's doing to my uncle. I even ... I even see what it's doing to you."

"To me?" said Carl, laughing as he put aside another stick. "Well, I can tell you straight out, T.J., No one sent me here. I come on my own. An' I thought I'd loosen up a little first so's we could have a little fun. I didn't expect you to be trying no soul-saving. But then that lady at yer church is

280

tryin' to make ya into a preacher, so maybe yer gettin' some practice in."

Carl handed T.J. one of the sharpened sticks. He gathered up the rest, along with the bat.

"You hunt, an' I'll spot," Carl said. "We'll need t'borry one a yer daddy's coal oil lamps or somethin'. The light is what makes 'em freeze up."

"Maybe you'd better hunt, Carl," T.J. said.

"Look, there ain't nothin' to it. You see a frog, you sneak up real slow and quiet, right? You shine that light in their eyes, then..."

He grabbed up a spear and thrust it into the empty air.

"You stick 'im!" Carl said.

8

It was getting warmer now with each passing day and, even though the water was still ice cold, T.J. could stand to wade in it. He and Carl both left their shoes on the bank and rolled up the legs of their trousers. The last rays of the sun were being put to bed on the far horizon.

They decided not to go gigging on the river, since it was too deep to spear effectively. They knew that, to keep the frogs from wriggling their way off the sticks, they'd have to push them through to the bottom. So they chose the creek that ran across the Latham property. It was early in the year, still, but T.J. had heard the frogs croaking for at least the past two weeks every night when he went to bed. He was glad the eerie silence of the winter nights was over at last. The crickets and frogs were like a little symphony that lulled him to sleep each night.

281

The creek varied in depth, from the ankles to the knees, but not much deeper. That was good, T.J. thought, because he liked to keep his testicles warm and dry. T.J. and Carl stalked through the cold water as silently as they could manage, with Carl fumbling with the sticks, baseball bat, and lamp, and T.J. crouching with just the one spear.

T.J. felt like an Indian and he wondered if someone his age, but red, might have engaged in this very same activity in this same creek some 100 or 200 years ago. He would find arrowheads in the creek and fields every so often and he kept them in a tin can under his bed. He'd collected about 50 of them through the years.

T.J.'s eyes darted back and forth, looking for the shiny eyes of the bullfrogs. Some of the frogs were as large as cats. The sunlight had faded away to nothing, however, and the trees hanging over the creek made it even harder to see.

"Why did you ask me how well I knew Hoke?" T.J. whispered.

"You're gonna scare off the frogs," Carl warned.

"But why did you want to know that?" T.J. said.

"Well, it's probably nothin' but talk. But Abijah has a friend in Rome who swore up an' down he'd seen Hoke the other day."

"Rome? Why would he be in Rome?" T.J. said, his eyes still scouring the waters and the banks.

"Well, that's just it. An' that's not the worst thing. This feller said he saw him with that girl, that Jo Ann. Said they was walkin' downtown and just a-laughin' and holdin' hands."

"What? But that doesn't make any — "

T.J. thought about this for a moment, then was overcome with a sense of dread.

282

"You mean Hoke and that girl are just scheming together to get Bije's money? How could Hoke do that to Bije after all Bije has done for him? That doesn't make any sense."

"That's what I said. I told Bije that the feller over in Rome prob'ly saw someone else. That couldn't 'a been Hoke. Where would he be stayin', anyhow? Y'all ain't got no family up there, do ya?"

"No," said T.J. "But he does have some friends from Rome."

"Well, I'm sure it ain't Hoke. That just doesn't sound like something Hoke would do. Does it?"

T.J. shook his head.

"I hope not," he said. "Now let's shut up and get us a frog."

They crept through the water for a good 100 yards before spotting anything at all. Every time they got to a bend in the creek, the croaks would cease until they passed by.

But then T.J.'s heart skipped a beat as he spotted the shiny eyes of his prey bulging out from the water. He tensed and gripped the stick tightly, motioning for Carl to shine the light in the needed direction. His feet were numb now from the cold, making it difficult to navigate the rocks, but he tried to step carefully and silently, almost motionless in his motion, imperceptible, invisible. But the frog appeared to be staring right at him with his huge, spherical eyes.

T.J. gripped the stick and slightly bent his knees, trying to get poised for action. He slowly, ever so slowly, raised it above the frog. He knew the tip was sharp enough to pierce the frog on contact. He stood there, silent as a rock, then tensed and lunged, thrusting the spear clear through to the creekbottom.

T.J.'s motion sent him tumbling into the water, but he hoped that at least he had the frog.

"Bring it up! Bring it up!" said Carl, readying the baseball bat.

T.J. pulled up the stick, but there was nothing on it except mud and moss. The frog had managed to hop away at the last moment and now it was nowhere to be seen.

"Damn!" Carl said. "You almost had it, too."

"We'll get one,' said T.J. standing up and wiping the mud from his hands. "Come on!"

They walked through the creek another 50 yards before T.J. spotted another one, this time perched on a log. Its throat was puffed out and on display. The frog had no awareness of their presence, or didn't care to acknowledge them.

It was only when T.J. got closer that he realized that the frog was a mutant. It had no eyes.

Carl looked sympathetic and shook his head, motioning for them to let it go. But T.J. crouched once more for action, closing in on the blind frog.

The frog continued to puff its massive neck and croak for a mate, although none would likely be interested in an eyeless suitor. T.J. wondered if the frog even had any way to know that he was different. Was there some form of frog teasing or exclusion? Could he have any way of sensing that there was even such a thing as sight?

The frog sat motionless, as though it were inviting T.J. to put him out of his suffering. T.J. knew the frog, at this close proximity, must be aware of his presence. T.J. must have made some sound, or given off some odor, to alert the frog. Yet the frog was unmoved.

T.J. raised up the spear and bowed his legs. Then, in one swift motion, brought the spear down with all his might, piercing the frog through its stomach and pinning it to the log. Its legs began to kick wildly.

"I got it!" T.J. said excitedly as the frog twitched and contorted its massive limbs.

"I got it!" he said again, twisting the spear into the frog's guts. A gooey substance began to spew out of the wound.

T.J. took the stick out and looked to Carl.

"Where's the bag?" he asked.

"Aw, shit," said Carl. "I forgot to bring one."

T.J. looked down at the frog, which was now twitching pathetically. It was shaking. It looked like it was in tremendous pain.

"Here. Hand me that bat," T.J. said.

"No, T.J. Don't," Carl said.

"Give it here," T.J. said. Carl handed the bat to him and T.J. raised it up and brought it down on the frog with a heavy *blump!*

The frog's left leg twitched twice more, and then all movement ceased. Now that he held the limp body in his hands, T.J. felt a little sorry for the frog. Why had he felt the need to kill this helpless, blind one? Was he that desperate to show Carl he could gig a frog?

T.J. scooped up the bloody, green corpse and stared at its massive, eyeless face. He wondered if frogs had any emotions, or any way of feeling at all. The frog was cold and bumpy.

"You hold onto it," he said, handing the frog to Carl.

"Where you goin'?" Carl asked.

"Give me the lamp. I'm going up to the house to get us a sack. I'll be right back."

9

When T.J. arrived at the house, Beryl was sitting out on the front porch, bathed in flickering lamplight, and Uncle Virgil's car was in the driveway.

"What're you and Carl up to at this time of day?" Beryl asked.

"Hunting for girls. Want to come?" T.J. teased. "How's Mother?"

"She's all right," Beryl said. "She's shut herself in her room with Erlene."

T.J. nodded.

"It might be a good idea if you go fetch Erlene and let her be by herself for a while," he said.

"Where's Carl?"

"He's down by the creek. Get on inside."

Beryl stuck her tongue out as T.J. walked to his father's shop.

He tried not to attract the attention of his father or Uncle Virgil, who were still working together wordlessly on the Maxwell. T.J. didn't know a car could contain so many parts. Metal components and fittings littered every corner of the shop and Tom and Virgil seemed in some form of deep trance as they stuck their fingers into the oily recesses of the engine.

"What you need?" Tom asked with a flat, disinterested tone that said, *"get it and get out."*

"I just need a sack," T.J. said.

"I just stacked some out by the crib," Tom said. T.J. nodded and went back out the door. As he walked out to the crib and grabbed a bag, T.J. looked up and saw that the stars were coming out at last. It was cool, not unpleasant, even though he was wet and muddy. He inhaled deeply, taking in the fresh spring air.

Then he heard the screams coming from the creek.

T.J. ran as fast as he could manage, holding the cumbersome lamp before him. When he got to the creek he thought he saw two pale, ghost-like figures race past, squealing. He held the lamp up higher and slowed his pace.

"Hello!" he said. "Hello there? Carl, is that you?"

"T.J., put that lamp away!" admonished a female voice from behind the bushes that lined the bank. Instead of putting the lamp aside, T.J. stepped forward and shined the light into the brush. He spotted the faces of two of his cousins, Uncle Victor's daughters, Dora and Eurinee, who lived on the opposite side of the creek. They were completely naked and shivering in the brush. T.J. almost didn't recognize them because of their hair. Beryl must have finally made good on her promise to give them permanents. Unfortunately, they weren't flattering.

"Hey!" T.J. said, but the light sent the girls scrambling back over the edge of the bank, seeking refuge. When T.J. ran up to the edge of the water, Carl was nowhere to be seen.

"What happened? What's the matter?" T.J. asked. He saw Carl's baseball bat lying in the water. As he slid down the bank to retrieve it, he stopped mid-way, spotting the frog they had killed, lying in the mud. He picked it up.

Before the girls could speak, Virgil and Tom came running up behind T.J.

"Son of a bitch!" Virgil said. "What happened!"

He looked at the naked girls, who were still too frightened to speak, and he slipped down the embankment to the waters. Virgil spotted the bat and picked it up.

"Where are your clothes?" he asked them.

"Go away!" screamed Dora.

"Did somebody try to hurt you?" Tom asked.

"Just go away!" Dora said again.

"Who was it?" Virgil said. "What happened?"

"It was Carl. Carl Bishop," said Eurinee. "He ran thataway."

"Shit!" said Virgil, grasping the bat in his fist and making his way back up the bank.

"That son of a bitch. I told you he was trouble, Tom."

"Wait!" said T.J. "We still don't know what happened."

"I think it's right clear, don't you?" said Virgil.

"But—"

"I know he's your friend, T.J., so you just stay here," Virgil said. "We'll handle this."

T.J. wondered what Virgil meant by "we."

"Wait!" said T.J., following the two men back to the Virgil's car. Tom ran inside to get the guns.

"We were frog gigging!" he said, holding up the dead frog to Virgil as evidence. Tom sprinted back out of the house and threw the guns into the back seat. T.J. tried to climb in after them.

"Stay here!" his father said.

"But I—"

"Let go of the car, T.J.! This doesn't concern you!"

T.J. relented and watched impotently as the two of them drove off. He stomped the earth and waved the frog corpse with his clenched fist.

288

"Shit!" he screamed.

He turned around and saw Beryl standing on the porch, arms folded, eyebrow arched.

"What did you just say?"

He flailed his arms.

"I said *shit!* Shit, shit, shit!"

CANTO XIV

And then a fair, saintly Lady calls to me, and I beseech her to command me.

Her eyes shine brighter than the Star; and she begins to say, gentle and low, with voice angelical, in her own language:

"O Poet, this lover of mine, and not the lover of fortune, upon the desert slope is so impeded upon his way, that he has turned through terror, and may, I fear, already be so lost, that I too late have risen to his succour. Bestir thee now, and with thy speech ornate, and with what needful is for his release, assist him so, that I may be consoled.

"Beatrice am I, and Love has moved me, which compelleth me to speak. Do what is right, Thomas, and when I shall be in presence of my Lord, full often will I praise thee unto him."

Then she pauses, and so I answer her:

"O Lady of virtue, thou alone through whom the human race exceedeth all contained within the heavens, so grateful unto me is thy commandment, to obey, if 'twere already done, were late; no farther need'st thou ope to me thy wish."

And so I put the hammer down and sit by the bed, and I cry in hopeless terror.

Chapter Fourteen

1

It didn't take long for Virgil and Tom to make their way back to the house. They went to Carl's home but no one there had seen him for some time. Then they drove to Bije's but he would not open the door. They peered in the window but could see no evidence that Carl was there.

Virgil kept the car running as he dropped Tom off at his house.

"Where are you going?" Tom asked.

"I'm going to get a little help. We might need it," Virgil said. Tom shook his head disapprovingly.

"Let's just keep this in the family, all right?" Tom said as he shut the car door. "All right, Virgil?"

"I'll be right back. Don't worry. It's all right."

He drove away and Tom stared after him for a moment before going back into the house. Beryl and T.J. stood on the front porch.

"Daddy, I think you should listen to what T.J. has to say," Beryl said.

"Where are the girls?" Tom asked.

"I went over to Uncle Victor's and Birdy came back and got them and wrapped them up and took them home," Beryl said. "But, T.J., tell Daddy what was going on. Please!"

"Dad, me and Carl were out frog gigging. That's why I needed that sack. That's why we had the baseball bat. I'm sure all of this is just a misunderstanding."

Tom nodded.

"How long were you up at the house? How long was he alone down there with those girls?"

"It couldn't have been more than five minutes, Dad," T.J. said. "I'm sure nothing could have happened. I didn't even see those girls when I left. I don't even know where they came from."

Tom thought about this for a moment and then nodded again.

"Well, you know Virgil's getting up his friends. The Klan, I guess," Tom said. "They're gonna be out there looking for him. I think the worst they'd do is flog him, but..."

T.J. looked at Beryl, who was growing pale.

"If you know where he is, son, you need to tell me," Tom said. "We've got to find him before they do. And we don't have a car."

"You already looked at his house, and at Bije's?" T.J. said.

"Yeah, that's the first place we checked."

"Then I don't know," T.J. said.

Beryl stood up.

"I know," Beryl said. T.J. and Tom both looked at Beryl, who seemed like she immediately regretted having said it.

"You?" T.J. said. Beryl nodded, ashen-faced, more scared than ever.

"I know where he is. Come on. I'll show you."

2

Tom and T.J. followed Beryl through the dark woods. Tom brought his oil lamp to light the way, although Beryl insisted they wouldn't need it.

Beryl walked as if she had navigated her way through this forest a hundred times in the darkness. She seemed to

293

know every dip and turn, every tree and passing branch, ducking and turning and high-stepping as if on cue.

"Come on," she said, getting frustrated at the slow pace of her father and brother.

"Where are we going, Beryl?" Tom asked. "There's nothing out here. We're wasting time."

"It's just another hundred yards or so," she said.

T.J. was shocked when they finally arrived at their destination. It was an old house, probably 100 years or more. The notches on the corners and the old puncheon floors told him this wasn't a typical white man's house. This was an old Cherokee or Creek Indian cabin, in the midst of a slow surrender to the encroaching woods. As many times as he'd been in these woods, T.J. had never come across it before, which seemed impossible. But it was overgrown with vines and trees, so it might be difficult to spot from far away, he reasoned.

"Carl's here?" T.J. said. "He's never shown me this place before."

Beryl pushed open the door, motioning for her father to come in.

"Be careful on that step," she said.

Tom shined his lamp into the old house and stepped inside. The hovel didn't look like it had sat abandoned for 100 years. Someone had cleaned it up. Someone was living here.

There was a pile of hay in the corner. T.J. could hear rasping in the darkness. The whole place smelled like whiskey.

Tom lit the northwest corner of the room. Carl was there, clutching his chest, with an empty liquor bottle beside him. He appeared wide-eyed and frightened. Carl looked over to Beryl with an expression of dumbfounded betrayal, but couldn't speak.

"I'm smotherin'," he said weakly.

Tom tossed his light around the room. Something glinted on the far side. He walked over and picked it up.

It was a photograph. Carl and Beryl sat nuzzled together in a kind of timeless idyll. Tom illuminated the far wall and saw some of Beryl's books on the floor and two dresses hanging by the fireplace. T.J. could sense the fury swelling in his father as he started to put all the pieces of the puzzle together.

"Dad, wait," T.J. said as Tom spun around and put down the lamp. He rolled up his sleeves and marched over to Carl, who lay cowering in the corner, helpless and out of breath.

"*Daddy!*" Beryl screamed as Tom knelt over and grabbed Carl by the scruff of the neck. He hoisted his limp frame up and looked directly into his eyes. Carl winced in a raspy, alcoholic daze.

Then Tom flung Carl over his shoulder and marched to the door.

"Get the lamp and shut the door," he said.

3

Tom managed to get back to his house with Carl before Virgil and his friends arrived. Lois had emerged from her room and had already put Erlene and Collier to bed, but Grady was waiting up with her and helping her do the dishes when Tom, Beryl, and T.J. arrived.

"Oh my Lord," said Lois. "What happened? Is he going to be all right? Carl?"

Tom took Carl into T.J. and Grady's bedroom and threw him down on the bed.

"Is he breathing?" Lois asked. "I don't think he's breathing, Tom."

Beryl started to cry as she stroked Carl's head. Then she stood suddenly and screamed. Tom slapped her and Beryl sank to the ground.

"Tom!" Lois shouted, slamming her husband's slight frame against the wall. "Don't you ever lay a hand on her!"

Beryl stayed there on her knees, crying, as Lois comforted her, while T.J. shuffled over to Carl, who started to cough. Apparently the screams had startled him back into consciousness.

"I need whiskey," he said. "I need more whiskey."

"Don't get it!" Tom said. "If that boy is going to drink himself to death, he's not gonna do it in my house. Does everybody understand me? Beryl, run and get some Vicks. T.J., get us some honey from the kitchen. Does ... does anyone around here — "

"Dad!" said Grady, bursting into the room.

"What?" said Tom.

"Virgil's here! He's got the Klan with him!"

4

Tom instructed everyone in his family to stay inside as he stepped out onto the front porch. Virgil was there with about 30 Klan members, most carrying lanterns or torches.

"Come on, Tom," Virgil said. "Let's find that son of a bitch before he skips town."

"He's not going to skip town," said Tom.

"How do you know that?" asked Virgil.

"I know because Carl is here with me."

Lois held T.J., Beryl, and Grady near to her as the men outside started to mutter and approach the house. As they closed in, stepping onto the porch, Tom held up his hands to fend them off.

"Wait!" he said. "None of you men are coming in this house."

Frank White scowled and nudged Virgil.

"You better talk some sense into your brother because we gotta straighten this boy out," he said.

"If you do, you'll kill him," Tom said. "You'll kill him, Virgil. I know y'all and you'll get carried away and kill him. He's just a boy. A scared boy. And he's sick."

"You mean drunk," said White.

"He shoulda thought about that before he attacked those little girls, Tom," said Virgil. "I thought you was on our side. Now step aside."

Tom stepped into his brother's path, but Virgil pushed him to the floor of the porch and motioned for his fellow Klan members to join him as he walked to the door. Lois backed up with her children against the far wall and grasped them tightly.

But then a voice called out calmly, authoritatively, from behind the throng. A lone figure, clad in a white night shirt, emerged from the darkness. It was Birdy.

She cut a path through the middle of the crowd like Moses parting the waters and ascended the steps.

"You men go home," she said. "Dora and Eurinee are fine. Carl didn't mess with them any. You hear me? No one messed with them. Go home."

That demanded an explanation, which she was more than willing to supply.

"We had a talk. My daddy, Victor, had a talk with them. They admitted they had been out skinnydipping, which they have been told repeatedly not to do. Carl came up suddenly and they were frightened and ran away, leaving their clothes. But he didn't touch them. He didn't lay a finger on them. This is all a misunderstanding, so please, just go. Go home."

The men began grumbling to themselves as they turned and started to disperse. But Tom, who was still splayed on the porch, spotted something as he lay there. It was his old crate, the one he'd used at the school for so many years. Someone had brought it to the porch and filled it with fishing gear.

Tom rose to his feet and dumped out the contents of the crate. Then he stepped onto it, turned to face the crowd, and raised his hands in the air.

"Wait!" he said. Everyone stopped and turned.

"Where are you going? There's still work left to do here, tonight," he said. Virgil looked confused. Lois cracked open the door behind him.

"Go back inside, Lois," Tom said. "I know what I'm doing." She didn't go back in, but she didn't speak up, either.

"Men! Do you not see the true evil at work here tonight? Why was this boy out there frog gigging in the first place? Why does he spend all his time playing fiddle and getting into trouble? I'll tell you why. It's the *liquor!* When are we going to finally admit to ourselves that we cannot tolerate this evil in our midst any longer? This boy nearly died tonight. The boy has asthma. And my brother had given him the mistaken idea that liquor can cure him of it! He's about drank himself to death on that account!

"And then this poor girl's father, my brother, Victor. He had a son, Woodrow, who I'm sure you all remember quite well. What did him in? They said it was a train, but we all know *whiskey was the true culprit*. He wouldn't have even been on those tracks if not for his drunkenness, his stupor. And what's led to his father picking up the bottle, if not his son's death? And what does Victor inform me of, just last Christmas? He informs me that he, too, is dying from it. Cirrhosis of the liver, the doctors call it. Alcohol. My brother, Taz, was drunk on the night he shot himself. The alcohol only made his despair at his hopeless medical condition all the greater. And my brother, Abijah, is also being robbed, not of his life, but of his very soul. And I ... *I committed great sin* while under the influence of my brother's liquor. I'm standing here telling you I'm a sinner, and I sinned *because of that whiskey!* I tell you, Satan himself is in our midst! We're all here and ready. We know where it is, do we not? We are many, and Abijah is just one man. If the law will not stop him, then we must do it. What do you say?"

Then men muttered amongst themselves, then stepped forward, one by one. They were all riled up to kick someone in the teeth tonight. For all that most of them cared, it might as well be Abijah Latham as Carl Bishop.

"I'm in. *Let's do it.*"

"I'm in!" said another hoisting his rifle.

"Me, too!"

"Not me!" said a voice in the back. "Abijah Latham's a good man. Better than this'un. What'd he ever do to make us do this thing? Supply the county with a little drink in hard times like these? I can't go along with this, fellers. Good night."

With that, about 10 men pulled away and followed the man out of the circle. But the rest appeared ready to do what had to be done.

"Come on then, gentlemen," said Tom.

Inside the house, T.J. pulled himself away from his mother.

"T.J.! Where are you going?"

"I'm going with them," he said.

"You most certainly are not!" said Lois. "Come back here!"

"I'm sorry, Mama," he said, opening the door. "I have to go."

T.J. stepped off the porch cut across the woods, hoping he could beat the men to Abijah.

5

T.J. was out of breath when he reached Abijah's house, but he arrived a minute too late. Abijah met the Klansmen out in the driveway, almost as if he already knew they were coming. Tom told the men to hold back for a moment as he approached his brother and laid a hand on his shoulder. Strangely, Abijah didn't object. He looked like a defeated man.

"Brother, we're not here for you, just for your still," said Tom. "Now step aside and we'll tend to our business, but we won't lay a finger on your other property."

"I'm not movin'," said Abijah. "But you folks go right on ahead. The still's down the hill there, over there by the river. It's covered up, but I recognize some of the faces out here this evening. They've been out here a time or two before. I'm sure they'll be glad to point it out for you."

Tom nodded and motioned for the men to follow. T.J. watched all the men file past Abijah as if he were the last sentinel of a forgotten race. He nodded to the ones he knew, but he seemed far away, like his mind was in another place. When the last man had passed by, Abijah stood there for a moment, staring into the empty night. Then he turned and walked back into his house and closed the door.

T.J. bolted out of the bushes and followed the men down to the still. His father had lost control of the men, who behaved like wild monkeys, chopping up and shooting everything in sight. First they lit into the still, dismembering it and tossing its remnants all about the woods. Then they uncovered the supply of liquor, already made and ready to be shipped out to customers. The men lined up the jugs, took out their pistols and rifles, and began to shoot them, firing-squad style.

BLAM! went one, exploding into shards and dust.

A mad dog, a ghost dog, her fur and skin white as death--

BLAM! went another.

--standing there, growling--

One of the men held up his hand, bent over, and started to lap up the liquor as it dribbled into the underbrush.

--all tooth, jaws snapping, head up, ravenous--

The bottles detonated, one by one, until none were left. The men cheered and hoisted their guns into the air.

But then there was another gunshot.

The men looked at each other quizzically. It sounded like the shot had come from Abijah's house.

"*Oh no,*" said Tom, running back up the hill.

T.J. tried to blend in with the crowd in the darkness as they followed his father up the hill. Tom raced to Abijah's

301

front door, which was standing wide open. Abijah was nowhere to be seen.

"*Bije! Bije!*" he screamed.

"Tom!" yelled one of the men from the garage.

T.J. watched as his father emerged from the house then ran to the garage, to Bije's Model A. T.J. spotted a contorted hole in the roof and a slumped-over figure in the front seat. Two men had opened the driver's side door.

"*No!*" said Tom as he tugged at the limp body of his brother. "Abijah! Somebody help! *Somebody help me!*"

CANTO XV

The Poet, he takes my hand, and he urges me to pray with him. I wipe my tears away and we bow our heads together.

"*Thou Virgin Mother, daughter of thy Son, humble and high beyond all other creature, the limit fixed of the eternal counsel-*
-"

"*Just get on with it,*" *I tell him. I have heard all of this before.*

"*But she is the living fountain-head of hope,*" *the Poet says. I cannot tell whether or not he is joking. He has changed through the years. He is far removed from his work.*

"*Hope is something I've left far behind, brother,*" *I tell him.*

He urges me to try once more. I bow my head.

"*In thee compassion is, in thee is pity, in thee magnificence; in thee unites whate'er of goodness is in any creature.*

"*Now doth this man, who comes from the lowest depth of the universe so far as here, does supplicate thee through grace for so much power that with his eyes he may uplift himself higher towards the uttermost salvation.*

"*And I, who never burned for my own seeing more than I do for his, all of my prayers proffer to thee, and pray they come not short, that thou wouldst scatter from him every cloud of his mortality so with thy prayers, that thy Chief Pleasure be to him displayed. Let thy protection conquer human movements.*"

303

And so I, who to the end of all desires am now
approaching, the ardour of desire within me ends. I glance up in a
half-hope, looking first at the roof, and then through it. And my
sight at this moment becomes purified, and I join my aspect with the
Glory Infinite.

O grace abundant, by which I presumed
  To fix my sight upon the Light Eternal,
  So that the seeing I joyously consume!

I see that in its depth far down is lying
  Bound up with love together in one volume,
  What through the universe in leaves is scattered;

Chance and necessity, and their operations,
  All interfused together in such wise
  That what I speak of is one simple light.

The universal fashion of this knot
  I think I see, since more abundantly
  In saying this I feel that I rejoice.

My mind in this wise wholly in suspense,
  Steadfast, immovable, in attentive gaze,
  And evermore with gazing growing enkindled.

In presence of that light one such becomes,
  That to withdraw for some other prospect
  It is impossible to ever consent;

Because the good, which object is of will,
  Is gathered all in this, and out of it
  That is defective which is perfect there.

304

Within the deep and luminous subsistence
Of the High Light appears to me three circles,
Of threefold color and of one dimension,

And by the second seems the first reflected
As Iris is by Iris, and the third
Seems fire that equally from both is breathed.

O Light Eternal, sole in thyself that dwells,
Solely knows thyself, and, known unto thyself
And knowing, loves and smiles on thyself!

As the geometrician, who endeavours
To square the circle, and discovers not,
By taking thought, the principle he wants,

Even so am I at this new apparition;
I wish to see how the image to the circle
Conforms itself, and how it there finds place;

But my own wings are not enough for this.

Here vigor fails the lofty fantasy:
But now turns my desire and will,
Even as a wheel that equally is moved,

The Love which moves the sun and the other stars.

I take up the hammer again and hoist it, filled with
overwhelming joy and love, such as I have never felt before.

305

Revelation

Chapter Fifteen

1

It was less than a week after they buried Abijah in one of the largest caskets T.J. had ever seen that T.J. noticed his father's earaches had returned, worse than ever. He'd also been losing weight at a worrisome rate. T.J.'s mother had sent Tom to Doc Sanford about it several times, but Tom insisted that the doctor could not help him. He went, anyway, to placate her, but he never bothered to fill any of the prescriptions.

Tom had asked T.J. to help plant peas in the cotton skips. The two of them hooked the new mule to the old wagon, but she wasn't Grace. She kept trodding on their efforts as they trudged along.

T.J. led the mule as his father tossed out the peas from the wagon. T.J. tried not to look at the Model A sitting in the driveway. Abijah had left it to Tom in his will, which he had drawn up the week before he killed himself. T.J. didn't know if he had left it to his father out of spite or because he really needed a car. He liked to prefer the latter, but he was almost certain his father didn't see it that way. He thought his father intended to sell it to pay off the Maxwell once and for all.

His father had been mostly silent for the past week and had rebuffed any attempts at consolation or conversation. The only thing that seemed to interest him was the fact that winter had been hard and the ground would not produce. "It's not going to yield, this year," he kept saying. "I just want it said up front, this ground is not going to yield a thing." T.J. felt the desperate need to ask him about his involvement with the Klan and what had happened that night long ago in

308

Milledgeville, when those men drove down to the state prison and took Leo Frank from his cell. It seemed like now was the perfect time to ask. His father was cornered and they would be here, planting, all day. He still didn't know what the right way might be to approach the subject. Better the wrong way than no way at all, T.J. finally decided, taking a deep breath.

"Dad. What happened back in 1915?"

"1915? I thought I told you," said Tom. "I've told you lots of times. I know I've told the story."

"I'm not talking about the story," said T.J. "I'm asking you what really happened that night. Willie explained it a little differently."

"Willie?" said Tom.

"And what were you and Mom fighting about that night?" T.J. asked. "What happened between you and that girl, Beatrice?"

"You know, T.J. -- you know Jesus was out in the wilderness for 40 days. How long are we ... how long ..."

T.J. heard something fall to the ground behind him. When he raced around to the back of the cart, his father was lying there on the ground, cradling his head.

"Dad?"

T.J. reasoned that it must have been his father's inner ear problems troubling him again. He had leaned over too far when throwing out the peas and tumbled into the dirt. But why wouldn't he respond now? His father's stare was empty and cold as he lay there on his back and watched the heavens blow by.

"Look, T.J.," he whispered.

"Dad, are you all right? Did you fall out?"

"Look," he said. "Look."

"Look where, Dad?"

309

"Up there. Look. It's the *Celestial City.*"

T.J. felt his father start to shiver.

T.J. peered into the sky but saw only clouds and the deep, deep blue.

"I don't see anything, Dad."

"It's right there, see? You see it? The Celestial City. Paul talked about it, son. Isn't it beautiful? Remember the poem? It's the new birth. To depart and be with Christ. It's far, far better." His father started to cry and shake. T.J. didn't know what to do besides lie there at his side, which he did, until his father could find the strength of body and mind to pull himself up out of the dirt one more time.

2

Later that afternoon, Tom cleaned himself up and drove the Model A into town. It was the first time he'd driven since the Maxwell went down.

Tom Latham stepped into Wallace's Store and plopped down a sackful of Irish potatoes on the counter.

"Hello, Mr. Wallace."

"Hello, Mr. Latham. I'm so sorry to hear about your brother. We all loved Abijah here."

"I know you did," Tom said. "Thank you."

"You gonna plant these Arsh potatoes or eat 'em?" said Wallace as he counted them up and bagged them.

"Well, I'll tell you," said Tom. "We're going to eat these potatoes for supper, and then I'm going to kill my family."

Wallace didn't even blink as he finished counting up the potatoes.

"Well," he said, "we all feel like that sometimes, don't we? That'll be a dollar twenty-five, Mr. Latham."

3

T.J. was pleased at suppertime, not only by the excellent meal but by his father's upbeat mood. Even his mother, who had barely spoken to him for the past few weeks, seemed in a forgiving mood, even though Tom had never, to T.J.'s knowledge, asked for forgiveness or even admitted to what had happened with Beatrice. Still, Tom seemed happy and confident for the first time in months. His mother had actually laughed tonight. Maybe everything would be all right, after all.

He noticed Grady had now taken up reading the Bible after the nightly meal. *He might even be further along than I am, now,* T.J. thought. *Maybe he'll be the pastor in the family, and not me.* After all, T.J. reasoned, Grady always talked about wanting to see the world. What better way to do that than as a circuit rider or missionary?

Erlene and Collier were playing under the table, which their father usually did not condone. For some reason tonight he was letting them get away with it, and their giggles gave away what a grand time they were having under there.

Beryl was the only sullen face at the table. Strangely, she was dressed in the Easter dress her mother had bought for her. T.J.'s father had given Lois some money and sent her to the store to buy the Easter clothes. Normally the children would not have been allowed to wear them until Easter, but Tom actually encouraged them to go ahead and put them on to model the clothes for the family. Tom complimented each

311

child, and especially the baby, Erlene, whom he gave a big, warm hug and cradled in his arms.

"You are so beautiful," he said, holding her and tickling her under her chin. She giggled and tucked her chin into her neck.

At the dinner table, Beryl cut a strange figure, sitting there with such a sour expression in such a splendid dress. T.J. knew she missed Carl, whom she was now forbidden to see. Tom had placed a lock on her door to keep her in at night. Even T.J. had been told to stay away from Carl's house. But he had learned something from Carl during these months he'd spent with him. He'd learned how to tell a little white lie and not feel too guilty about it.

"Mama," said T.J. "if you don't mind, Homer Wilson's having a little get-together across the road after dinner. We might play cards or whatever. Old Maid, I mean. Do you mind if I go?"

"You're coming back before 10, aren't you?" Tom said with a little concern.

T.J. nodded.

"Yes sir," he said.

"I don't know," said Lois. "The Wilsons just moved in here a month ago. I don't know his parents too well."

"Let him go, Lois," said Tom. "But, T.J. I've got that churn sitting out on the porch, and I want you to bring it in and set it by the fireplace when you come in, you hear? So it'll clabber morning, so we can make the butter. Don't forget, all right? You understand?"

T.J. agreed and headed out the door to Carl's house.

"Don't worry," he said. "I won't forget this time."

4

Carl was still recovering from that night when he had nearly smothered and drank himself to death. He hadn't much energy but had decided to go out hunting today with his dog, an old bluetick hound his father had inherited from a friend. He and the dog had both wandered through the forest until they were lost, he told T.J. As night approached, he became frightened. At last he came to a little clearing, ringed by ancient oaks, with a fallen chestnut log straddling a small spring in the middle of it. Carl could feel another asthma attack coming on, and here he was, out in the middle of nowhere. Carl said a beam of light had shone down through the trees as he sat on the log and took a drink of spring water.

"I had gone about as far as I could go," said Carl. "And that dog put its head in my lap and was just a-pantin', just like I was. And I could feel another attack a-comin' on. I looked down at my feet, down by that ol' chestnut. I guess the blight got it. An' I noticed, outta that stump, there were some fresh ones a'comin' up. Little itty-bitty chestnut saplin's. So you know what I did, T.J.? I got down on my knees. I got down on my knees and I started to pray to my God."

Carl told T.J. he made a promise right there in those woods, on that holy spot of ground.

"I promised to leave all my drankin' and bad ways here in Haralson County," he said. "I'm a-leavin' this place, T.J., and I'm a-gonna take Beryl with me, if she'll have me. We'll go to Atlanta or somewheres, T.J., and start up a family. And I'll leave all the women and the sangin' and the drankin' behind. Because I love her, T.J. And I'm a saved man, now. I have accepted the Lord Jesus Christ as my Lord and Savior. I have accepted him into my heart and soul. And he brought me out of those woods, T.J. He brought me out. And do you

313

know what he's gonna do fer me? He's gonna cure me of this asthma. I know he will. I'm a man of the Lord, now, not of the world."

T.J. didn't know what to say to this. It sounded to him like Carl had experienced some kind of revelation. T.J. had waited all his life for a revelation, for God to reach out to him. Perhaps he was not worthy. Perhaps Mrs. McConnell was wrong about him, as everyone had been so wrong about Carl. You could never really tell about people, T.J. thought.

"I'm happy for you, Carl," he said. "I hope everything works out for you."

"With the Lord guiding you, T.J., you cain't go wrong. I'm on the straight path, now. You'll see. And your family will see. It's all gonna be differnt."

T.J. convinced Carl to play some Old Maid with him before he left. He stopped by Homer Wilson's house on the way home to cover his bases in case his parents were to ask the wrong kinds of questions, but he didn't stay long.

When he got back home, everything was still and dark. Everyone must have gone to bed, he thought. A little early for the parents to turn in, he thought.

T.J. walked into the den, then remembered what his father had told him about the churn.

"Almost forgot," T.J. said, admonishing himself.

He walked back outside and picked up the churn, then placed it carefully beside the fireplace.

"There," he said. "See? I remembered."

When T.J. walked into the bedroom, he saw Grady asleep, with a Bible splayed across his chest. When he picked it up to put it away, some papers fell out onto the bed. T.J. reached over to pick them up and laughed as he recognized

314

them. They were his pictures of Louise Brooks. Even the missing nude.

"You little booger," he said, smiling, tucking the pictures back into the Bible and putting it away.

As he moved to his bed, T.J. tripped over something. He looked down and saw that the cork Grady had put into the floor had finally popped out. He wondered what had become of it.

T.J. got into his nightclothes and went to sleep, thinking of what Carl had told him. So Carl was saved by grace. When would T.J.'s day of salvation come? He wondered how and when it would happen, and what it would be like to be baptized. He longed for the time when he could accept Jesus Christ with his whole heart. He wanted it so much, like he wanted nothing else. But he didn't know how to make it happen. He would just have to have faith, like everyone said. The day would come, in its time. He trusted that the Lord had a plan for everything. Everything that happened had a special purpose. He would have his day.

Then T.J. pulled up the covers and went to sleep. As he drifted off, he wondered what he had ever done with that frog he had killed.

5

T.J. awoke with the yellow lamplight piercing straight through his skull, pounding his brain matter.

He threw his hands up instinctively as something cold, hard and unforgiving rained down on his hands and head. His fingers gushed like crushed tomatoes under the scarred metal of the ballpeen hammer. T.J.'s legs tangled in the bedsheets as a scaly, dry fist grasped his hair and twisted it to

315

steady him, and he lost consciousness for a moment as another round of blows pounded his head.

When T.J. awoke, he wasn't sure how much time had elapsed. He wasn't even sure of who or where he was as all consciousness seemed to narrow into a tiny point, centered on the back of his throbbing skull. But the heavy footsteps he heard in the hallway snapped T.J. back into sentience, and he felt his head, which was drenched in a warm wetness. T.J.'s dulled instincts told him to rush out of the house as fast as his legs could carry him, but he couldn't do that. Not yet.

"Grady!" he said, moving to his brother's bed and flinging back the bedsheets. But his brother would not move. The white moonlight revealed black pools and smears of blood on the white sheets and pillow.

Then the dark figure with the lamp was upon him again, silent and deadly, swinging with the force of judgment. T.J. slapped his father as hard as he could against the wall, then he grabbed his pillow and ran to his parents' room.

"*Mama!*" he screamed. He looked down and saw her lying there, eyes open, with a dark smudge across her cheek. Erlene lay curled up beside her, with a damp, hairy tangle where her head should have been. They were wrapped in one another's arms, in a quiet and fearful embrace.

Where was Collier?

T.J. galloped out of the room as the figure with the lamp pursued him. He tripped and fell in the hallway. When he got to his feet he saw his sister Beryl lying there. She grasped her head like she was trying to hold its constituent pieces together. Beryl flailed with her other arm, swimming across the hall through a pool of her own blood.

"T.J.! It's Daddy. *He's killing us all,*" she said. "*He's killing us all!*"

316

T.J. grasped her free arm as he got back on his feet and dragged her across the floor. He managed to lift her to his chest as more blows from the hammer fell, then he crumpled. He tumbled through the door and down the steps of the front porch, landing on the mercifully soft ground as Beryl screamed and clutched her head. T.J. didn't know if Beryl would make it. She was injured much worse than he was. He gave her his pillow. It was all he had.

"Wrap this around your head!" he said.

T.J. could see Tom's face now. There was nothing of his father in it. This was a different face, enraptured, impenetrable, and dark and malevolent as Nature. He vanished back into the house.

"We have to run, Beryl. Can you run?"

She shook her head and collapsed. A gunshot rang out and T.J. was looked for immediate cover. The glint of Abijah's Model A shone like a beacon in the moonlight. T.J. shoved his sister over the door and then climbed in as gunshots thumped the metal and dirt around them. T.J. winced as he pulled the door shut with his pinky. His other fingers were crushed beyond any use.

T.J. saw his father descend the stairs. He lowered and aimed the gun.

T.J. didn't have the keys. He kicked the gear shift into neutral. The car drifted down the hill, slowly at first, agonizingly so, and then with steadily gathering speed.

He saw the shadow figure of his father give chase for a moment, then stop. He fired one shot, and then another. Beryl covered her ears with the pillow and screamed. Something fell out of the pillowcase into the seat beside T.J. It was the gold nugget. T.J. placed it in his lap and clutched it like a talisman.

317

T.J. clung onto his sister as the car continued to pick up speed, careening down the hill, until finally he couldn't see his father anymore. When he did reappear in the doorway, in a kind of silhouette, there was a final gunshot, and T.J. thought he saw Tom's shadow slump to the floor.

The car continued to race down the hill and onto the Eaves Bridge Road. It would remain dark for several more hours, but soon the morning would come, T.J. thought, and he would just have to put his trust in something, pray that they would not strike a tree or fall into the river, as the momentum of the automobile carried them farther and faster. He looked down once more at his sister, who was still in her Easter dress. She had worn it to bed. It was bloody, but it could be washed clean in time for Easter. T.J. thumped himself for having such an absurd thought. But what thoughts were appropriate? How should he think? The whole world was on fire, everything was lit with pain. Was it wrong to think his sister would live to see Easter? How had this happened? Who had allowed this to happen? Hadn't he remembered to put the butter churn beside the fireplace? What test had he failed? What had he done wrong? What was the Plan, the Purpose here? *Fur and skin white as death, all tooth, jaws snapping--*

T.J. looked once more in the mirror but saw only his own unrecognizable face, christened in blood. The dimly-lit road stretched out toward Mt. Kilimanjaro. It was somewhere out there, if only he could drive far enough. T.J. let go of the steering wheel and he prayed.

AFTERWORD

Tom Latham was my great-grandfather.

Much of this book is true, but not all of it. I streamlined and compressed the story, changed the order of some of the events, and combined characters when necessary. In some cases names were changed. Sometimes I just made stuff up. (As Mark Twain falsely attributed to Herodotus, father of history: *"Very few things happen at the right time, and the rest do not happen at all. The conscientious historian will correct these defects."*)

I spent many long days with Terry Jones Latham, my great uncle, in the early-to-mid 1990s, recording his version of the events related here. I also recorded Carl Bishop's version of the events, and those of a number of other relatives. Sometimes these versions were in conflict with one another. This book is based on those recordings.

The Confederate-related history is taken from various family stories that have been passed down to me. Most of the details of these stories came from the Pollard side of the family, rather than the Lathams, and involved Pollard family members, most of whom also lived in Haralson County.

The minstrel show material for the "daints" comes from a comedy routine originally developed by Gid Tanner and the Skillet Lickers, which served as the inspiration for some of my grandfather's informal performances.

The material for the Cantos was derived primarily from the Longfellow translation of Dante's *Divine Comedy*.

Collier was found hiding in his mother's bedsheets. He was unharmed and he lived to be an old man. Tom, Lois, and Erlene were pronounced dead at the scene. Grady and Beryl were taken to a Cedartown hospital and were given only a small chance for survival. Beryl lived. Grady did not.

Beryl and Carl married, moved to Atlanta, and had five children. Carl took a job with a mill, and then later at the Ford Motor Company. He stopped drinking. He had asthma until the day he died. Beryl and Carl were my grandparents.

T.J. studied theology and put his skills as a preacher and construction worker to use when he moved to California as a missionary, building Baptist churches throughout the mid-20th century. While out west he married a Haralson County woman he met there by chance and together they adopted a daughter. T.J. returned to Georgia as an old man and died alone while wandering outside his home in the dark on one especially cold winter night in 1997.

Nothing is left of Latham Town today except for an old house and the Philadelphia Church Cemetery. Most of the Lathams are buried there.

This story is incomplete.
Experience the rest:
acoldcoming.blogspot.com

20610451R00189

Made in the USA
Lexington, KY
15 February 2013